Urban Memo⌐

CW00357571

Urban Memory: History and amnesia in the modern city brings together ideas about memory which bear upon the architectural and urban experience. It presents a critical and creative approach to the theorisation of memory, and focuses this burgeoning area of studies on the actual forms of the built environment in the modernist and post-industrial city.

Urban memory was a key theme for many leading modernist writers and social thinkers. Conversely, modernism in architecture often seemed to erase memory from the city. More recently the two have come together, and cities that were once centres of intensely forward-looking modernist culture are now focused on commemoration. This can also be seen in the growing number of architects specialising in monuments to trauma, the nostalgic collaborations between conservationists and developers, and the ever-increasing number of museums and amenity groups.

This book analyses these patterns, showing that the dynamics of history and memory pervade our 'post-urban' and post-industrial cities as never before.

Contributors approach the theme from the overlapping fields of architectural history, art history, cultural studies, sociology, fine art, critical theory and psychoanalysis. Particular focus is on post-industrial Manchester, but the book also includes studies of contemporary Singapore, New York after 9/11, contemporary museums and art spaces, and memorials built in concrete. The book is illustrated with images of architecture, art works, views of cities, and maps, and includes ten specially commissioned pieces by leading contemporary artists Nick Crowe and Ian Rawlinson.

Mark Crinson is an art and architectural historian interested in colonialism, urban theory and contemporary art. He has published three other books and from 2000 to 2002 was co-director of the AHRB-funded research project 'Urban Memory in Manchester'.

Urban Memory

History and amnesia in the modern city

Edited by Mark Crinson

Routledge
Taylor & Francis Group

LONDON AND NEW YORK

First published 2005 by Routledge
2 Park Square, Milton Park, Abingdon, Oxon, OX14 4RN

Simultaneously published in the USA and Canada
by Routledge
270 Madison Ave, New York, NY 10016

Routledge is an imprint of the Taylor & Francis Group

© 2005 Mark Crinson, selection and editorial material; individual chapters, the contributors

Typeset in ITC Charter by Keystroke, Jacaranda Lodge, Wolverhampton
Printed and bound in Great Britain by TJ International, Padstow, Cornwall

British Library Cataloguing in Publication Data
A catalogue record for this book is available from the British Library

Library of Congress Cataloging in Publication Data
A catalog record for this book has been requested

ISBN 0–415–33405–5 (hbk)
ISBN 0–415–33406–3 (pbk)

Contents

List of illustrations

Artists' pages by Nick Crowe and Ian Rawlinson are placed between each chapter.

Illustration credits

The authors and the publishers would like to thank the following individuals and institutions for giving permission to reproduce illustrations. We have made every effort to contact copyright holders, but if any errors have been made we would be happy to correct them at a later printing.

a^{2}0 7.1

Carne, Sarah, *High Noon*, 2002 9.7

Chodzko, Adam, *Remixer*, 2002 9.4

Chodzko, Adam, *The Georgies' Centre*, 2002 9.5

Coley, Nathan, *I Don't Have Another Land*, 2002 9.3

Crowe, Nick and Rawlinson, Ian, *Explaining Urbanism to Wild Animals*, 2002 9.6

Eliasson, Olafur, *Weather Project*, 2003–4 6.4

Forty, Adrian 4.1, 4.2, 4.3, 4.4, 4.5, 4.6

getforme.com 7.3, 7.4, 7.5

Gten Photography & Design 3.2, 3.3, 3.4, 3.5, 5.4, 5.5

Himid, Lubaina, *Cotton.Com*, 2002 2.1, 2.2

Leach, Neil 8.1, 8.2

Phillips, John 7.6

Sebald, W.G., *The Emigrants*, London: Harvill Press, 1997 1.1

Trafford Park Development Corporation, publicity brochure 5.3, 5.6

Wentworth, Richard, *An Area of Outstanding Unnatural Beauty*, 2002 9.1, 9.2

Williams, Richard 6.1, 6.2, 6.3, 6.4, 6.5, 6.6

Contributors

Mark Crinson is Senior Lecturer in Art History at the University of Manchester. His publications include *Modern Architecture and the End of Empire* (2003), *Empire Building: Orientalism and Victorian Architecture* (1996), and (with Jules Lubbock), *Architecture or Profession? 300 Years of Architectural Education in Britain* (1994).

Nick Crowe and **Ian Rawlinson** have worked collaboratively since 1994. Their work explores issues around urban space and the social, cultural and economic forces that shape our experience of it. Previous projects include architectural adaptations to a bridge in central Manchester, a durational performance work for Lower Manhattan Cultural Council and a planning application for a metal fenced ghetto around the Oval cricket ground, London. Characterised by a playful engagement with contested sites, their practice has recently involved playing recordings of construction sites to ecosystems in the Cheshire/Manchester greenbelt for their 2002 work *Explaining Urbanism to Wild Animals*. Their 2003 work *Two Burning Bushes*, based on the biblical/quranic account of the manifestation of God, was filmed in an overgrown industrial wasteland near Old Trafford. Depicting two bushes burning with a fire that does not consume them, after a tour of the UK the film was shown at PS1 MOMA, New York.

Adrian Forty is Professor of Architectural History at the Bartlett, University College London. His publications include *Objects of Desire: Design and Society since 1750* (1986), *Words and Buildings, a Vocabulary of Modern Architecture* (2000), and (with Suzanne Kuechler) *The Art of Forgetting* (1999).

Graeme Gilloch is Senior Lecturer in Sociology at the University of Salford and a former Humboldt Foundation Research Fellow at the Johann Wolfgang Goethe University of Frankfurt am Main. His main publications include *Myth and Metropolis: Walter Benjamin and the City* (1996) and *Walter Benjamin: Critical Constellations* (2002). He is presently writing an intellectual biography of Siegfried Kracauer.

Jane Kilby is a Lecturer in the Department of Sociology at the University of Salford. Her research interests include trauma, memory, and the representation of violence and victimisation. She has a forthcoming book on the cultural politics of childhood abuse.

Neil Leach has taught at a number of institutions including the Architectural Association, London, and Columbia University, New York. He is the author of *The Anaesthetics of Architecture* (1999), *Millennium Culture* (1999) and *China* (2004); editor of *Rethinking Architecture* (1997), *Architecture and Revolution* (1999), *The Hieroglyphics of Space* (2002), *Designing for a Digital World* (2002); co-editor of *Digital Tectonics* (2004); and co-translator of *L B Alberti: On the Art of Building in Ten Books* (1988).

Claire Pajaczkowska is Reader in Psychoanalysis and Visual Culture at Middlesex University's School of Arts. Her books *Perversion, Ideas in Psychoanalysis* and *Feminist Visual Culture* were published in 2000. As Leverhulme Research Fellow 2002–2004 she is writing on the Sublime in the culture of everyday life.

John Phillips is Associate Professor at the National University of Singapore. He is co-editor of *Reading Melanie Klein* (1998), editor of *Contested Knowledge: A Guide to Critical Theory* (2000), and co-editor of *Beyond Description: Singapore, Space, Historicity* (2004).

Paul Tyrer is interested in questions of identity and space, and in particular in psychoanalytical ways of understanding the subject in the city. He was Research Associate at the University of Manchester, working on the AHRB project 'Urban Memory in Manchester'.

Richard Williams is a Lecturer in History of Art at the University of Edinburgh and is the author of *After Modern Sculpture* (2000) and *The Anxious City* (2004).

Urban memory –
an introduction

Mark Crinson

Something seems to have happened to cities and their relation to the past recently. Even if they agree on little else, there is a consensus among leading urban theorists that some epochal change has been afoot. Never before have there been so many amenity groups, preservation societies, genealogists, museums, historians amateur and professional, conservation areas, and listed buildings. The past is everywhere and it is nowhere. We seem at times overwhelmed by the oceanic feeling of a limitless archive, of which the city is the most physical example and the 'memory' of our computers is the most ethereal yet the most trusted, and at others afflicted by a fear that the material traces of the past might be swept away, taking memory with them. Wiping, computer failure, demolition, redevelopment: all seem inter-changeable threats. Meanwhile, as if in compensation, 'musealisation', even 'self-musealisation', extends collecting activities to almost any kind of object and any kind of recorded memory.[1] Memory is both burden and liberation.

'Post-modern urbanism' or even 'posturbanism', as it has come to be called, treats the past as something to be quoted selectively, something already deracinated: the 'villaging' of city centres to evoke lost or mythical forms of public life, historic buildings that are little more than the carcasses of former functions, loft spaces with cleaned brick and stripped interiors filled with new fittings, 'historic interiors' that are preserved as if in aspic, façades saved while their inners are gutted and completely rebuilt, and new museums established in old mills, steelyards and power stations. Some of this is *nostalgie de la boue*, or memory with the pain taken out, and the paradox of this is that it works in a context where deprivation has increasingly become peripheralised in the post-industrial city, while in other parts of the world slumdom has increased as never before. Residents of slums now make up one-third of the world's urban population, some 921 million people forming a truly Dickensian prospect in the most rapidly expanding cities of the world. As Mike Davis writes, 'They are the gritty antipodes to the generic fantasy-scapes and residential theme parks . . . in which the global middle classes increasingly prefer to cloister themselves.'[2]

This book attempts to analyse the characteristic forms, experiences and spaces of modern urban memory. Its materials are some of the artworks, novels, buildings, events and city spaces that articulate the contradictions and potentials of our current urban concerns. Before this examination can develop, however, the job of this Introduction is to provide some basic understanding of the relation between memory, urban memory, and history. This will be done by summing up some of the main reference points for this present volume rather than providing unnecessary potted accounts of the chapters that make it up.

In our everyday understanding of memory the term encompasses two closely interlinked aspects: the first is of a residue of past experiences that has somehow stuck or become active in the mind, and thus in our sense of ourselves, while other experiences have been forgotten; the second is of an ability or faculty by which we recollect the past. The sense of process or mental machinery is common to both aspects of the term and seems to derive from another and older sense of memory as a structure of rhetoric. Also common, although this is more modern, is the sense of memory as a subjective matter; one would have to modify it (memorial) or add a qualifier (collective memory) to make it look outwards from the self. 'Urban memory' does not yet have the same everyday understanding, though it is getting there. Urban memory can be an anthropomorphism (the city having a memory) but more commonly it indicates the city as a physical landscape and collection of objects and practices that enable recollections of the past and that embody the past through traces of the city's sequential building and rebuilding. The problem with memory in contemporary usage is that it has become not so much a term of analysis as a mark of approval, and this happens even in much recent academic literature where it is often uncritically appropriated and used in an untheorised way to conjure up the metahistorical.[3] Memory, then, has come to be associated with such notions as the authentic, personal, subaltern, auratic and humanised, as opposed to such matters as the mass media and globalisation, which are deemed to be agents of amnesia. Accordingly urban memory seems to indicate cities as places where lives have been lived and still felt as physically manifest, shaping what is remembered beyond the discourses of architects, developers, preservationists, and planners. But it is also often strategically mobilized by those professions.

The implied polarity of memory in such schemes is history rather than amnesia. Perhaps the source for this pitting of memory against history is the work of the sociologist Maurice Halbwachs, especially his book *La*

Mémoire Collective (1950). Halbwachs saw history as an instrumental and overly rationalised version of the past, by contrast with memory which was intimately linked with collective experience. Memory, for Halbwachs, bound groups of people together, recharging their commonality by reference to the physical spaces and previous instances, often a founding moment, of that collective identity. But clearly the collective nature of Halbwachs's memory made it amenable to the collective spatiality that is the city. These specific resonances with the city are clear in the following passage:

> When a group is introduced into a part of space, it transforms it to its image, but at the same time, it yields and adapts itself to certain material things which resist it. It encloses itself in the framework that it has constructed. The image of the exterior environment and the stable relationships that it maintains with it pass into the realm of the idea that it has of itself.[4]

There is little of class consciousness here and still less of historical specificity, but there is much Hegelianism.

Among others, the architectural theorist Aldo Rossi took up Halbwachs's ideas and most recently they have been re-energised by the architectural historian Christine Boyer. In Rossi's *The Architecture of the City* (1966), a book with enormous influence on architecture, and written as a rebuttal to the modernist redevelopment of European cities after the Second World War, the human body and the city are seen as similar in being the creation of a unique set of experiences. A city remembers through its buildings, Rossi argues, so the preservation of old buildings is analogous with the preservation of memories in the human mind. The process of urban change is the domain of history, but the succession of events constitutes a city's memory and this is the preferred psychological context for making sense of the city. Identity, it follows, is the sum of all the traces in the city but likewise if development sweeps buildings away then memory loss and identity crisis threaten and the city loses its typology (its memory forms), and can no longer act as a kind of guide or exemplar for the people living in it. In Boyer's updating of this, the collective project and social order that is city building are seen to have been dissipated over the past twenty years by what she calls the 'pictorialization of space and time' through a 'matrix of well-designed fragments . . . fictional styles of life and imaginary behaviours'.[5] In this vision, history has repressed the subjective and instrumentalised the past, the modernist city is itself washed from the slate of memory, and we have lost the interpretative means to 'translate memories and traditions into meaningful contemporary forms'.[6]

A related version of the contrast between history and memory has appeared in the French historian Pierre Nora's series of volumes on *lieux de mémoire*. History, which, according to Nora, is a distanced practice based in the archive and its documentary evidence and relics of another era, is always about analysis and critical discourse reconstructing and representing the past. However, memory, as with Halbwachs, is part of what makes a community and, as such, is

> in permanent evolution, subject to the dialectic of remembering and forgetting, unconscious of the distortions to which it is subject, vulnerable in various ways to appropriation and manipulation, and capable of lying dormant for long periods only to be suddenly reawakened.[7]

But again memory evokes loss, indeed, the very triggering of memory is a symptom of the disappearance of close organic communities living in continuity with their pasts, in other words, Halbwachs's 'collective memory'. Memory of this kind, for Nora's postmodern history, no longer exists: instead, '*Lieux de mémoire* exist because there are no longer any *milieux de mémoire*.'[8] To put it differently, because memory has been eradicated by history and the bonds of identity are broken, *lieux de mémoire* have come into being in compensation, as sites devoted to embodying or incarnating memory and entirely reliant on the 'specificity of the trace' for which we feel a superstitious veneration.[9] While including such things as historical figures, books, emblems and commemorative events, *lieux de mémoire* are also buildings, monuments and places. One might find examples of *lieux de mémoire*, for example, in the kind of decontextualised monument that is identified with the modern city, either removed from its surroundings and positioned in some new synthetic context or having its surroundings removed from around it so that it achieves a previously unconsidered prominence.[10]

Another element is brought into these polarised concepts of history and memory if we consider modernism. In a sense, it matters less that history is challenged by memory – it has, after all, endured and benefited from many similar challenges to its authority – as that memory challenges a notion central to modern urbanism, its very forward-looking or utopian trajectory; the promise inherent in modernism. If memory obeys periods, then urban memory in the traditional city, as Anthony Vidler has suggested, was 'that image of the city that enabled the citizen to identify with its past and present as a political, cultural and social entity'.[11] In such a city, monuments functioned by metaphorical tropes to remind the citizenry of their relation to past deeds and events and to indicate their relation to utopia. Memory was thus a rhetorical form whose patterns were mapped across spaces and objects. Later, in what Vidler suggests can properly be called urbanism, urban memory became self-mirroring as the city became constructed as a memorial of itself, cutting out great areas to provide a memory theatre in its very heart.[12] But later still, modernism sought to erase memory from the city, a highly destabilising idea but one that was nevertheless in dialectical opposition to the preceding urbanism. In this epochal schema we have now entered another memory period in which the modernist city which negated memory creating a 'presence of absence' is now itself remembered by the postmodern or posturban city and the older city is now 'a haunting absence, not a haunting presence'.[13]

Some have called this present situation a crisis of memory. This may be a particular version of a crisis that has been more often identified with the nineteenth-century city, or with the post-war period, but also with modernity in general.[14] The crisis of memory that pervades the work of many of the key modernists from Baudelaire and Proust to Freud and Benjamin,[15] and the ground for which is the individual's experience of urban change, continues to play a central role in the fictions of contemporary writers like W. G. Sebald and Paul Auster. But whereas in the nineteenth and early twentieth century this concern was based on a sense that there had been some seismic rupture separating the present from traditional forms of memory (like the Renaissance theatre of memory), in the present postmodern or postindustrial moment there is another watershed that has been passed, identified with a loss of continuity with the nineteenth-century city and sourced either to some traumatic moment of conflict or to some economic shift in the character of the city. The 'abstraction in consciousness' that Benjamin found in Baudelaire's poetry,[16] or the 'blasé attitude' that Georg Simmel found in the Berlin crowds, each of course symptomatic of the breakdown of what Halbwachs called collective memory, are transformed into another form of distance in the contemporary city.

The differences can be summed up by contrasting passages from Proust and Sebald. In Proust, past and present are connected neither by wilful collective commemorations nor by conscious memorising but by individual acts of involuntary memory triggered by the senses. One famous instance of this occurs when the narrator trips accidentally on cobblestones on his way to a party:

> almost at once I recognized the vision: it was Venice, of which my efforts to describe it and the supposed snapshots taken by my memory had never told me anything, but which the sensation which I had once experienced as I stood upon two uneven stones in the baptistery of St Mark's had, recurring a moment ago, restored to me.[17]

This trigger or trip opens memory to a magical, even archetypal, image, decanted, free of anxiety and of temporality itself and evoking a honeyed sense of loss. But this is also an account that foregrounds forgetting almost as a function of modern experience ('the supposed snapshots').

Where Proust conceived of memory as an involuntary and sensuous mode of compensation ('time embodied'), for Sebald, memory is a representational form. Neither history nor memory seem directly accessible in Sebald's work. History is epitomised by a panorama of the Waterloo battlefield: 'It requires a falsification of perspective. We, the survivors, see everything from above, see everything at once, and still we do not know how it was.'[18] Monuments seem insincere and pointless:

> Near Brighton, I was once told, not far from the coast, there are two copses that were planted after the Battle of Waterloo in remembrance of that memorable victory. One is in the shape of a Napoleonic three-cornered hat, the other in that of a Wellington boot. Naturally the outlines cannot be made out from the ground; they were intended as landmarks for latter-day balloonists.[19]

Memory is epitomised by aimless wandering, here in post-war Berlin:

> If I now look back to Berlin . . . all I see is a darkened background with a grey smudge in it, a slate pencil drawing . . . blurred and half-wiped away with a damp rag. Perhaps this blind spot is also a vestigial image of the ruins through which I wandered in 1947 when I returned to my native city . . . for a few days I went about like a sleepwalker, past houses of which only the facades were left standing, smoke-blackened brick walls and fields of rubble along the never-ending streets.[20]

Eventually he finds a cleared site where the bricks saved from the ruins have been stacked in neat rows in which 'the thousandth brick in every pile was stood upright on top, be it as a token of expiation or to facilitate the counting' and where the bricks in serried rows seem to reach as far as the horizon.[21] Berlin's bricks have the most minimum signifying potential ('a token of expiation') marking calculated amnesia and memory-less renewal.

There are no more obvious markers of memory in a city than its monuments and no more obvious sites for crises of memory.[22] Monuments are usually paid for or at least sanctioned by the state and represent what must be remembered according to established power, although they can also stand for challenges to that power. Monuments can themselves often be subject to memory-wiping operations by insurgent groups (such as the destruction of the Vendôme Column by the Paris Commune) or, most obviously, if they offend the sensibilities of a newer regime. It could be said that contemporary technology like television, video and the Internet brings in an extra dimension here by allowing for repetitions of the operation (as with the pulling-down of the statue of Saddam Hussein in Baghdad) so that the wiping of memory is itself memorialised in favour of a new dispensation.

Monuments can also suffer from a more pervasive amnesia. As the events or persons that they memorialise lose relevance or lack the rekindling operations of history, so monuments join the life of the street, brought into the extensive time of the everyday, the necessarily ignored. Freud's understanding of monuments was as 'mnemic symbols' originally built to mark particular traumatic experiences like the death of a queen (Charing Cross) or the Great Fire of London (The Monument). In that sense, Freud says, they resemble hysterical symptoms. But if every Londoner were to stop in front of these monuments in the same state of deep melancholy experienced by their builders, then the city would be full of neurotics and hysterics.[23] (It might be full of them for other reasons too, such as personal projections of traumatic memories onto familiar monuments.[24]) But Freud stops short of any modernity-as-trauma view, any medicalisation of the loss of urban memory. There is a necessary distancing from the past, he says, an absorbing and deadening of its violence, in order to deal with what is immediate and real. And this, contrarily, is why the Surrealists found so much potential in the monuments of Paris.

If anything, though, we might say that the true urban hysteric is the tourist (or perhaps the architectural historian) who seeks out these monuments and their forgotten meanings. This is why Benjamin and Ruskin distrusted Rome, as the epitome of the imperial city filled with monuments: 'perhaps in Rome', Benjamin wrote in 1929,

> even dreaming is forced to move along streets that are too well paved. And isn't the city too full of temples, enclosed squares and national shrines to be able to enter undivided into the dreams of the passer-by, along with every shop sign, every flight of steps and every gateway? The great reminiscences, the historical frissons – these are all so much junk to the *flâneur*, who is happy to leave them to the tourist.[25]

Ruskin found Rome too full of rubbish, of classical sites with little resonance for him, and of an alien popery, and preferred the decayed, 'savage' and time-wracked Gothic of Venice, whose buildings seemed 'lamps of memory' washed by streams of humanity and records of the touch and thought of their makers.

Monuments have become particularly troubled in the contemporary city through several factors: a sense of democratic participation in public space while that space becomes increasingly privatised and commercial; a lack of aesthetic consensus; and a sense of shame about colonial pasts, military adventures and other such previously commemorated events. Arguably, the role of the monument has migrated to the commemorative function of architecture, and to a category we could sum up by the words 'trace' and 'fragment'. These latter bring us back to the work of Walter Benjamin who was scathing about the true meaning of official monuments as commemorations of cruelty and barbarism.[26] The quotation from Benjamin cited earlier continues:

> And he would be happy to trade all his knowledge of artists' quarters, birth-places and princely palaces for the scent of a single weathered threshold or the touch of a single tile – that which any old dog carries away.[27]

Benjamin's attitude to such traces, which is similar in some respects to Ruskin's appreciation of the architectural detail as an embodiment of those who made and used the building, has licensed a contemporary attitude towards building materials in which it is common to find memory located in a wall surface or chipped paintwork or some other material trace or fragment. Memory is understood in these instances to be a presence as if an older discourse locating memory in the structures of the human form has now been transferred to the structures made by humans.[28]

But for Benjamin the notion of 'shock' was central to modernity and with the unassimilable stimuli of shock came memory and amnesia; both were intimately bound up with the experience of the modern city. The fragment was understood as having a dynamic role as a random element to do with moments and discontinuities, plucked or dug out from the illimitable archive that is the city and joining with others to suggest fleeting but critical insights (which are also shocks) into the past as well as a sense of a lost continuity. And this is only one aspect of Benjamin's complex understanding of urban memory, which encompassed metaphors of archaeology, the labyrinth, writing, the family tree, and optical devices. Another aspect is the idea that architecture is itself the memory-space of the collective, so that, most famously, the Paris arcades are the memory traces of the collective unconscious of nineteenth-century capitalism.[29]

Within the current memory industry there is a privileged area that deals with the Holocaust and similar collective traumas, both because these experiences seem particularly definitive for modernity, or at least the turn from a utopian version of it to one based on loss, and because in relation to them memory is the return of the repressed.[30] A subset of this overlaps with what we broadly call urban memory. Here not only is the monument seemingly reinvigorated through a new job of relating to trauma, but also the professional and intellectual character of an architect like Daniel Libeskind is itself a contemporary phenomenon in which the architect has become a specialist in this kind of work. Libeskind's architecture raises trauma-reflection to a fine art by designing buildings whose main function is to materialise and redeem traumatic experiences and provide the new monuments of the contemporary city: evoking the loss of Berlin's Jews or the catastrophe of the World Trade Center. Though such buildings address hugely important moments, they cannot avoid absorption into other agendas. The World Trade Center design, for instance, is also about restoring the US financial centre to its 'rightful place in the world', according to New York's mayor, and proclaiming 'what the freedom of America stood for', according to Libeskind.[31] Libeskind's work in Berlin and New York amounts to a highly sophisticated rhetoric for conserving memory, or, more facetiously, 'a Museum of Knotted Handkerchiefs'.[32]

Libeskind's architecture is a public manifestation of work which has often been done with less fanfare, especially when the issue has been not about memory but about amnesia. This is most interestingly the case with the almost totally destroyed cities of the losers in war: Japan and, particularly, Germany. In the latter, the process of *Vergangenheitsbewältigung*, to use its appropriately convoluted German term, meaning coming to terms with or even overcoming the past, has entailed successive policies of either wiping away unpleasant memories,[33] especially in the form of undesired architecture, or commemorating the fate of the victims. Both have had urban implications, ranging from erecting *faux* historic buildings to replace those destroyed by war, to designing modernist buildings as if Germany had rapidly rejoined a family of nations, to the saving of material relics as testimonies to the end of bad objects like the Berlin Wall, to proposals to retain urban wildernesses caused by wartime destruction and Cold War politics as 'prairies of history' and to the intense and resourceful debates about the appropriate function and form of Holocaust memorials.[34] A city like Berlin, once one of the centres of an intensely forward-looking modernist culture, now proclaims itself primarily a palimpsest or 'memory space'.[35]

Berlin and Manhattan may perhaps be extreme cases but the dynamics of history and memory, commemoration and amnesia, seem as never before to pervade our contemporary cities. To capture what he calls 'posturbanism', Vidler uses an image of merged urban domains without memory maps:

> We wander . . . surprised but not shocked by the continuous repetition of the same, the continuous movement *across* already vanished thresholds that leave only traces of their former status as places. Amidst the ruins of monuments no longer significant because deprived of their systematic status . . . walking on the dust of inscriptions no longer decipherable because lacking so many words, whether carved in stone or shaped in neon, we cross nowhere to go nowhere.[36]

Although more a description of the dystopian cities of certain recent films than of any actual city, nevertheless this sparks resonances with many existing cities.

Manchester is one of these and it is more than just any example in this current book, which comes in part out of experiences, research and debate about it. It has particular importance in the writing of W.G. Sebald who found its relation to its past had profound correspondences even with his sense of irrecoverable loss in cities hollowed out by war or genocide. Like Sebald, the French novelist Michel Butor also found this distinct sensibility aroused by Manchester. The city in Butor's *L'emploi du temps* (1957) constantly conveys a sense of its archetypal status, yet it is also at the same time post-something: *after* the labour of many industrial hands, *after* a time when the meaning of its monuments could be deciphered. It is also the city without boundary, a maze traversed by a latter-day Theseus and constantly haunted by the uncanny, in which maps and the plotted routines of detective stories are tantalising but ultimately useless keys to the city's codes. The estrangement of the narrator from the city is itself an epitome of the city's tearing and scattering of memories.

As Vidler suggests, the sense of the edge is different in such posturban cities and the associated notion of fragments or traces is different too.[37] Instead, and this is not necessarily written negatively, 'the margins have entirely invaded the centre and disseminated its focus'.[38] Everywhere is interstitial; the architectural array is fragmented; regeneration seems image-thin. As in our museums so in our cities, the hope of juxtaposition takes over from the logic of the map. We are not so sure that memory has a place in the contemporary city and that is why it is talked about so much.

Acknowledgements

I would like to acknowledge the help of my present and past colleagues at the University of Manchester who formed the 'Urban Memory in Manchester' research team: Helen Hills, Natalie Rudd, Frank Salmon, and Paul Tyrer. That project was supported by a generous grant from the Arts and Humanities Research Board. In addition, thanks to Rebecca Duclos for her research assistance, to Richard Williams for comments on some of the chapters, to Gten Photography & Design for their expertise, to Caroline Mallinder for believing this could be a book.

Finally, I would like to thank Nick Crowe and Ian Rawlinson for adding another dimension to the book through their artists' pages. They describe their work as an attempt to create caesuras between the chapters of the book which would enable the reader to reflect on the questions being raised on a more 'human' scale: 'By bringing the entire thrust of the work down to these small, incidental moments we were hoping to open up a space for the consideration of individual usage within the larger context of contemporary urban experience.'

Notes

1 Andreas Huyssen, *Present Pasts: Urban Palimpsests and the Politics of Memory*, Stanford, CA: Stanford University Press, 2003, pp. 24, 32.
2 Mike Davis, 'Planet of Slums: Urban Involution and the Informal Proletariat', *New Left Review*, 26, March–April, 2004, pp. 13–14.
3 See Kerwin Lee Klein, 'On the Emergence of *Memory* in Historical Discourse', *Representations*, 69, Winter 2000, pp. 127–50.
4 Halbwachs, as quoted in Aldo Rossi, *The Architecture of the City*, Cambridge, MA: MIT Press, 1982, p. 130.
5 Christine Boyer, *The City of Collective Memory: Its Historical Imagery and Architectural Entertainments*, Cambridge, MA: MIT Press, 1996, pp. 2–4.
6 Ibid., p. 28.
7 Pierre Nora (ed.), *Realms of Memory: Rethinking the French Past*, trans. by Arthur Goldhammer, New York: Columbia University Press, 1996, vol. 1, p. 3.
8 Ibid., p. 1. Something of the same distinction runs through Marc Augé's concepts of 'anthropological place', a social space which bristles with meaningful monuments, and 'non-places', spaces essentially of passage where history is the spectacle of 'places of memory': Marc Augé, *Non-Places: Introduction to an Anthropology of Supermodernity*, London: Verso, 1995.
9 Nora, *Realms*, pp. 8–9.
10 I am thinking here, for instance, of the shifting of monumental fragments to make the building for the École des Beaux Arts in Paris, and the isolation of certain gates and towers in French colonial cities: see David Van Zanten, *Designing Paris: The Architecture of Duban, Labrouste, Duc, and Vaudoyer*, Cambridge, MA: MIT Press, 1989, pp. 71–83; and Gwendolyn Wright, *The Politics and Design of French Colonial Urbanism*, Chicago: University of Chicago Press, 1991, pp. 85–160.
11 Anthony Vidler, *The Architectural Uncanny: Essays in the Modern Unhomely*, Cambridge, MA: MIT Press, 1992, p. 177.
12 Ibid., p. 179.
13 Ibid., pp. 182–3.
14 See Boyer, *City*, p. 26.
15 See Richard Terdiman, *Present Past: Modernity and the Memory Crisis*, Ithaca, NY: Cornell University Press, 1993, p. vii.
16 Ibid., p. 37.
17 Marcel Proust, *Remembrance of Things Past*, vol. 3, trans. by C. K. Scott Moncrieff, Terence Kilmartin and Andreas Mayor, London: Penguin, 1981, pp. 899–900.
18 W. G. Sebald, *The Rings of Saturn*, London: Harvill, 1998, p. 125.
19 Ibid.
20 Ibid., pp. 177–8.
21 Ibid., p. 179.
22 Street-naming might also be mentioned here. See, for example, on how street names can create a mythology of Englishness or memorialise anti-colonial insurrection: S. Appleby, 'Crawley: A Space Mythology', *New Formations*, 11, 1990, pp. 19–44; and Zeynep Çelik, 'Colonial/Postcolonial Intersections: *Lieux de mémoire* in Algiers', *Third Text*, 49, Winter 1999–2000, p. 69.
23 Sigmund Freud, *The Standard Edition of the Complete Psychological Works of Sigmund Freud*, vol. XI (1910), London: Hogarth Press, 1957, pp. 16–17. As Freud tells us elsewhere, 'hysterics suffer mainly from reminiscences': Ibid., 2, p. 7.
24 See Stephen Kite, 'The Urban Landscape of Hyde Park: Adrian Stokes, Conrad and the *Topos* of Negation', *Art History*, 23:2, June 2000, pp. 205–32.

25 Quoted in Amit Chaudhuri, 'In the Waiting-Room of History', *London Review of Books*, 26: 12, 24 June 2004, p. 3.

26 See Graeme Gilloch, *Myth and Metropolis: Walter Benjamin and the City*, Cambridge: Polity, 1996, pp. 73–5.

27 Chaudhuri, 'Waiting-Room', p. 3.

28 On this older, late nineteenth-century discourse, see Matt K. Matsuda, *The Memory of the Modern*, New York and Oxford: Oxford University Press, 1996, pp. 9–10.

29 On Benjamin and memory, see particularly Gilloch, *Myth*; and Sigrid Weigel, *Body- and Image-Space*, London: Routledge, 1996.

30 Klein, 'On the Emergence', pp. 138–9.

31 *Guardian*, 28 February 2003.

32 The term is borrowed from Terdiman, *Present Past*, p. 16.

33 Gavriel D. Rosenfeld, *Munich and Memory: Architecture, Monuments, and the Legacy of the Third Reich*, Berkeley, CA: University of California Press, 2000, pp. 1–4.

34 Among a growing literature, see James Young, *The Texture of Memory: Holocaust Memorials and Meaning*, New Haven, CT: Yale University Press, 1993; Brian Ladd, *The Ghosts of Berlin: Confronting German History in the Urban Landscape*, Chicago: Chicago University Press, 1997; Mélanie Van Der Hoorn, 'Exorcizing Remains: Architectural Fragments as Intermediaries between History and Individual Experience', *Journal of Material Culture*, 8: 2, 2003, pp. 189–213.

35 Huyssen, *Present Pasts*, p. 77.

36 Vidler, *Architectural Uncanny*, p. 185.

37 Ibid., p. 185.

38 Ibid., p. 186.

Barun Raj
takes off his jacket and logs
onto his workstation at
H & H Computers,
F/14, Bima Nagar,
Sanatorium Lane,
Andheri East, Mumbai.

Chapter 1

Trauma and memory in the city

From Auster to Austerlitz

Graeme Gilloch and Jane Kilby

Homo Ferber

> Manchester has taken possession of me for good. I cannot leave.
> I do not want to leave. I must not.[1]

These puzzling words are spoken by the reclusive artist Max Ferber, the fourth
and last of the enigmatic figures portrayed in Winfried Georg Sebald's *The
Emigrants*. It is the autumn of 1966 and the narrator, 'Sebald', has recently
arrived in Manchester to take up a teaching post at the University. He seeks
to escape the tawdriness of his hotel room and the tedium of the British
Sunday by undertaking long, aimless walks across the bleak post-industrial
Mancunian cityscape. 'Sebald' wanders past empty soot-blackened buildings,
abandoned mills, deserted factories and warehouses, dreary streets on the
point of demolition, and desolate expanses awaiting redevelopment (Figure
1.1). Mid-1960s Manchester is half-ruin, half-building site. On one of these
perambulations, he chances upon Ferber's ramshackle studio, occupying a
derelict building somewhere amid the disused docklands near Trafford Park.
They become regular acquaintances – during the next three years 'Sebald'
meets with Ferber almost every week, either at his studio or at a nearby

The Emigrants

Max Ferber

stand around them or skip about, restless shadowy figures. On that bare terrain, which was like a glacis around the heart of the city, it was in fact always and only children that one encountered. They strayed in small groups, in gangs, or quite alone, as if they had nowhere that they could call home. I remember, for instance, late one November afternoon, when the white mist was already rising from the ground, coming across a little boy at a crossroads in the midst of the Angel Fields wasteland, with a Guy stuffed with old rags on a hand-cart: the only person out and about in the whole area, wanting a penny for his silent companion.

It was early the following year, if I remember correctly, that I ventured further out of the city, in a southwesterly direction, beyond St George and Ordsall, along the bank of the canal across which, from my window, I could see the Great Northern Railway Company depot. It was a bright, radiant day, and the water, a gleaming black in its embankment of massive masonry blocks, reflected the white clouds that scudded across the sky. It was so strangely silent that (as I now think I remember) I could hear sighs in the abandoned depots and warehouses, and was frightened to death when a number of seagulls, squawking stridently, all of a sudden flew

out of the shadow of one of the high buildings, into the light. I passed a long-disused gasworks, a coal depot, a bonemill, and what seemed the unending cast-iron palisade fence of the Ordsall slaughterhouse, a Gothic castle in liver-coloured brick, with parapets, battlements, and numerous turrets and gateways, the sight of which absurdly brought to my mind the name of Haeberlein & Metzger, the Nuremberg *Lebkuchen*

◇ 158 ◇

◇ 159 ◇

transport café, an improbable Anglo-African eatery 'which bore the vaguely familiar name of Wadi Halfa'.[2]

'Sebald' marvels at Ferber's eccentric artistic technique – brush in hand, he applies paint rapidly and thickly to the canvas, scratches it off, and then paints over once more. Armed with his charcoal sticks, Ferber launches himself into furious bouts of activity, producing a frenzy of lines and figures which are then either rapidly buried under more and more layers of frantic scribbling, or are smudged and blurred by the artist's blackened fingers. Little survives beyond the next morning when almost everything is wiped away with a 'woollen rag already heavy with charcoal'.[3] Ferber's Sisyphian work consists of repeated moments of energetic expression and almost instantaneous obliteration and erasure, such that at any particular point one is unclear as to whether one is witnessing the act of creation or an 'exercise in destruction'.[4] Consequently, the few images that do survive resemble pictorial palimpsests:

> He might reject as many as forty variants or smudge them back into the paper and overdraw new attempts upon them; and if he then decided the portrait was done, not so much because he was

1.1
Double page spread from W. G. Sebald, *The Emigrants*

convinced that it was finished as through sheer exhaustion, an onlooker might well feel that it had evolved from a long lineage of grey, ancestral faces, rendered into ash but still there, as ghostly presences, on the harried paper.[5]

But all this matters little to Ferber. He now understands that what appears on the paper or canvas is less significant than the by-products of his labours – the drips of paint that accumulate on the studio floor and congeal with the charcoal dust of innumerable sketches and erasures:

> This, said Ferber, was the true product of his continuing endeav-
> ours and the most palpable proof of his failure. It had always been
> of the greatest importance to him, Ferber once remarked casually,
> that nothing should change at his place of work, that everything
> should remain as it was, as he had arranged it, and that nothing
> further should be added but the debris generated by painting and
> the dust that continuously fell and which, as he was coming to
> realize, he loved more than anything else in the world.[6]

Ultimately, Ferber's pictures are only an excuse, an alibi for this other process, his real labour of love, the 'steady production of dust'.[7] 'Sebald' leaves England in 1969 but returns a year later to take up a post at the University of East Anglia. Ferber becomes an indistinct memory. In November 1989 'Sebald' spots a painting bearing Ferber's signature in the Tate Gallery and, shortly after, chances upon a Sunday colour supplement feature on the artist himself. Intrigued by the painting[8] and by the sparse biographical details provided by the magazine article – in 1939 the 15-year-old Friedrich Maximilian Ferber had been sent from Munich to England by his parents who were subsequently deported and murdered by the Nazis around 1941 – 'Sebald' returns to Manchester and revisits his old acquaintance. He arrives just as the rede-velopments of the 1970s are now themselves on the point of destruction: the concrete crescents of Hulme and elsewhere are about to be bulldozed and a new, post-post-industrial cityscape is to rise in its place:

> The buildings that had been put up to stave off the general decline
> were now themselves in the grip of decay, and even the so-called
> development zones, created in recent years on the fringes of the
> city centre and along the Ship Canal to revive the entrepreneurial
> spirit that so much was being made of, already looked semi-
> abandoned.[9]

The Wadi Halfa is no more but 'Sebald' finds Ferber at work in his old studio 'and as I crossed the threshold it was as if I had been there only yesterday'.[10] In the course of the next three days, Ferber relates his indistinct memories of his provincial German childhood and early youth in the 1930s. In marked contrast, he remembers, with an uncanny precision and sense of detail, as if it really *were* only yesterday, the 17th May 1939, his mother's fiftieth birthday and the day of his sorrowful departure from the Oberwiesenfeld airfield. Ferber presents 'Sebald' with his mother's handwritten memoirs, a manuscript which he has read twice but which has proven too painful for him. These memoirs form the basis of the second half of 'Sebald's' narrative as he presents an abridged version of the poignant story of Ferber's mother, Luisa Lanzberg, as a girl and young woman. But this is not enough for 'Sebald' – he feels compelled to return to southern Germany so as to follow up the traces of Ferber's long-dead family.

But let us stay with Max Ferber. When he finished school in Kent in the mid-1940s, Ferber came to Manchester in preference to moving with his Uncle Leo to New York. His reason for this decision was simple: he thought that Manchester, a city about which he knew next to nothing, where he knew no-one, where there were no associations or connections, this city would allow him to start a new life, without a past, without memories.[11] Manchester meant nothing to him and this was his hope. He soon realised his mistake: 'inexperienced as I was, I imagined I could begin a new life in Manchester, from scratch; but instead, Manchester reminded me of everything I was trying to forget'.[12] Ferber became another immigrant worker in a city of immigrant workers, another German-Jewish refugee moreover, in a city whose industrial past was imbued with Jewish and especially German-Jewish culture. He became another exile in a city of exiles. He came to Manchester 'to serve under the chimney' as Ferber puts it,[13] to labour unremittingly in a city whose industrial skyline of chimneys and smokestacks could not but call to mind the industrialisation of death in the extermination camps. The chimneys are now all gone, the 'primordial landscape' of production has vanished, but he remains amidst the now desolate cityscape, an urban environment whose degradation corresponds to his own enduring inner desolation and despair. He has now lived in Manchester for nearly fifty years: the city has gradually taken possession of him for good, has become his 'destiny'.[14] This is why he cannot, he must not, he does not want to leave it.

Ferber's artistic activity, his continual creation and obliteration of images, is extremely suggestive. It is analogous in the first instance to the continual processes of construction and demolition as cycles of urban renewal, for the city itself, too, is, of course, nothing other than a palimpsest of past and present forms. In the city, as in Ferber's pictures, the traces of what has been remain, former figures linger as ashen ghosts. And the charcoal dust which engrains Ferber's fingers and layers the floor of his studio, corresponds to the soot and grime that have coated the city's buildings and nestled in their crevices and niches. Both city and artist are indelibly marked by their years of toil. Indeed, Ferber's practices are a metaphor for his relationship with the city: it is an environment which, against his expectations, against his hopes, prompts the work of memory, calls to mind precisely that which he seeks so desperately to erase, the images in all their pristine clarity of the traumatic events which have brought him here. For Ferber, Manchester is the memory-free memory-filled city he is unable to leave because his identity is bound to this place.

In *The Emigrants*, and particularly in the figure of Ferber, Sebald presents and articulates the intricate and ephemeral constellations formed by memory, urban space, exile, and individual and collective loss, a complex of themes which have preoccupied a number of key writers on the modern metropolitan experience, especially real German-Jewish émigrés such as Walter Benjamin and Siegfried Kracauer. Benjamin's famous studies of Charles Baudelaire and Marcel Proust, in particular, foreground the manifold connections between urban life, memory and trauma, trauma understood here not as the experience of specific catastrophic events, but rather in a more general sense as the very condition of city-based existence, as 'shock'. 'Shock experience' [*Schockerlebnis*] is a key, if highly ambivalent, concept for Benjamin. It is characteristic of the *flâneur*, the aimless stroller in the city for whom the anonymity, alienation and amnesia engendered by the swirling metropolitan crowd and the overstimulation of the human sensory system bring both pain and pleasure. Shock experience is the very fragmentation of experience itself and the concomitant diminution of memory. Shock is also the signature experience of the new media and, in particular, film, a medium that eliminates the contemplation of auratic distance and challenges the cinema-goer with a new immediacy and dynamism. Shock accompanies the modern shattering of traditional cultural and aesthetic experiences, categories and notions of self. Shock experiences, be they cinematic, be they metropolitan – and for both Benjamin and Kracauer, the two are inextricably intertwined – leave scars in the human unconscious which are the source of our most enduring and profound reminiscences. Benjamin notes in his semi-autobiographical reflections on Berlin: 'It is to this immolation of our deepest self in shock that our memory owes its most indelible images'.[15] The *flâneur* is transformed here into a figure of remembrance, one for whom the cityscape itself acts as a stimulus for memory, as a 'mnemonic' device. The places, edifices and signs composing the urban environment are saturated with earlier associations and these act as a series of prompts to the present-day, perambulating pedestrian. Shock is not merely the cause of urban forgetfulness, but rather is the response to moments of sudden, unexpected recognition, the very jolts given to us by memory itself.

Siegfied Kracauer's highly suggestive 1932 essay 'Street without Memory' presents precisely such a momentary jolt, one which sets in train a series of musings on the relationship between memory, obliteration and the changing face of the cityscape, on what one might term the 'dialectics of disappearance'. Before catching a train, Kracauer pops into one of his favourite cafés – rather different from the Wadi Halfa one suspects – on the Kurfürstendamm, one of Berlin's main shopping streets, only to discover with surprise that this establishment has gone. Kracauer must make do with another bar, one that proves far too garish for his taste. A year or so later, Kracauer is suddenly struck by the disappearance of this second café – a sign left in the window informs passers-by that the space is now to rent. He reflects upon this seemingly banal, commonplace experience of urban transformation:

> Elsewhere, the past clings to the places where it resided during its lifetime; on the Kurfürstendamm it departs without leaving so much as a trace. Since I have known it, it has changed fundamentally again and again in no time at all. The new businesses are always brand new and those they expel are always wholly obliterated.[16]

On the Kurfürstendamm – and it is not insignificant that this is a locus of consumption, fashion and leisure – the new eradicates the old seemingly without residue, and it does so with greater rapidity. For Kracauer, the fate of the cafés thus brings into focus distinctive features of our experience of the modern cityscape: how 'Perpetual change erases memory';[17] how the endless quest for novelty merges into the flow of undifferentiated, empty time; how the past is consigned to oblivion by the present, and, perhaps most importantly, how it may fleetingly reappear as an irruption that disturbs, gives a shock to, today's passer-by. There both is, and is not, a palimpsest of forms in this sense. The trace – that which remains in the present – is not architectural, it is not in the city as such; rather, it is in Kracauer's memory of this space. And it is ironically precisely the act of obliteration – the present absence of the former cafés – that brings them so vividly to mind. Demolition, erasure, brings with it a sudden appreciation of what is no longer there. The void is also a mnemonic. The Kurfürstendamm may well be without memories, but Kracauer is most certainly not.

Ferber is no *flâneur*, however – it is Sebald whose urban odysseys lead him to traverse the bleak Mancunian cityscape, one on the point of demolition, one about to vanish irrevocably, one offering itself to the gaze of the *flâneur* 'at the moment of ceasing to be'[18] as Benjamin puts it, at 'last sight'. There is another figure in Benjamin who does correspond to the enigmatic artist: one who waits patiently and faithfully for the long-lost wanderer's eventual return and who fills the intervening hours and days with interminable labours: Penelope, wife of Odysseus, the weaver who at night unravels the threads on which she has worked during the day. Sebald draws on this image too: in *The Rings of Saturn* (1998), he recalls a visit to a house in Ireland occupied by the eccentric Ashbury family – a suggestive name in itself – and observes how the three daughters, Catherine, Clarissa and Christina, spend their days at home engaged in sewing and dressmaking even though they had long abandoned any pretence to earn a living through clothes-making. Indeed, so dissatisfied are they with most of the products of their handicraft, 'they mostly undid what they had sewn either on the same day, the next day or the day after that'.[19]

Significantly, Benjamin invokes the figure of Penelope in his 1929 essay on Proust as part of his consideration of the *mémoire involontaire*, the sudden, fortuitous, fleeting remembrance of the forgotten past occasioned by some contingency, some chanced-upon correspondence in the present:

> the important thing for the remembering author is not what he experienced, but the weaving of his memory, the Penelope work of recollection. Or should one call it, rather, a Penelope work of forgetting? Is not the involuntary recollection, Proust's *mémoire involontaire*, much closer to forgetting than what is usually called memory? And is not this work of spontaneous recollection, in which remembrance is the woof and forgetting is the warf, a counterpart to Penelope's work rather than its likeness? For here the day unravels what the night has woven.[20]

This fabrication of memory, the continual ravelling and unravelling of threads, not only accords with the repeated production and erasure of images practised by Ferber, but also with Sebald's own literary technique. The long, flowing sentences and multiple clauses of Sebald's texts suggest a seam-lessness and continuity at odds with the fragmentary patchwork of stories and memories that he stitches together. This disparity itself is characteristic of Proust in which labyrinthine sentences belie the fleeting thoughts that set them in train. But the contradiction, such as it is, is only superficial: 'Sebald' describes his own writing as the remains of a restless frustration with his powers of expression. Committing Ferber's story to paper in the winter of 1990–1,

> was an arduous task. Often I could not get on for hours or days at a time, and not infrequently I unravelled what I had done, continuously tormented by scruples that were taking tighter hold and steadily paralysing me. These scruples concerned not only the subject of my narrative, which I felt I could not do justice to, no matter what approach I tried, but also the entire questionable business of writing. I had covered hundreds of pages with my scribble, in pencil and ballpoint. By far the greater part had been

crossed out, discarded, or obliterated by additions. Even what I ultimately salvaged as a 'final' version seemed to me a thing of shreds and patches, utterly botched.[21]

It is, of course, precisely in this 'botchedness' that Sebald's text remains true to its subject. Sebald presents us with his own palimpsest – his shreds and patches are textual counterparts to Ferber's precious dust.

From the New World

Chance and the contingencies of memory; walking in the city as both remembrance and amnesia; the instability and fragility of the self in the face of catastrophe and loss; the quest for anonymity and seclusion; the practice of writing and the complexities and sensitivities posed by traumatic narratives – these preoccupations of Sebald find a New York echo in the work of Paul Auster. Both writers focus less on how the city itself constitutes a site of shock, and more on how traumatic experiences are lived through in urban space, how misfortune leads to a life out of place, out of time, an 'extraterritorial' life haunted by shadows and ghosts. In Auster this takes both fictional and autobiographical form. The semi-autobiographical reflections and musings of *The Invention of Solitude* (1982) are prompted by the death of his father and the ensuing collapse of Auster's marriage. Personal bereavement and loss also act as the fundamental points of departure for the characters which people Auster's novels: in *The Music of Chance* (1990), for example, Nashe hits the road and seeks oblivion behind the wheel after his father dies and his wife walks out on him; *The Book of Illusions* (2002) opens with David Zimmer lost in a self-destructive drinking binge following the death of his wife and two sons in a plane crash; Anna Blume arrives *In the Country of Last Things* (1987), in a post-apocalyptic New York, to search for her brother William who has vanished; and the first page of *City of Glass* (1988), the initial part of Auster's *New York Trilogy* (1988), informs us that Daniel Quinn's wife and son have died.

For Quinn, the author of trashy detective stories, New York has become a site of oblivion, of an amnesia which enables him to engage in the joyless, mechanistic process of putting words on paper. Quinn can write only 'by flooding himself with externals, by drowning himself out of himself'.[22] To erase his memory and eradicate himself, he becomes a metropolitan *flâneur*:

> New York was an inexhaustible space, a labyrinth of steps and no matter how far he walked, no matter how well he came to know its neighbourhoods and streets, it always left him with the feeling of being lost. Lost not only in the city, but within himself as well. Each

time he took a walk, he felt as though he were leaving himself
behind, and by giving himself up to the movement of the streets,
by reducing himself to a seeing eye, he was able to escape the
obligation to think, and this, more than anything else, brought him
a measure of peace, a salutary emptiness within . . . By wandering
aimlessly, all places became equal and it no longer mattered where
he was. On his best walks, he was able to feel that he was nowhere.
And this, finally, was all he ever asked of things: to be nowhere.
New York was the nowhere he had built around himself, and he
realized that he had no intention of ever leaving it again.[23]

Quinn can no more leave New York than Ferber can leave Manchester. Nor
can Anna Blume escape the nightmarish cityscape that New York has become.
While Quinn seeks to obliterate the memories of the past which torture him,
Blume's narrative is testimony to how an imaginary, catastrophic future comes
to destroy the very possibilities of remembrance. As she makes her painful
way, 'one step at a time'[24] around the dystopian urban environment – a city
that is falling apart, collapsing into dust – she becomes the unsentimental
witness to the last things.

Blume's thoughts and memories – of her lost brother and of the
person she has left behind and for whom she writes – are all she has left to
hold on to, even though they slow her down in a city where speed is of the
essence. And this applies to writing too. In the country of last things, words
crumble into dust along with the cityscape in which they once had meaning:

Everyone is prone to forgetfulness, even under the most favourable
conditions, and in a place like this, with so much actually disap-
pearing from the physical world, you can imagine how many things
are forgotten all the time. In the end, the problem is not so much
that people forget, but they do not always forget the same thing.
What still exists as a memory for one person can be irretrievably
lost for another, and this creates difficulties, insuperable barriers
against understanding. How can you talk to someone about air-
planes, for example, if that person doesn't know what an airplane
is? It is a slow but ineluctable process of erasure. Words tend to last
a bit longer than things but, eventually they fade too, along with
the pictures they once evoked.[25]

Blume's narrative is written in an already archaic language. As witness to the
last things, she is their historian. Hers are the last words.

This notion of bearing witness amid traumatic circumstances, of
the unfolding of individual memory as history rather than just (auto)biog-
raphy, is central to *The Book of Memory*, the second part of *The Invention of*

Solitude. Here, paradoxically, a particular kind of amnesia becomes the precondition for genuine remembrance:

> Memory, then, not so much as the past contained within us, but as proof of our life in the present. If a man is to be truly present among his surroundings, he must be thinking not of himself, but of what he sees. He must forget himself in order to be there. And from that forgetfulness arises the power of memory. It is a way of living one's life so that nothing is ever lost.[26]

This shift from a self-preoccupied inwardness to an acute sensitivity to the external world and attentiveness to the words of the other are characteristic of both Sebald and Auster. For these writers, the self, the author, is destabilised, dispersed and disavowed through a number of shared techniques: the intricate interlacing of autobiographical reflections, biographical accounts and historical anecdotes; the endless transgressions of the boundaries between the fictional and the 'real'; the complex fluctuation between narratives and narrators such that one is frequently led to question: who is it that is now speaking? who is this 'I'?[27] For Auster, the practice of *flânerie* promises the dissolution of the autonomous, bounded subject and this in turn brings a heightened sensitivity to the contingency of the city and the circulation of memories. Auster discovers this not in his beloved New York but rather in Old Amsterdam:

> All during the three days he spent in Amsterdam, he was lost. The plan of the city is circular (a series of concentric circles, bissected by canals, a cross-hatch of hundreds of tiny bridges, each one connecting to another, and then another as though endlessly), and you cannot simply 'follow' a street as you can in other cities. To get somewhere you have to know in advance where you are going. A. did not, since he was a stranger and moreover found himself curiously reluctant to consult a map. For three days it rained, and for three days he wandered around in circles . . . He wandered. He walked around in circles. He allowed himself to be lost . . . It occurred to him that perhaps he was wandering in the circles of hell, that the city had been designed as a model of the underworld, based on some classical representations of the place. Then he remembered that various diagrams of hell had been used as memory systems by some of the sixteenth century writers on the subject . . . And if Amsterdam was hell, and if hell was memory, then he realized that perhaps there was some purpose to his being lost. Cut off from everything that was familiar to him, unable to discover even a single point of reference, he saw that his steps, by

> taking him nowhere, were taking him nowhere but into himself. He
> was wandering inside himself, and he was lost. Far from troubling
> him, this state of being lost became a source of happiness, of
> exhilaration. He breathed it into his very bones. As if on the brink
> of some previously hidden knowledge, he breathed it into his very
> bones and said to himself, almost triumphantly: I am lost.[28]

Auster's triumph here is not that of a self-indulgent narcissism but rather
a realisation that in losing ourselves we discover the world and in it the
presence of others:

> even alone, in the deepest solitude . . . he was not alone, or, more
> precisely, that the moment he began to try to speak of that soli-
> tude, he had become more than himself. Memory, therefore, not
> simply as the resurrection of one's private past, but an immersion
> in the past of others, which is to say: history one both participates
> in and is a witness to, is a part of and apart from.[29]

And in the cities of post-war Europe this history, in which one is cast as
participant and witness, is the catastrophe of the Holocaust and the post-
Holocaust world. To this end, Auster, to his surprise, but not ours, finds his
way to Anne Frank's house. Referring to himself in the third person (as other),
Auster recalls:

> He stood in [her] room, the room in which the diary was written,
> now bare, with the faded pictures of Hollywood movie stars she
> collected still pasted to the walls, he suddenly found himself cry-
> ing. Not sobbing, as might happen in response to a deep inner pain,
> but crying without sound, the tears streaming down his cheeks, as
> if purely in response to the world. It was at that moment, he later
> realised, that the Book of Memory began.[30]

At this point, Auster is compelled to bear responsibility for the memory of
Anne Frank among others. The fact that he encounters Anne Frank motivated
by little more than a curious whim and the memories this sets in train, might
render him a tourist of history, but this does not, altogether, distract from
the significance of his discovery, for it is a discovery foretold: childhood,
seclusion, traumatic history, the act of witness and the practice of writing – all
these come together in this figure.

There are other maps to the city of Amsterdam, among them Albert
Camus's novel *The Fall* (1956). Camus's narrator also figures the concentric
canals of Amsterdam as an allegory for hell, and as such, is also concerned
with the problem of finding one's historical bearings in a post-Holocaust
Europe. Once again, the canals of Amsterdam are not merely an allegory for

the hell of remembering, but also require the remembering of a hell by virtue of the fact that they circumnavigate the pre-war Jewish Quarter, a centre that was systematically destroyed during the Occupation. For Shoshana Felman and other Holocaust scholars, more generally, finding one's way in contemporary politics and ethics requires an encounter with 'actual history', a history that stands at the centre of Amsterdam and Europe. To this end, the geometrical/geographical/literary/allegorical allusion to the circularity of Hell in Dante also makes reference to the historical erasure of the Jewish population of Amsterdam. As Felman points out, this reference to the task of remembering a hell (on earth) is itself easily missed by the reader of *The Fall* since it appears in the narrative 'to be itself disorientingly peripheral', mentioned in passing at the beginning of the novel when the narrator, who had just met his interlocutor in a bar, offers to show his companion the way back to his hotel:

> 'Your way back? . . . Well . . . the easiest thing would be for me to accompany you as far as the harbor. Thence, by going around the Jewish quarter you'll find those fine avenues with their parade of streetcars full of flowers . . . Your hotel is on them.
> *'I live in the Jewish quarter or what was called so* until our Hitlerian brethren made room. What a cleanup! Seventy-five thousand Jews deported or assassinated; that's real vacuum cleaning. I admire that diligence, that methodical patience. When one *has* no character one has to apply a method.'[31]

Whether by accident or design, the canals of Amsterdam make it easy to wander around in circles and thereby avoid the centre (of European history), a risk clearly run by Auster who could have so easily missed Anne Frank's house – or so he would have us believe. Felman contends that for Camus and his narrator in *The Fall*:

> we might choose to bypass certain quarters of our history . . . And yet the way back home passes through that one place – that one hell – we want most of anything to avoid: the Jewish quarter. Ultimately, then, the question becomes what does it mean to inhabit the exterminated Jewish quarter of Amsterdam (of Europe).[32]

Waiting rooms

What does it mean, then, to find one's way in a post-Holocaust Europe? This is the question and predicament that Sebald grapples with in *Austerlitz*. His last novel is precisely the story of how finding one's way back home requires passing through hell – the hell of surviving the exile and trauma resulting from the Holocaust. Jacques Austerlitz is the melancholy figure who strives to retrace his steps. In many respects, Ferber is the prototype of Austerlitz: Austerlitz, too, is a Jewish émigré, reluctant to know his past, immersing himself instead in the obsessive activity of his work. Austerlitz, however, is not an artist bent on the constant erasure of his images but rather an architectural historian, whose immediate task is to preserve the details of history against disappearance. Significantly, then, Austerlitz is a writer preoccupied with the past, his work being to archive the urban landscape, to document the physical details of the European city, both monumental and incidental. Unlike Ferber, who cannot bear to leave Manchester, Austerlitz never stops travelling, criss-crossing Europe with a precise and vigilant eye for the minutiae of the past. He absorbs history, drinking it in, committing to memory untold detail. Meticulously documenting everything that he sees, constantly taking photographs, he misses nothing. And so it is a bitter irony that he refuses any knowledge of the Holocaust and the impact it has had on European history, his own history included:

> Inconceivable as it seems to me today, I knew nothing about the conquest of Europe by the Germans and the slave state they set, nothing about the persecution I escaped . . . As far as I was concerned the world ended in the late nineteenth century. I dared go no further than that, although in fact the whole of history of the architecture and civilisation of the bourgeois age, the subject of my research, pointed in the direction of the catastrophic events already casting their shadows before them in time.[33]

Austerlitz wilfully blots all this out – 'I was clearly capable of closing my eyes and ears to it' – and allows the accumulation of nineteenth-century detail to function as 'a substitute or compensatory memory'.[34]

Austerlitz functions in a state of unknowing and as such is clearly distinguished from Auster, who seeks to be lost. Auster somewhat disingenuously stumbles upon the sites of past catastrophe and is moved to tears by them; Austerlitz himself is the bearer of this very catastrophe. Traumatised by his forced exile from Prague at the age of four, when his mother had secured a place for him on a *Kindertransport*, he has no memory of his life as a child and no knowledge of the Holocaust. Growing up as an orphaned child in the bleak and dour landscape of Bala in Wales, under the name of Dafydd Elias, Austerlitz is unable to access his past and remains oblivious to his own history. 'Since my childhood and youth', Austerlitz muses,

> I have never fully known who I am. From where I stand now, of course, I can see that my name alone, and the fact that it was kept

from me until my fifteenth year, ought to have put me on the track of my origins, but it has also become clear to me of late why an agency greater than me or superior to my own capacity for thought, which circumspectly, directs operations somewhere in my brain, has preserved me from my own secret, systematically preventing me from drawing the obvious conclusions and embarking on the inquiries they would have suggested to me. It hasn't been easy to make my way out of my own inhibitions, and it will not be easy now to put my story into anything like an order.[35]

Austerlitz's amnesia paradoxically enables him to embark upon, but never realise, a history of European architecture, one that makes no reference to the rise of Nazism and the impact it had on his childhood. This act of omission is made all the more peculiar, moreover, because he has a particular fascination with the architecture of railway stations, which are perhaps the ur-symbol of the Holocaust, of what made the mass deportations and annihilations possible. But Austerlitz's fascination is a myopic one. He does not, cannot, will not see that the waiting rooms of the European railway stations served to deliver a people to their exile and death, even though professionally he links railway stations to death and insanity: he discovers that Broad Street Station was built on burial grounds and Liverpool Street Station on the grounds of what used to be Bedlam. Without the knowledge of his own past, Austerlitz is thus unable to see the symbolic significance of this genealogy, where the foundations of modernity and the possibility of progress lie in the systematic destruction of life. It is as if he has walked away from his past without memory and without psychic injury. With regard to his exile and the Holocaust, Austerlitz is and draws a blank. In order to contemplate his project, he has had to forget himself, his family and his people.

If the genealogical significance of the modern railway system escapes Austerlitz, it did not, however, escape Freud, whose attempt to understand the void left by trauma turns on an insight related to railways:

It may happen that someone gets away unharmed, from the spot where he has suffered a shocking accident, for instance a train collision. In the course of the following weeks, however, he develops a series of grave psychical and motor symptoms, which can be ascribed only to his shock or whatever else happened at the time of the accident. He has developed a 'traumatic neurosis'. This appears quite incomprehensible and therefore is a novel fact. The time that elapsed between the accident and the first appearance of the symptoms is called the 'incubation period', a transparent allusion to the pathology of an infectious disease . . . It is the feature one might term latency.[36]

If the railway accident of the nineteenth century provided us with the modern meaning of trauma, the Nazi use of the railway system has taken our understanding of accident and trauma to the limit. In the letter, though, it was the very efficiency of the rail network – and not its breakdown or failure – that engendered mass death and trauma. For Austerlitz, the efficiency of the railway system in the form of the *Kindertransport* meant a double escape – both in mind and body – but at a deep cost:

> It was as if an illness that had been latent in me for a long time were now threatening to erupt, as if some soul-destroying and inexorable force had fastened upon me and would gradually paralyse my entire system. I already felt in my head the dreadful torpor that heralds disintegration of the personality, I sensed that in truth I had neither memory nor the power of thought, nor even my existence, that all my life had been a constant process of obliteration, *a turning away from myself and the world.*[37]

Trauma scholars such as Cathy Caruth, Shoshana Felman and Dominick LaCapra have extended Freud's initial insight in their attempts to conceptualise the Holocaust and its impact. To this end, latency (the idea of delay) replaces repression (the idea of wish-fulfilment and the Oedipal complex) in the conceptual economy of traumatic memory. As a consequence, then,

> pathology cannot be defined by either the event itself – which may or may not be catastrophic, and may not traumatise everyone equally – nor can it be defined in terms of a distortion of the event, achieving its haunting power as a result of distorting personal significances attached to it. The pathology consists, rather, solely, in the *structure of its experience*, or reception: the event is not assimilated or experienced fully at the time, but only belatedly.[38]

Importantly, as Caruth makes plain, this means that the very possibility of knowing traumatic history becomes a function of future recognition, it is only ever known in connection with another time and space. History is bound to turn up later, no matter how successfully the Nazis tried to clean up. Traces will always remain. Debris will always be found.

Significantly, then, Austerlitz's memory is triggered by a visit to Liverpool Street station. Having destroyed all of his work – doubting, like Ferber, that he has captured the essence of what he sees; frustrated, like Sebald, at the failure of his writing – Austerlitz is overcome by an ensuing panic. Unable to sleep at night, he takes to wandering the streets of London, invariably finding himself drawn, as dawn gathers, to Liverpool Street station. He recalls how, sitting in the station, he 'felt at this time as if the dead were returning from their exile and filling the twilight around [him] with their strangely slow but incessant to-ing and fro-ing'.[39] With the line between the dead and the living increasingly blurred, Austerlitz is attracted by the activity of a shabbily dressed porter cleaning the concourse in an especially laborious fashion. Following the porter for no apparent reason ('To this day I cannot explain what made me follow him'),[40] Austerlitz finds his way into the former ladies' waiting-room, 'the existence of which, in this remote part of the station, had been quite unknown to me'.[41] Hidden behind scaffolding and about to be demolished, the waiting-room is part of the old station, with an architecture and interior design belonging to an earlier time, one of those anachronistic edifices that, as Louis Aragon puts it, 'were incomprehensible yesterday, and that tomorrow will never know'.[42] Utterly entranced by his discovery, Austerlitz finds 'scraps of memory' drifting

> through the outlying regions of [his] mind . . . In fact I felt, said Austerlitz, that the waiting-room where I stood as if dazzled contained all the hours of my past life, all the suppressed and extinguished fears and wishes I had entertained.[43]

And finally it is in this enraptured state that Austerlitz sees himself as a boy of five waiting to be picked up by the two strangers who would become his adoptive parents. Here, then, Austerlitz begins to remember and it is an excruciating experience: he finds himself sent mad as memories are restored to him. Time and again, he has to recover himself in order to discover himself. Relying on his skills as a historian he does, however, slowly piece his past life together, tracing his early life in Prague – whence he returns and meets his former nursemaid. He learns the fate of his mother, who perished in Theresienstadt, and painstakingly, hopefully, hopelessly seeks the image of her face in the surviving documentary film footage of this hellish urban concentration camp.

Sebald's *Austerlitz* is a profound meditation on memory and the need for historical knowledge, which culminates in the description of the new Bibliothèque Nationale in Paris. Desperately trying to trace the fate of his father, Austerlitz visits this new library in the hope of discovering precisely where his father disappeared. Unlike the old Bibliothèque Nationale in the rue Richelieu – where, in the course of his former architectural researches, Austerlitz had made himself very much at home – the new Bibliothèque Nationale, situated near the old marshalling yards of the Gare d'Austerlitz, is distinctly forbidding: 'unwelcoming if not inimical to human beings, and runs counter, on principle, one might say to the requirements of any true reader'.[44] Everything about the architecture and the logic of the library appears absurd, and must have been devised 'on purpose to instil a sense of insecurity and humiliation in the poor readers'.[45] As a consequence, Austerlitz finds the library hopeless:

At any rate, as far as I myself was concerned, a man who, after all, had devoted almost the whole of his life to the study of books and who had been equally at home in the Bodleian, the British Museum and the rue Richelieu, I for my part, said Austerlitz, found this gigantic new library, which according to one of the loathsome phrases now current is supposed to serve as the treasure-house of our entire literary heritage proved useless in my search for any traces of my father who had disappeared from Paris more than fifty years ago.[46]

Tormented and anguished by his failure, Austerlitz is approached by one of the library staff, Henri Lemoine, who confesses that he also finds the library ludicrous and infuriating, as if 'the official manifestation of the increasingly importunate urge to break with everything which still has some living connection to the past'.[47] Following their chance meeting and a casual remark by Austerlitz, the librarian takes him to the 18th floor where they can see the entire urban spread of Paris. But the experience, in keeping with the interior logic of the library, is unsettling:

We were standing only a foot behind the glass panels which reach all the way to the ground. As soon as you looked down . . . the pull exerted by the abyss below took hold of you forcing you to step back. Sometimes, so Lemoine told me, said Austerlitz, he felt the current of time streaming round his temples and brow when he was up here, but perhaps, he added, that is only a reflex of the awareness formed in my mind over the years of the various layers which had been superimposed on each other to form the carapace of the city. Thus, on the waste land between the marshalling yard of the Gare d'Austerlitz and the Pont Tolbiac where this Babylonian library now rises, there stood until the end of the war an extensive warehouse complex to which the Germans brought all the loot they had taken from the homes of the Jews of Paris.[48]

Austerlitz's search for his past ends here at the top of this 'Babylonian library', perched high above the site where so many cultural treasures were once amassed, meticulously examined and catalogued by art historians and experts, and then carefully packed for their journey east to the collections of eminent Nazis, an impressive cargo indeed in comparison to the impoverished children who had made their uncomfortable and uncertain train ride in the opposite direction a few years earlier. Austerlitz, then, is left with no satisfactory conclusion, no comfortable destination, no safe haven. The past – and the knowledge we build of it or on it – will always pull us into its vortex and the visions it offers will always repel us, reminding us that remembering the past is a demanding, necessary, endless, tortuous task. Memory provides neither a simple nor a guaranteed passport to our history.

Terminus

Memories can attach themselves to anything, they are not subject to the exercise of will, are not to be bounded and contained, are not to be circumscribed, prescribed or proscribed, encouraged or erased. It is precisely when memories seem most endangered that they present themselves most profoundly and powerfully to us. Perhaps this is why the issue of urban memory seems so acute in the context of the post-industrial city. We fear we are in the city of last things, but we must remember, too, that it is only 'at last sight' that they speak most eloquently to us. The old warehouses in Paris are gone and a pristine, glistening monument to western culture and civilisation now occupies the space. For the reader of Sebald, however, this imposing new edifice can now only ever call to mind what it has replaced, what is no more. Memories, individual, collective, may remain blurred, disfigured like Ferber's drawings, but this is to miss the point. In the dialectics of demolition, there will always be the debris, the loose threads, the drips, the dust – these are the remains of last things, these are what we must come to love most of all, these are the stuff of which memories are made.

Notes

1 W. G. Sebald, *The Emigrants*, London: Harvill, 1997, p. 169.
2 Ibid., p. 162.
3 Ibid.
4 Ibid., p. 180.
5 Ibid., p. 162.
6 Ibid., p. 161.
7 Ibid., p. 162.
8 The improbable title of this painting – *G. I. on her Blue Candlewick Cover* – is a double joke. First, when 'Sebald' initially arrives at the Arosa Hotel in Manchester, his landlady Mrs Gracie Irlam (G.I.) is clad in a dressing gown of pink 'candlewick', a material whose strange nomenclature he finds rather puzzling. Second, his visit to the Tate in 1989 was with the intention of seeing Paul Delvaux's *Sleeping Venus*, an interesting contrast to the Mancunian landlady.
9 Ibid.
10 Ibid., p. 179.
11 'I did not want to be reminded of my origins by anything or anyone,' Ferber explains. Ibid., p. 191.
12 Ibid.
13 Ibid., p. 192.
14 Ibid., p. 169.
15 Walter Benjamin, *One Way Street and Other Writings*, London: Verso, 1985, p. 343.
16 Siegfried Kracauer, *Strassen in Berlin und Anderswo*, Berlin: Das Arsenal Verlag, 1987, p. 17.
17 Ibid.
18 Walter Benjamin, *The Arcades Project*, Cambridge, MA: Harvard University Press, 1999, p. 833.
19 W.G. Sebald, *Rings of Saturn*, London: Harvill Press, 1998, p. 212.
20 Walter Benjamin, *Illuminations*, London: Collins, 1973, p. 204.
21 Sebald, *Emigrants*, pp. 230–1.

22 Paul Auster, *New York Trilogy*, London: Faber and Faber, 1988, p. 61.

23 Ibid., pp. 3–4.

24 Paul Auster, *In the Country of Last Things*, London: Faber and Faber, 1987, p. 5.

25 Ibid., pp. 88–9.

26 Paul Auster, *The Invention of Solitude*, London: Faber and Faber, 1982, p. 138.

27 Commenting on *The Invention of Solitude*, Auster observes, 'I don't think of it as an autobiography so much as a meditation about certain questions, using myself as the central character': *Hand to Mouth: A Chronicle of Early Failure*, London: Faber and Faber, 1998, p. 276. He goes on to explain his eschewal of the first person singular in the text:

> In order to write about myself, I had to treat myself as though I were someone else. It was only when I started all over again in the third person that I began to see my way out of the impasse . . . In the process of writing or thinking about yourself, you actually become someone else.
>
> (Ibid., p. 277)

It is only in his fiction that Auster allows himself the first person singular.

28 Auster, *Invention of Solitude*, pp. 85–7.

29 Ibid., p. 139. Here, then, Auster confirms the insight of Tztvetan Todorov when he asserts that, 'The other remains to be discovered . . . [a fact] worthy of astonishment, for man is never alone, and would not be what he is without his social dimension': cited in Howard Marchitello (ed.), *What Happens to History: The Renewal of Ethics in Contemporary Thought*, London and New York: Routledge, 2001, p. 123. This, of course, is also a historical dimension.

30 Auster, *Invention of Solitude*, pp. 82–3.

31 Quoted in Shoshona Felman and Dori Laub, *Testimony: Crises of Witnessing in Literature, Psychoanalysis and History*, London and New York: Routledge, 1992, p. 188.

32 Ibid., p. 189.

33 W. G. Sebald, *Austerlitz*, London: Penguin Books, 2001, p. 197.

34 Ibid, p. 198.

35 Ibid, pp. 60–6.

36 Freud cited in Cathy Caruth (ed.), *Trauma: Explorations in Memory*, Baltimore, MD: Johns Hopkins University Press, 1995, p. 4. Ian Hacking also notes:

> The railroad is . . . an epic symbol of the psychologization of the trauma . . . The railroad created the [modern nineteenth-century] accident. Cuttings caved in, boilers exploded, and trains went off the rails. There was not just a wholly new kind of accident, the railway accident. The railroad fixed the very idea of an accident with its modern meaning. The word has always meant, among other things, something that happens by chance or is uncaused. . . . But our present specific meaning – something sudden, bad, harmful and destructive – derives almost entirely from the railway accident.
>
> (Ian Hacking, *Rewriting the Soul: Multiple Personality Disorder and the Sciences of Memory*, Princeton, NJ: Princeton University Press 1995, p. 185)

37 Sebald, *Austerlitz*, p. 174.

38 Caruth, *Trauma*, p. 4.

39 Sebald, *Austerlitz*, p. 188.

40 Ibid., p. 189.

41 Ibid.

42 Louis Aragon, *Paris Peasant*, London: Picador, 1987, p. 29.

43 Sebald, *Austerlitz*, pp. 192–3.

44 Ibid., p. 386.

45 Ibid., p. 389.

46 Ibid., p. 393.

47 Ibid., p. 398.

48 Ibid., pp. 400–1.

Diego Gaston,
the loss adjuster
who works on the top floor of
the headquarters of Mexico's
largest cement manufacturer
in San Pedro Garza Garcia,
rubs his aching eyes.

Chapter 2

Urban memory / suburban oblivion

Claire Pajaczkowska

Every memory has a mother hidden within its folds, and it is this state of being hidden that characterises the nature of forgetting and loss. The 'unremembered maternal' as a precondition for representation in art, as a form of unacknowledged work in urban space, and as the suburban 'other' of urban memory, is the subject of this chapter. It is an explanation of what it means to forget, and how it feels to be forgotten. To explain is, etymologically speaking, to unfold (*ex planere*). I have, in this chapter, explained the obvious, and yet the surface of this text, in its process of explaining and unfolding, remains concealed, hidden and inexplicit.

In other words, this chapter explores the dysfunctional amnesia that impedes recognition of the links between subjective and historical realities. My hypothesis is that the consciousness and memories of difficult and shameful experiences are avoided or repressed and the ensuing gaps in the continuity of thought are filled in with ideas, images and thoughts that are altogether more pleasant, less doubtful and more certain. The dialectic of contradiction between the hidden and visible thoughts is a dynamic requiring active maintenance, a dynamic which takes up energy that might otherwise be available for transforming and making history. This hypothesis is an application of Freud's early theory of memory, to which I then bring the concepts of narcissism, cathexis,[1] and thoughts on the relationship between ideas and emotions, public and private representation, urban and suburban memory.

Using structuralist concepts of culture, particularly the idea that representational worlds function through structures of antinomic conceptualisation, I discuss some of the 'structuring absences' that generate patterns of textuality, where texts are the fabric of collective memory, or history.[2] This enables us to consider historical and spatial experience as textual experience, and I give examples of this connection by discussing three texts, one a site-specific installation by Lubaina Himid, the second, a brick wall that was built in Deptford, and the third, W.G. Sebald's novel *Austerlitz*. These three texts of art, architecture and literature are each analysed as memorial metatexts, which indicate the relation between subjective and collective remembering. Himid and Sebald explicitly reveal the process by which painful realities become forgotten and voided from history. Himid's art uses the textual idiom of painting to recollect the fragments that indicate the integral part played by slavery in the economic history of industrial Manchester, and culture's use of art to clothe that history. She considers her presence in the here and now in relation to the absence of representations of the labour of black women slaves in 'the archive'. This reconnection of links that are needed to give meaning to her presence as an artist are links that she asks her spectators to make in considering the relationship between the component parts of her installation. The metaphor of archaeology as a practice of uncovering and disinterring is related to Himid's techniques as a painter, particularly in the use she makes of scratching paint to uncover hidden surfaces and material. The disinterring of the textual is the process I shall use in order to consider the links between the moods of urban and suburban consciousness. Sebald's writing is an exploration of the experience of forgetting and the uncovering of repressed memories, as this process is materialised in language and speech. The novel is a powerful testament to the fact that meaning depends on relationship, and that the emotional void left by repression of painful emotion is the active cause of dysfunctional memory. Sebald's novel gives a sophisticated account of the interaction of political and personal dynamics of memory, and shows how these are played out across the urban landscapes of Europe. Sebald's writing produces, for his readers, the feeling of being known, which the author then extends into a shared knowledge of the unthinkable pain of subjective experiences of lives destroyed by the Holocaust. The textual and narrative structure rests on the presence of a narrator who absents himself from dramatic presence in order to be a medium of transmission for the presence of another. Writing becomes a frame, a boundary, a container. The man with the authority of writing, which is the authority of the representational world of history, inverts the active expression of his subjective presence into the passive receptivity of listening to the voice of a man whose history has been forgotten because it is too troubling for our consciousness. In a different, literary, form Sebald pays attention to the activity of forgetting, the damage done to consciousness through this absence, and the work of remembering and recollecting, through a relationship to another. The analysis of a brick wall in Deptford gives a more detailed account of the interaction of personal experience of emotions such as grief and mourning, with the large-scale historical events of the First World War.

Following these investigations into the patterns of memory and oblivion within the urban, I go on to suggest that there is a replication of this structure in the relation between the urban and the suburban. Contemporary culture shows that while the urban is conceived as a space that is full of historical meaning, the suburban is represented, and experienced, as a dystopic void, an absence of historic significance. It is suggested that this void is also a symptom of forgetting, particularly a kind of childhood amnesia that is generated by the growing significance of suburbia in contemporary childhood. The popular association between suburbia and 'boredom' is explored as a trope of the regulation of affect and meaning discussed in relation to urban memory and amnesia, but this form of dystopic void differs significantly from the popular association as it refers to an aspect of latency culture, an adolescent moment of waiting and anticipating the replication of a lost past in the present. With Sebald's novel as a point of reference the structure of remembering and forgetting of suburbia is related to the Oedipal drama and to unconscious triangulation. Is this, suburban, oblivion central to a less dysfunctional, more optimistic and pregnant genre?

How does the collective world of history, embodied in the symbolic, representational world of textual spaces such as those of narratives, bricks and mortar, and art, affect our experience of everyday life and our awareness of our own subjective dynamic of avoidance, repression and remembering? Is it the lost past, re-encountered in the textual spaces of buildings, stories and art, that gives meaning to present-day reality?

Art and urban memory

I want to look in detail at the installation Lubaina Himid made in 2002 for the gallery at CUBE (Centre for Understanding the Built Environment) in Manchester's Portland Street, as part of the *Fabrications – New Art & Urban Memory in Manchester* exhibition (Figure 2.1). Modern in its references, it relates also to the decorative arts, to industrial manufacture and to the absent history of slavery as an invisible component of the textile industry in industrial Manchester. As a series of one hundred 'modern paintings' fixed to the atrium wall of the gallery it seems to invite a formalist approach. However, the formalist aesthetics of 'significant form' are evidently incapable of comprehending the significance of the work which pushes the boundaries between textual presence and absence. I return to discuss formalist aesthetics of early

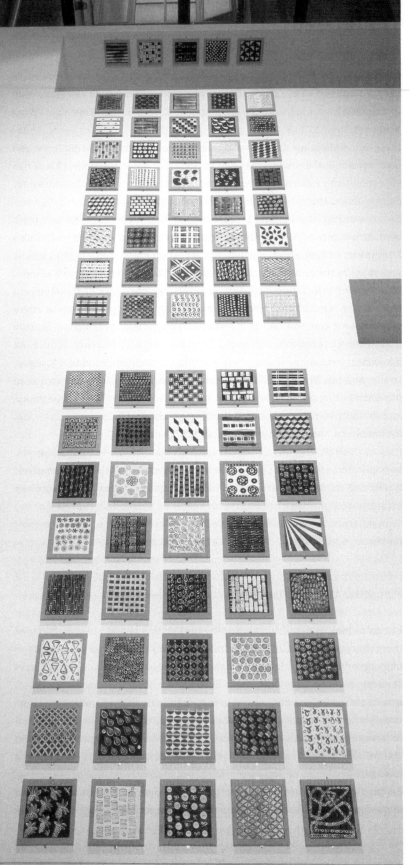

2.1
Lubaina Himid,
Cotton.Com,
2002

twentieth-century British modernists as the discourse of a conservative middle class, when, in a later section, I analyse the architectural meaning of a wall in Deptford. In place of the limitations of formalist aesthetics we find a materialist analysis of the emotional presence of culture that locates the origins of textual meaning in the symbolic connections that underlie both psyche and history. Architecture is then seen as the materialisation of attitudes, just as narrative is seen as the material trace of relations, and art as the fabrication of 'linking'.[3]

CUBE in Portland Street is an exhibition space, gallery and RIBA bookshop that occupies the first two floors of a large, mid-nineteenth-century building that combines Italianate columns with a Palazzo-style entrance. The whole street, like others in this district, consists of these impressive, solid, red brick buildings that were built as places for the display and sale of the fabrics produced in the mills and factories. Intended as showcases where wholesalers could come to see samples of the range of textiles in production and to place orders, they were also the administrative headquarters of the industries. Sometimes mistakenly identified as the mills themselves, they were spaces of display, a temporary interlude within the process of importation, unloading, transporting, unbaling, spinning, spooling, dyeing, weaving, printing, buying, selling and exporting in the textiles industry of nineteenth-century Manchester. Not only was Manchester among the first of Britain's industrial cities, and the centre of its cotton textile industry, its dominance in the imperial trade was such that, in Australia, even to this day the haberdashery and 'whites' departments of department stores which sell sheets and domestic linens, are called, colloquially, the 'Manchester' department.

The warehouse at 113 Portland Street is neither a dark satanic cotton mill, nor a dockside warehouse. It was built to represent the power and solidity of the industry, to impress clients and flatter the owner's fantasy that being a wealthy industrialist had secured him a place of architectural and cultural merit within classical civilisation. The entrance doors set above street level are reached by ornate stone steps with extravagant brass handrails. The doorways are grand but signify power rather than display, they speak more of bank than palace. The street presence is forbidding, without windows or signs, with an aloof distance from street life altogether. This reinforces the elevating function of the stairways to the entrance doors, the purpose of which is to remove the visitor from proximity and vulgarity towards refinement through textiles and their denotation of interior domestic space. These were the spaces for displaying samples to show prospective buyers. The upper floors were the offices where an entire hierarchy of managers and their clerks maintained the administration of the industry. Portland Street was the zone of the interface between production and consumption, away from the potential of class struggle in the factory, from noise, from smoking chimneys and from all evidence of the labour that produced the fabrics destined for the luxurious and soft domestic interior. The clean, tidy, pretty fabric samples were symbolically lifted and elevated from their origins in industry, printed with flowers, ornamental or abstract designs, displayed to connote only the ideas that would harmonize with the domestic interior. Like drapes and curtains, the fabrics served the function of concealing, of setting a stage for another scene far removed from their origins as raw materials and the process of their production. The tactile lure of fabric was severed from the associations that link touch to manual labour, or to ideas of contagion, contamination or dirt. It connoted only the right kind of proximity, the feminine touch of soft furnishings, the clothing and draping of the home.

Now largely used as office space, the buildings in Portland Street retain their meaning as existing at the interface of industrial production and consumption. So this is an inspired location for an art gallery. The rooms betray no domestic or industrial scale but were designed for display. The spaces at CUBE have been linked by an interesting but unobtrusive series of ramps and stairs that, in places, maximise the opportunities to use atrium walls rising over the height of two storeys for maximum display. The neutralisation of spatial reference to history and location is further underscored by the name of the gallery, which replaces historical specificity with Euclidian geometry. The complex interconnections of systems of production and exchange are emptied out from the white space, intended to be an abstract frame, an imaginary cube which circumscribes the references that real space might confer on objects within it. Lubaina Himid's *Cotton.Com* is a piece that is directly site-specific, a response to the material history of 113 Portland Street, as it was before it became a gallery. *Cotton.Com* is set dynamically and confidently in the interstitial space between past and present building, between historical and conceptual space. It was commissioned for an exhibition in the gallery, but speaks of the building's function before its post-industrial reincarnation as a recreational and cultural space.

Using the atrium wall which spans two floors of the building, a hundred canvases about ten inches square are fastened to the wall with brass plates, in horizontal and vertical rows, making a vertical, rectilinear grid. The grid formation allows for five canvases across the horizontal axis, each square separated by a gap of about two or three inches, and some thirty or so along the vertical. These canvases look as if they are being classified rather than paraded. They offer themselves up to our gaze as objects of knowledge and curiosity rather than as picturesque or pleasurable paintings. The grid structure in which they are placed infers taxonomy or classification, as of artefacts rather than art. But it is not at all apparent what the object of curiosity might be. What are we supposed to know? Is it something we can count? Is it something that will be revealed if we look long enough at the cryptic surfaces of the paintings? The orderliness is simultaneously reassuring and enigmatic.

The piece is imposing in its scale, but otherwise is tidy and modest, apparently unassuming and undramatic. The paintings are on canvas stretched over square stretchers, in what seems to be the traditional technique of the oil painting (Figure 2.2). The canvases are primed with either white or black paint to within a margin of an inch or so of the edges of the stretched surface; this leaves a border of raw, unprimed cotton canvas around each of the squares of painting. They are monochrome with a layer of either white or black Liquitex paint applied evenly across the canvas up to the margin. Each has a different pattern applied by brush or scratched into the surface layer of paint. The effect of these deep black and white squares applied in even rows to a high wall is to conjure the illusion of ceramic tiles, especially the Islamic tiles familiar to us from nineteenth-century Orientalist interiors. There is a comfortable sense that this is what one might expect from a prestigious display in a period building. It is unsettling to find that these are not ceramics or craft objects, but are small square oil paintings that belong to a different category of wall coverings altogether. But there are so many of them, that

2.2
Lubaina Himid,
Cotton.Com,
2002

this completely removes any sense of the aura which is associated with uniqueness. Furthermore, some of these pictures seem to have been made by someone scratching at wet paint with a sharp implement, leaving white lines as the primer coat is revealed beneath the gouged topcoat. This technique, known as *sgraffito* in oil painting, is one that is associated with modernism and its citations of the neo-primitive.

We all know that oil painting was developed in order to allow painters to achieve new effects of luminosity by applying semi-translucent layers of coloured oils over a white or pale undercoat. Oil painting allowed a highly developed technique of draughtsmanship to be rendered in a style of painting that counterposed a flat and varnished surface with an exceptional level of illusionism and transparency. The height of nineteenth-century realism, the form preferred by the bourgeoisie, oil paintings were the most desirable of *objets d'art* for homes of taste and respectability. Like the eighteenth-century landowner's view over his picturesque garden, and the twenty-first-century loft dweller's view over the docklands, the nineteenth-century 'man in the boardroom' felt more pleased with himself if he saw himself in oils, up there on the wall. Even following the revolution of modernism, the meaning of painting still retains a lot of its nineteenth-century heritage for most people. So when we see these little black and white squares replicating themselves across a large gallery wall we are surprised. They could have been scratched by a child or by another 'primitive' artist. Entailing the exact inversion of the sophisticated techniques of applying successive layers of colour over primer, this is an anti-painting. Scratching designs is a technique reminiscent of Paleolithic art rather than bourgeois realism. Stubbornly retaining their status as paintings yet deliberately overturning the conventions of painting, these canvases intrigue and affront.

Then we also see that the designs that are gouged are simple linear motifs showing flowers, stars, seashells, spirals, in abstract patterns. There is evidence of the rhythmic movement of the hand and arm, in the physical activity that produced these marks. The patterns are repeated within the canvas as if in poetic imitation of mechanical reproduction. They may be contemporary in style but they refer, unmistakably to the prints that decorated the textiles from the mills, and the presentation of the hundred paintings as 'taxonomic samples' refers us to the original presence of samples of fabric within this building in Portland Street. Here is another challenge to the auratic in art. Surely there is no difference here between pattern-making and painting, and this is a final insult to the distinction that must be made between art and decoration, in order to secure the position of art as occupying the apex of a hierarchy of visual culture. In fact, the whole piece is hovering precipitously on the edge that separates art from interior design, its denigrated younger sister.

Lubaina Himid clearly enjoys playing with these elements of art and its history, but her work also reaches beyond this into a very different and uncharted space. The canvas that we are shown as the literal and figurative 'material' underlying a painting is a reminder that a painting is referred to as *une toile*, a metonymic trope which serves to emphasize the masterly significance of what lies, precisely, on top of the canvas, the painting itself. What remains unspoken and 'immaterial' is the most important part of the object, and to render it unspoken is to pay tribute to its sublime nature. It is beyond words. It is the 'stuff that dreams are made of'. But here in the offices of the cotton trade we are aware of another material base that underlies the painting, and for which the canvas is a metaphor. We are aware that the two ways in which hands are put to work, in art and in manufacture, are qualitatively different categories of human labour. The structure of industrial manufacture, as described by Marx, using the Manchester textile industry as his example, is used to transform use value into exchange value, and thereby obscure the value of the wage labourers' work. How is the politics of class contradiction to be integrated with the experience of an artist who is also a black woman?

The brass plaque in Lubaina Himid's *Cotton.com* suggests another perspective on the political economy of unpaid labour in Britain's industrial revolution, and one which was invisible to Marx and Engels. The plaque is an exaggeration of the names, dates and dimensions that traditionally accompany a painting in a gallery. It could also be a name plate of a building or a prestigious space. It has a sentence engraved on it which reads 'He said I looked like a painting by Murillo as I carried water for the hoe gang, just because I balanced the bucket on my head.' The statement seems to be from a woman, one of the slaves who worked on the cotton fields of Carolina, USA, one of the sources of the raw materials imported, via Liverpool, to Manchester in the nineteenth century. If the class politics of Marx fail to take into account the value of the unpaid labour of slave workers in America, this exists as a level of the unspoken infrastructure of labour on which the capitalist triumphs of industrial Britain were based. The structural position of such labour as invisible renders its history liable to be cast into oblivion, just as the fabric of the canvas that underlies the painting is liable to become invisible and unrecognised. Lubaina Himid is doing more than 'baring the device' in a modernist idiom, she is suggesting that it is the work of the artist to restore such repressed materialities to vision and consciousness. The cryptic sentence, the reported speech of an imaginary slave, is also unmistakably the speech of an objectified, muted, other. Structured as an 'I' made self-conscious by a man addressing her, commenting on her appearance to him ('He said that I looked like a painting by Murillo'), the position of her to-be-looked-at-ness, infers her femininity. Murillo's paintings often feature picturesque peasants and children in poignant scenes that represent the underclass as 'noble savage'. The male spectator, whose gaze is compared to that of Murillo, is occupying a position of dominance as his statement conveys an educated familiarity with Spanish painting, and a sense of aesthetics which perceives the ability to work, to balance a bucket on the head, as an attribute of grace and beauty. The ability to idealize and aestheticize a slave woman's work, without valuing and renumerating it as labour, is an essential element of the fetishistic structure of an Orientalist and 'primitivist' visual culture. The reference to Murillo suggests the equation of black slaves with European peasants, and both can be rendered picturesque through the emphasis on appearance and the simultaneous denial of history.

We are suddenly made aware of Himid's predicament as a black woman artist commissioned to make a piece for the *Fabrications* exhibition. While there are many ethnic subcultures in evidence in contemporary post-industrial Manchester, and the city's Tourist Information flags the 'Chinatown' district near Portland Street as an area of particular interest because it frames its cultural otherness as an urban picturesque, Himid has chosen to represent the absence of the recognition of the labour of black women within the historical documentation of Manchester's urban past. Of course, a social historian might say that there were few black women in nineteenth-century Manchester. And the artist who remains alive to the reality beneath empirical facts replies that it is precisely absence from the record of the presence of industrial power that enables the illusion of 'profit' to be upheld. This absence would be all the more troubling were it not concealed by a disguised presence, a sort of para-amnesia, veiling the trauma of an absence. Art is what veiled the troubling absences in history by offering the presence of a picture to conceal the absence of thought. The fantasy of a statuesque peasant, in a painting by Murillo, is the veil that is draped over the wound in the historical account of the economic function of America's black slavery in Manchester's past. And it is a fact that is not easily reconciled with the visual culture of Manchester's proletarian history. This is not a gratuitous act of remembering and excavating the absent structure of industrial history, but is a material component of Lubaina Himid's presence in the CUBE building. Her presence in the exhi-bition is to make evident and visible the 'structuring absence' in the narrative of urban memory, showing that memory has its counterpart in oblivion. If Lubaina is in the exhibition as the only black woman artist, and she wonders 'Where are all the other black women?', as well she might, she inevitably arrives at the fact of absence, and the history of the erasure and veiling of that absence. There is then a network of relations restored between the domestic workers of the nineteenth century to whom the textiles were destined, and the slaves whose unpaid labour made the price of the raw materials of the industry capable of sustaining the profits that fuelled the industry. Himid suggests that a central idea in this work was that of communication and dialogue between the black cotton slaves in Carolina and the white cotton workers in Manchester, 'I imagined each of these exploited peoples writing emails and text messages to each other, telling each other of their conditions and their lives.'[4]

Himid's work has taken some of the most painful and troubling aspects of the CUBE site, and restored them from oblivion to consciousness. In the empty white geometry of a blankness that symbolises forgetting, Himid has found, and made visible the relationships that link art, cloth, industry, labour, manufacture, patterns, decoration, display, domestic labour, slavery and femininity. Unlike the simple rectilinear grid which presents paintings in an orderly and tidy way, these relationships are complex and various, puzzling and troubling. It is the triumph of Himid's piece that she has held together these thoughts and allowed us to think them through her work. Himid writes that

> It is also important to note that the work also commemorates the part actually played by the workers of Manchester in the abolition of the slave trade. They wrote to Lincoln to offer their support, he wrote back to say that he realized and understood the sacrifice they were making by giving their support. Everyone knew that it would ruin the industry. There is a monument to Lincoln in Manchester, in Lincoln Square, on which this letter from him to them is reproduced. I have actually chosen to represent the absence of the recognition of a solidarity between oppressed workers. Until the solidarity is recognised, the oppressors have duped us all.[5]

A city wall

The city wall is the real or imaginary boundary that demarcates urban space from the outskirts. From Roman walls that separated the necropolis from the metropolis, perfectly preserved at Pompeii, to the symbolic boundaries of the roads that circumnavigate major cities such as the *périphérique* in Paris, the need to represent boundaries is ubiquitous. In Pompeii the separation of the world of rationality and social order from the realm of the dead is significant in the way that the Word separates light from dark in Genesis. What is attributed to the realm of darkness is represented in the Villa of Mysteries, the rites of passage that societies use to mark out time and experience. The world of urban order is no less irrational than its counterpart in the necropolis; the two great spaces for public assemblies, the forum and the stadium, one rectangular, the other curvilinear, are the *recto* and *verso* of the meaning of public exhibition. The first allows people to meet together addressed as citizens, and the other to gather together a mass audience for spectacular cruelty and pleasure.

The ring roads of modern cities offer citizens the freedom to access and leave the city autonomously. The M25 that circumnavigates London has its own mythology. Many of the myths refer to the paradox of a motorway that goes 'nowhere', in circularity without destination:

> Nobody can decide how long the road is, somewhere between 117 and 112 miles. By the time you have driven it, you don't care. You should be way out in another eco-system, another culture: Newport (Mon), or Nottingham, or Yeovil. The journey must mean something. Not a wearied return, hobbled to the point of origin.[6]

The endlessness of the motorway experience, which neutralises all regional difference to a uniform familiarity of motorway signage, is at the core of this joke. Drivers, centred by the apparatus of automobilia, once extruded from the matrixial womb of the city are carefully encased in another envelope of protection through the visual environment of motorway signage. The 'Mothercare' of the road, motorways allow infantilised drivers to become kings of the road through an experience that combines the automatism of hypnotic action with the realities of death. Fortifications of mediaeval city walls are recapitulated in the carapace of driving around the ring road. The enemy is less an invading civilisation than a disruption to the libidinal economy of citizenship itself. Road rage is the invading barbarian that lives on the threshold of civilised morality. Judging from the popular comedies that use it as the setting for sitcoms and humour, the remedial 'anger management course' meted out by judges as corrective treatment for such rage, is the contemporary equivalent of being physically and publicly restrained in stocks.

The wall has particular meaning for demarcating inner from outer spaces. It has the symbolic significance of a line. It is the element of signification from which an entire alphabet and lexicon of architectural meaning is built. The wall is the first test of the skill of the bricklayer. Like the Word of God in Genesis, its function is to demarcate. This is a function that is quite different from its function as elevation, surface or display of significance. This is so deeply, and implicitly, understood in cities that the high brick walls that characterised the street experience of the Isle of Dogs and Deptford, before they became 'Docklands' vistas of waterways and apartments, once bore the simple grafitti 'Millwall', to which had been added 'Brick Wall'. This dialogue of naming, identification and demarcation remained on the wall of Creek Road next to the Deptford Arms for decades.

I want to explore the meaning of another brick wall in Deptford.

It was a periphery wall of a housing estate, and functioned as bearer of the history of the residents and also of the oblivion of that history.

The London housing estates that spread from Tottenham through Hackney to Tower Hamlets, are monuments to the fantasy that the working classes are undifferentiated masses, needing to be controlled through being separated and itemised into nuclear units. The housing built before the 1980s is almost entirely a relentless industrial Enlightenment regimentation of communality that functions as a display of the 'taming' of the unknown. The repeated blocks, unvaried and uniform, are showcases of the bourgeois domination over its fantasy of working-class labyrinthine unknowability, chaos, proximity and 'dirt'. The repeated architectural trope of glass, white concrete and expanses of mid-blue ceramic tile speak loudly of the need for a visibly cleansed exterior, entirely available to the gaze of the onlooker. No privacy, no secrecy, no darkness, no surprises, no unknowable spaces that are shaped by the logic of the inhabitants, but only the shapes, colours and vistas that satisfy the curiosity and anxiety of the spectator/planner. Only the cars with personalised number plates transgress the utopian vision of a modular uniformity that has cleansed the warren of urban streets that housed the proletariat before the wars. In the inter-war council housing block of Crossfields Estate in London's Deptford, the red brick, five-storey blocks were designed as vertically layered streets, with front doors lined up along continuous 'balconies' leading to the communal rubbish chutes and staircase. Each block was built with a footprint of the three sides of a square, and the grass that filled the space between the verticals was intended to be a lawn. It was not so much the uniformity of the grid of blocks that was alienating as the curious obviation of the history of the inhabitants. Built to be 'Homes for Heroes', the ordinary men and woman who had won the 1914–18 war, there was one detail of the architecture that was at once obvious and yet a sign of a hidden amnesia or repressed history. To form the fencing that marked the boundary of the housing estate, the council's architects had found no reason not to use up a surplus of First World War medical stretchers, sturdily and indestructibly manufactured from steel. The stretchers were about 6 feet long and when laid end to end, their handles cemented into 4-foot high brick pilasters, several hundred of them entirely encircled the dozen housing blocks of the estate. There was something shocking, ignoble, if not contemptuous, about using the deathbeds of millions of young men as garden fencing. The presence of the stretchers and their indestructibility, a tribute to British engineering and manufacture, are in inverse ratio to the absence of young working-class men to survive the 1914–18 war. Perhaps it was felt, by the council architects, that it was a 'waste' to throw away this medical military surplus. Maybe it was thought that adapting the technology of war for uses in peace-time reconstruction was morally commendable. I doubt that the process by which the decision to build the boundary wall from stretchers was minuted and documented, there was something very 'unthought' about it. The effect was to demonstrate a very visible disrespect for the losses of the working class, by assuming that the urban proletariat must be insensible to the emotions that the middle classes experienced as devastating. Public culture offered historical respect to the Great War in war poetry, war memorials, the traditions of the poppies and the two-minute silence on Armistice Day. In the way that ideology has traditionally worked to invert the structural reality by projecting disowned aspects of the self onto an ideological other, the gross insensitivity of the designers was projected onto the council tenants, who were then stereotyped as being too robust to experience significant effects of mourning, loss, trauma or pain. There is still an assumption that the unity of the proletariat is cemented through the manic cultures of football, beer, cheerful humour and work but not through the ties of compassion and the shared experience of loss and the hidden injuries of class. The encircling wall embodies the invisible structure of a class war that continues to divide the nation long after the trauma of the world wars.

Here is an interesting dialectic between the public memorialising of war and the design of everyday life in which an unthinking oblivion testified to the hegemonic inability to sustain painful memory. As James Young has pointed out in relation to Holocaust memorials, the building of a memorial may serve to focus attention on just one place, thereby relieving the culture of a more widespread and individuated historical memory.[7] Although the local war memorial nearby proclaimed the national tragedy in public terms, with a sculpture and a white stone pediment, the stretchers around the housing estate suggested that the collective need to honour the dead of the working class is limited to laying a wreath at the memorial once a year, like the Queen, on Armistice Day, and does not extend to thinking about the quality of their everyday lives and housing. The working class is deemed insensible to the finer emotions expressed by Siegfried Sassoon and the war poets of the officer classes. The rehabilitation homes for shell-shocked officers in Edinburgh's Craiglockhart already had the baroque statuary and extravagant grounds felt necessary to heal the shattered nerves of the officer class, but down in Deptford, the practicality of the stretchers is a profound metaphor for the supposed 'practicality' of the working class, too 'handy' to throw away and not quite real enough to think about. The metonymic relation that connects the stretchers to the proletariat is found in the obviation of the symbolic or emotional significance of an object and a subsuming of this beneath the signification of its functional use. This is the exact inversion of the structure of meaning in the work of art, in which an object's functional significance is reframed as symbolic through the thought of the artist.

The ideology of formalist aesthetics that was the philosophy of Bloomsbury and remained hegemonic in Britain in the first half of the twentieth century, asserted that it was the 'disinterestedness' of the spectator's relation to the art object that guaranteed the purity of the aesthetic response. Roger Fry thought it impossible for people with too close an engagement with everyday life to have the capacity for this response to pure form, due to their proximity to the world of work and its utilitarian relationship to the environment and its objects. This was the officer class, that saw themselves as the curators of the aesthetic sensibility and culture in Britain, and it is this class that saw no contradiction in the symbolism that the building of Crossfield Estate offered its inhabitants. British modernism has always suffered from its lack of suffering, as Perry Anderson noted, the British middle class has been unable to change its identification with the upper classes, has never become revolutionary and has tended to maintain the contradictions, anxieties and proprieties of this unquestioned allegiance.[8] The boundary wall of the Crossfields Estate provided by the middle class for the working class, demonstrates the mysterious evaporation of thought that occurs when the middle classes are presented with their historical and emotional relation to the working class. This mysterious phenomenon, however, is like weather, capable of being understood through appropriate tools and scientific methods of description and analysis, as a consciousness retreating from the demands of emotional effort, a retreat that is concealed by the blankness that disguises the fear of being overwhelmed and rendered helpless. The thought withdrawn, action becomes compulsive and automatic, the unthinking grossness of middle-class narcissism. Here is an interesting dialectic between the obvious, the visible and what has been cast into oblivion, what is being kept from thought. This is the sense in which the supposedly benign social democratic principles of post-war town planning exists on a spectrum which also spans the Enlightenment architecture that produced the panopticon.[9]

The significance of the architecture of the penal system has been meticulously documented and incisively analysed by Robin Evans,[10] and more recently explored by Sebald in his novel *Austerlitz*, in which the protagonist's experience of visiting eighteenth-century military fortified buildings is connected to his unconscious knowledge and memory of the experience of the Holocaust in Second World War Czechoslovakia. This experience is described as a physical encounter with walls that either contain and protect, or constrain and entomb. The protagonist is an architectural historian whose profession is an expression of the depth of significance, attributed by Sebald, to the built environment as the medium of twentieth-century history. In this observation, and in his representation of this relationship between building and history, Sebald is accurate and profound.

In the city wall there is a dyadic logic that might have fascinated Lévi-Strauss or Barthes and has captivated Mary Douglas,[11] a logic that opposes the city to its otherness. Foucault demonstrated how the concept of city walls functioned to maintain the concept of the mental health of the body politic, expulsion from the walls being a ritual cleansing of criminality or lunacy.[12] This predicament of the suburb as beyond the boundaries of the city, the outside of the inside, raises questions of the nature and function of the liminal. The boundary is a notional state before it is manifested in architectural or material form, and it remains, primarily, a psychic and representational reality that assumes the material and historic power ascribed to it by culture and society. It is the cultural analysis of boundaries and their function as divisions between categories of existence that can throw light on the para-amnesias that punctuate our concept of suburbia. Whatever lies at the edge of a distinguishing division is especially susceptible to becoming anxiogenic, as Edmund Leach observed.[13]

Suburban oblivion

Why is it that suburban life is characterised, or caricatured as a void? Examples of stereotypic suburban dystopia abound, and it is difficult to find examples of representations of real suburban life as lived in Britain.[14] There are plenty of stereotypes, both idealist and denigratory, and these, split ideas, both share a fantasy that the suburb is eventless, either ideally safe or wretchedly boring. The idealist fantasy is that everyone can start a new life as bourgeois homeowner of a semi-detached home with front and back gardens, in the clean air and leafy crescents of the suburbs. The significance of front gardens cannot be overestimated as they represent the space of a correct distance between home and street, usually absent in the urban, a distance which defines respectability through the absence of vulgar proximity. It is respectability conferred through property that is the hallmark of this ideal. The negative fantasy is that the suburbs are barren wastelands where the rebellion of teenagers finds only the *anomie* of deracinated parents with whom triangulation fails, leading to drugs, Goths, Punks, serial killers and housewife-mothers on antidepressants. It is a curiously unsexy place despite the cultures of seduction and display, fast cars and conspicuous wealth, that flourish there, as if the suburban is pre-sexual and immature, masquerading as adult. The suburb is also conceived as a feminine-wifely, especially maternal, space where women are perpetually pregnant, and men are somehow emasculated, reduced to going out to work, driving away, or absenting themselves to the shed. This is the opposite of the modernist idealisation of the metropolitan experience of anonymity and individuation, where the crowd gives birth, paradoxically, to the individual. In the suburb the boundary between individual and family is conceived as amorphous and indistinct, a matrixial web from which the adolescent must escape in order to become a real self. This may, in part, represent a vestige of the matrilineal working-class kinship that characterised the urban proletariat, or it may be a particular, historic form of post-war family structure in which the place of the father was not always stable. Notwithstanding the development of the suburb as the realm of the housewife, featuring boutiques, beauty salons, hair stylists and gyms, the femininity of the suburban is a strangely indistinct and pre-Oedipal gender as if the concept of sex itself was absent. As Miranda Sawyer observes, in her analysis of 'wife-swapping' as suburban sexual culture, the exhibitionistic display of sexual activity is curiously onanistic and profoundly asexual. The lack is what creates the grounds for melodrama as the 'desire to desire'.[15]

The idealised stereotype of the inter-war British suburb, a period when Greater London expanded in size by 400 per cent through its suburban development, is enshrined in the children's comic strip Rupert Bear, whose home town, Nutwood, is somewhere between Wimbledon Common and Pinewood Studios. The nostalgia for an imaginary rural past is fused with the fantasy of a new social mix of classes, figured as species in the comic strips. Alien cultures are imagined within the lexicon of an idealised empire, exotic Chinese Tiger Lily and her magician father. The idealised upper-middle classes are figured in Ottoline the girl otter, and Bill the badger with his Eton collar. The negative fantasy has recently gained widespread circulation in the Harry Potter stories and films, where Harry's alienated existence in Acacia Avenue with his adoptive family is the motivation for his quest for his true Wizard parentage accessible only through the magical world of Hogwarts. It is the daytime world of the suburb, with its tyranny of boring relatives, the desperate aspiration towards gentility that is counterposed to the night-time world of magnificent, sublime and unknowable forces, compelling children and adults, ogres and magical creatures set in endless grounds of changing scenery. This is a popular replication of a template that finds innumerable imprints in adult as well as children's literature. It is the blandness and the blankness of that daytime, overlit, interior that mark it as dystopic. It is without shadows and dimension. The absence of fear and mystery transforms endlessness of suburbia into a blank panic of claustrophobia, familiar enough to the national psyche to have made Harry Potter into a household name. What is it about the experience of suburban living that makes people want to cast it into oblivion? Over 75 per cent of Britain's population grew up in the suburbs, in circumstances that their parents' generation considered less deprived than those of their own childhood. What is it about young people's experience of boredom that indicates the experience of a privileged childhood?

Once again, surprisingly perhaps, we take Sebald's *Austerlitz* as a text that explores the dynamics of memory and forgetting in relation to embodied memories that are experienced through symptoms of language, the bodily sensations of emotion and of illness, and the urban and suburban environments of England and Eastern Europe. Sebald explores the complex relationship between memory and narrative, a relationship that unifies the subject in language. A reflection on the effects of dislocation and denial on memory, the novel explores the need to integrate fragments of memory into an adequate account of origins, and this account must be both personally inclusive and historically accurate. The narrative has to connect inner experience, personal idiosyncrasy and particular feelings, with external, collective memory, or history. This protagonist, whose story, told to the narrator, is the narrative of the novel, has the name 'Austerlitz' which is, in turn, the name of the novel. It is the name of the father that has been lost to the son and whose journey is to find and understand the name and its disappearance. The framing discourse is that of a nameless narrator recounting to the reader, *verbatim*, the account of a life as it was told to him. It is an extraordinarily moving device for a German novelist to tell the story of a Czechoslovakian Jew without appropriating the tragedy for himself, and through a meticulous observation of the boundaries of separateness that does not preclude compassion and empathy. The novel is an account of how one man can listen to another, testament to the power of receptive hearing as a capacity that has been made invisible, unrecognised, in contemporary masculinity. The masculine ideals of action and independence which analysts such as Klaus Theweleit have identified as the emotional basis of *Freikorps* militia find their antithesis in the character of the receptive narrator with no name. The narrator, who is the author's gift to the reader, is an instruction in the art of listening, receiving, and being moved by an other's life journey. It is the narrator's receptivity, and by extension the reader's too, that provides the psychic space for the rebuilding of the shattered elements of a life that has been devastated by loss, separation, denial and oblivion. Billeted to a childless couple in Wales during the Second World War, the protagonist, a boy from Prague who arrived at Liverpool Street station by *Kindertransport* train, learns a new language, is given a new name and develops an amnesia that blanks out his early experiences of love and loss. When he reaches the age of 18, a teacher tells him of his original name and the circumstances of his arrival in Britain. As Austerlitz traces his origins, and searches for his parents, making the journey back to Prague, he re-experiences the blankness, leaden sense of alienation, inexplicable physical illnesses, fear, aphasia, insomnia, impotence, anxiety and hopelessness, and begins to find the cause of the conflicts and dislocations that underlie these symptoms. One key clue is the protagonist's strange experiences that seem to be acoustic hallucinations, and symptoms of psychosis, hearing and understanding strange languages, but which are revealed to be his mother tongue, his first language that has been repressed and forgotten and which has become an unconscious memory. Both description of a historical predicament for thousands of refugees, and metaphor for the state of being lost between meaning and symbol, the voyage of self-discovery is simultaneously a 'talking cure' as Jacques Austerlitz entrusts his narrative of intolerable pain to the narrator and implicitly to the reader. A series of 'donors', feminine, associated with knowledge, archives, learning and books, lead him to the home of Vera, a friend who had looked after him as a boy when his parents were at work.[16] The narrative then becomes the narrator's tale of listening to Austerlitz who is listening to Vera's testimony of the dissolution of his family and home, and the details of his mother's deportation to a concentration camp.

The new life for the refugee Austerlitz in Britain must be lived, without the blankness of amnesia, and this is the real predicament that the reader is invited to share with the narrator and author, who have, in turn, received it from 'Austerlitz'. The book demonstrates, by its textual structure, as well as in its themes and narrative, that only by the community created through communication, shared language, speech, writing, culture, can we bear the knowledge of our histories and destinies.

Sensitive to the meanings of urban environment, memory and history, the novel attributes different states of mind to different built environments. A provincial town in rural Wales is a false start, a suburb of Prague is a void, a spa town is the impossibility of sexual love, the city is the true origin. Metropolitan, modern, civilised, political and cultural, family life is contained in the city so that the city is textually located as the space of origins. The novel refers to two narrative episodes that occur in the suburban zone. The first is that related to the narrator by Austerlitz describing his journey to a state archive in which he will learn of his original family's address. The archive is located in a building in the suburbs and the journey there is associated with a desperate wandering through a wilderness of unremitting, uniformly comfortable houses which convey bleakness. The desolation is indicated by the anonymity of the suburban houses that each contain a family; the houses are unidentified and threatening in their vastness of number and undifferentiated uniformity. Every household is loathsome because it is not 'home'. The narrative locates origins in the city, and death and dystopia in the suburbs. The suburban zone contains necessary information, but is not the destination which entails the reconnection of information to meaning. Only knowledge of lived experience can give meaning to information or data, and the archive provides data alone which must be reunited with its origins in the city. The suburb is equated with the emptiness of data that has been severed from its lived origins. Is this a historical comment on the deracination of an entire class that became severed from its roots in metropolitan life?

The second incident is the factual reference to Theresin, the concentration camp which was located in the fortified military village built in the eighteenth century. Connected to the idealisation of Enlightenment ideology and associated with the history of military and penal architecture that the narrator recounts throughout the narrative, the camp exists at one stage as a parody of the suburban model village. The idiom of utopian garden-cities such as Bournville, Port Sunlight, Letchworth and Welwyn Garden City in nineteenth- and twentieth-century Britain, has elements of the rational ideology of planning and control also found in the housing estates of East London, described above. The suburban episode of Theresin in the Sebald novel is its historical transformation into a holiday camp, for the purposes of the propaganda exercise that results in filming the arrival of the International Red Cross. The transformation of the camp into a fictional *mise-en-scène* is related by Austerlitz to the narrator, and rests on the washing of the streets, re-clothing the inmates and advertising fictional concerts to imply the respect for culture. A particularly sinister icon noted in the documentary film that Austerlitz watches at the archive, is the parasols at the café tables posed to simulate carefree holiday ambiance. It is possible to identify connections between the 'suburbanisation' of Theresin and the ideology of compulsive cleaning that haunts the culture of suburbia, and the manic need for visible orderliness that subsists the planning of the working-class housing developments in welfare state Britain. The connection between the systematic sadism of the Holocaust and other more ordinary forms of perversion such as rigid imposition of ideals, has been explored by Janine Chasseguet-Smirgel who notes the recurring features of the compulsion to clean and purge in the 'Malady of the Ideal'.[17] The idealised, narcissistic ego is contrasted to the excremental other who is then targeted with extermination, and pursued in systematic and psychotic ways.

As well as being the oldest manifestation of ethnic 'cleansing', anti-semitism continues to be one of the most powerful of its expressions. The etymological origins of matter in *mater* indicate the emotional and psychic economy which has created the suburb as the 'proper' space for what Mary Douglas calls the dirt of 'matter out of place', the maternal uncanny.[18] The characterisation of the suburb as a feminine zone is also ubiquitous. The bourgeois ideal of a wife as mother at home is projected onto British suburbia in a way that has rendered it a place of the maternal uncanny in innumerable texts. Like all aspects of the maternal, it is destined for repression and oblivion in the adult psyche.

Is the maternal always destined for oblivion? It is primal repression that places 'desire of the mother' under the bar of the 'name of the father', the signifying process, thereby inaugurating the chain of desire that is, simultaneously, the chain of meaning within language and signification. The point of origin will always be a point of loss. The imaginary plenitude of maternal connection is lost to the word that originates and divides, the word that symbolises. The symbol with its ability to connect word and meaning, signifier and signified, is what proffers us the union that we use to atone for the loss of the first union. The symbol with its secondary connectedness is what allows us to enter the social, political and historical world of community and communication. The first union is separated from the second, rediscovered, symbolic reunion by a gap. This gap may be represented by a wilderness, an impossible wait, or frustration, a rite of passage, a journey across water or through difficult terrain. The psychic equivalent is the state of latency, a state represented as 'nothing happening', in which the Oedipal dramas are over and repressed and before the real-life drama of love and work begin to recapitulate the original infantile drama. The significance of suburban oblivion is complex and contradictory, containing historical voiding of contradiction as we find in urban memory. The political axis of this oblivion relates to the denial of class contradiction, which had been evident in the growth of urban space during Britain's industrial revolution. The paradox of the development of the suburbs is that they both promised an *embourgeoisement* for the nascent middle class, and for the working classes relocated after the two world wars, and that this promise was realised at the expense of a real relationship to history. It was made possible only by trying to inhabit a middle-class fantasy. However, the suburban space, which is one in which most childhood is lived in the twentieth century, is also a space of psychic boundaries. It seems that the suburban is a psychic space of the pre-Oedipal with all its benign and malignant fantasies, and the urban represents a psychic point of Oedipal triangulation with a past and a future, with the axis of time rather than the *topos* of space. If so, this would go some way towards explaining why the suburban is a picturesque and imaginary space whereas there is a language and vocabulary for representing and exploring the city.

The privilege of latency as a childhood phase in which 'nothing happens', sometimes called the 'trauma of eventlessness', is an index of a realm of unknown possibilities.[19] Boredom means latency and latency is a pregnant silence quite different from the mute silence of oblivion.

If modern childhood is, by and large, lived in the suburbs, is it the idea of the urban that represents both industrial past and post-modern future? If the maternal matrix of the suburb is the ground from which the adult must individuate and form a distinct self, is this a journey that necessarily entails an encounter with the urban as a space of history and the social sphere of adulthood?

Claire Pajaczkowska

Notes

1 Cathexis is the investment of an idea, or object, with meaning. The meaning can be positive or negative. It derives from the Freudian theory of libido, which ascribes an aim and a pressure to the component drives that then invest themselves in, or cathect, an object, or representation.

2 The structuring absence is a concept introduced by Louis Althusser to account for the dynamic of historical oblivion that underlies the continuous presence of ideology. It allows us to think of texts as fulfilling the fantasy of a continuous presence without gaps or aporia. The structuring absence is function of ideology as 'answers for which there are no questions', as elaborated in Althusser's essay on 'Ideology and the Ideological State Apparatus', in *Lenin and Philosophy*, New York: New York University Press, 1971.

3 British psychoanalyst Wilfred Bion described psychotic denial as an 'attack on linking': see Gerard Bleandonu, *Wilfred Bion: His Life and Work*, London: Free Association Books, 1993.

4 Letter from Lubaina Himid, 2 June 2004.

5 Ibid.

6 Ian Sinclair, *London Orbital*, London: Granta Books, 2002, p. 6.

7 See James E. Young, *Textures of Memory: Holocaust Memorials and Meaning*, New Haven, CT: Yale University Press, 1993.

8 Perry Anderson, 'Components of the National Culture', in Robin Blackburn and Alexander Cockburn (eds.), *Student Power*, London: Penguin, 1969.

9 Michel Foucault's well-known analysis of the ocularcentrism of Jeremy Bentham's design for the multi-purpose panopticon prison has given rise to a considerable secondary literature, and can be found in his *Discipline and Punish: The Birth of the Prison*, trans. A. Sheridan, London: Penguin, 1977. The analysis of how power is embodied in this building design once widespread in the design of hospitals and prisons, rests on the analogy of building and imaginary body, in which the eye is metaphorically placed as the centre of consciousness and surveillance.

10 See Robin Evans, *The Fabrication of Virtue: English Prison Architecture 1750–1840*, Cambridge: Cambridge University Press, 1982.

11 Mary Douglas, 'The Uses of Vulgarity', in *Thought Styles*, London: Sage Publications, 1996, pp. 1–20.

12 Michel Foucault, *Histoire de la Folie*, Paris: Gallimard, 1961.

13 See Edmund Leach, 'Animal Categories and Verbal Abuse: Anthropological Approaches to Language', in R. Jakobson (ed.), *New Directions in the Study of Language*, Cambridge, MA: MIT Press, 1971.

14 Miranda Sawyer gives a detailed and fascinating account of the culture of Manchester's Wilmslow suburb. Analysing the role of the car and driving in these affluent suburbs, she also analyses the function of heritage culture, social clubs, wife swapping, Women's Institutes, and family life as components of a complex cultural anthropology of suburbia. Without this perspective it is impossible to understand the meaning of the urban. See Miranda Sawyer, *Park and Ride: Adventures in Suburbia*, London: Lyttle Brown and Co, 1999.

15 'Women's pictures' were a popular genre, making explicit reference to the suburban context of the spectator. Contemporary genres of popular cinema that now make these references are Horror and Science Fiction in which the suburbs frequently feature as the initial *mise-en-scène*, and therefore narrative point of origin of the fiction. See Mary Ann Doane, *The Desire to Desire: Melodrama and the Women's Film of the 1940s*, Bloomington, IN: Indiana University Press, 1987.

16 See Vladimir Propp, *Morphology of the Russian Folktale*, Houston, TX: University of Texas Press, 1968.

17 See Janine Chasseguet-Smirgel, 'Reflections on the Connections between Perversion and Sadism', *International Journal of Psychoanalysis*, 59:1, 1978; *Creativity and Perversion*, New York: Norton, 1984; and *The Ego Ideal: A Psychoanalytic Study of the Malady of the Ideal*, New York: Norton, 1985.

18 See Mary Douglas, *Purity and Danger*, Harmondsworth: Penguin, 1966.

19 Adam Phillips, *On Kissing, Tickling and Being Bored*, London: Faber and Faber, 1993, pp. 71–82.

The Station Master
at the main train station
in Guangzhou enters his office
and puts
a fragment
of track
onto his desk.

Chapter 3

Clocking off in Ancoats

Time and remembrance in the post-industrial city

Mark Crinson and Paul Tyrer

'For sale' signs go up, car parks are laid out on the empty sites. Hoardings appear along the road. The windows of the mills are boarded and scaffolding rises above the pavement. On one side of the bridge the canal is choked with rubbish, on the other side its banks are cleared for new building. Ancient machinery stands idle while new paving is laid over the cobblestones. Brick walls are everywhere, some crumbling, some newly cleaned. A city that has been one thing becomes another.

This chapter focuses on some foundational issues concerning the contemporary urban life and urban forms that are exemplary of the post-industrial or post-Fordist city. These terms themselves presume some cultural and historical specificity. They point to cities that have in some fundamental way been established or crucially shaped by the impact of modern industrialism and have gone through some almost equally far-reaching change in the recent past involving de-industrialisation through the emergence of new technologies or the relocation of production.[1] These processes are familiar, indeed, the constant dismantling and remaking of the industrial city are seen as essential parts of capitalist industrialisation. But what really concerns us here is the remaindered industrial city and its transformation through neglect, gentrification and the rediscovery of the past through conservation, as well as its restyling and regeneration through the importation of new functions and new investment monies. In accounts of de-industrialisation the coterminous reshaping of architecture and urban space tends to be treated as illustrative of larger processes rather than as having their own dynamics and even their own distinctive role to play in affirming or disaffirming the notion of the 'post-industrial city'. The questions that we are interested in focus on these dynamics and centre on the representation of change and the political imperatives of preservation.

Our attempt to address these issues has led us to make close empirical studies of several areas in one of the most iconic and once most awesome of all early industrial cities – Manchester. In Trafford Park, as we show elsewhere in this volume, 'memory' has been used to aestheticise and co-opt the past into new forms of place-making. Motivated by development capital, one part of the area in particular celebrates the defeat of the past at the same time as it appears to mourn it. Remembrance has thus taken on some of the characteristics that Pierre Nora, in his work on *lieux de mémoire*, described as 'history' rather than 'places' and 'environments' of memory. For Nora, the latter were not static but constantly shifting and altering. When, however, they become subject to contemplation, they also become alienated from us, objects for the study and re-presentation of history. Memory survives, if it survives at all, in the form of traces or residues, fetishes of the past or bureaucratic orderings of certain venerated phenomena. The tokens and remnants of industrialisation, in a curious displacement of old Romantic tropes, have taken over the places of cottages, country houses, medieval churches, and the landscape of woods and fields; the sublime remade as the picturesque. In another area, Whitworth Street West, the old railway arches that are a characteristic feature of Victorian Manchester, have provided interstitial spaces which Helen Hills and Paul Tyrer have compared with the arcades of Paris. Just as those arcades were regarded by Walter Benjamin as emblematic of consumption and privatisation in nineteenth-century Paris, so the railway arches are emblematic of post-industrial Manchester.[2] The recent conversion of these arches to café-bars and design outlets has featured a retention of their industrial and working-class appurtenances as the new loft-living middle classes that use them seek also to hive off their associations with the illegitimate and the marginalised.

Manchester, it has often been said, had a central role in giving form to, and predicting the course of, the forces of modernisation that emerged in the nineteenth century. The area that is the subject of this chapter, Ancoats, holds a specially privileged place in Manchester's history as a crucible of that city's transformation. It became seen as a classic space of industrial production created by and for industry, and a classic slum, and as such it was the source of dystopic images of the intensely claustrophobic, inhuman and alienating effects of modernisation. Ancoats was the first industrial suburb and therefore was high on the itinerary of any industrial spy, social reformer, or serious nineteenth-century commentator on industrialism.[3] It was the collision of forces, the energy of building and engineering works (largely without the intervention of architects), the sublime sights, the new manufacturing discoveries and the new organisation of spaces and of people in and between those spaces – a suburb unplanned but driven by the logic of profit – together with all the consequent noise, squalor and filth, that fascinated these visitors. And Ancoats, except for one or two crumbs cast by philanthropic conscience, seems to have been bypassed by the new civic order that transformed Manchester's centre in the second half of the nineteenth century.[4]

It is, of course, curious that Ancoats's spatial abstractions, enhancing the functional specificity and mechanical efficiency of its mills and dismissing nature and the past from its environs, are now themselves the focus of so much memory-talk. By contrast, in the liberal governmentality of the Victorian industrial cities public memorialisation was a function more typically associated with city squares, public parks, libraries, museums and particularly cemeteries, where memory was enshrined in objects as well as in practices of visiting.[5] But Ancoats also became a paradigmatic case of de-industrialisation, memory-loss, and the post-industrial reconception of the city.[6] In such influential recent polemics as Richard Rogers and Anne Power's *Cities for a Small Country*, Ancoats is used to typify both decline and the potential for regeneration, its 'fragmented streets, abandoned housing and derelict land' are the quintessential case of urban decline, awaiting the magical powers of a newly healing and beautifying architecture.[7] These powers have worked their magic in recent images of Ancoats as an area of waterside leisure activities and tree-lined canals, bathed in the light of Canaletto's Venice.[8] But Ancoats is not yet an area of white-collar work and consumption, its mills are not yet dismantled or filled with high technologies processing information. From its conservation bodies to its absentee landlords, from its depopulated streets to its refurbished warehouse lofts, from its place-less retail park to its newly-named areas of regeneration, Ancoats provides rich evidence of the contested and contradictory nature of urban memory in the early twenty-first century. It has two characteristics in particular, shared with Trafford Park, that may have critical relevance for our understanding of the post-industrial city. One is that it was denuded of residents in the last decades of the twentieth century. The other is that it has had certain elements of its urban form protected while other elements are being dramatically reshaped.

In what follows, we interpret contemporary Ancoats through several different but intersecting viewpoints. First, we present a topographical sketch of its present physical state. This is followed by a discussion of the attempts to re-establish or import a sense of place to its public spaces, and then by a consideration of how heritage bodies have negotiated Ancoats's past in the face of current development. The last two sections show how the resultant pacts, compromises and unresolved juxtapositions can lead us to a new understanding of the area's material presence and, more speculatively, even of how it presents its relation to the past and to the future.

Incoherence and the temporalities of development

One particular area of Ancoats might be taken to demonstrate its contradictions with acute clarity. Great Ancoats Street is a continuation of the old sheep-roving road into Manchester from one of its satellite towns, Stockport. The now (sometimes) six-lane road is part of an inner ring of roads that once skirted the old centre, supplying a transport route into and around it, but it also acts effectively as a barrier or boundary between old Manchester and its first industrial suburb, Ancoats. Beneath the road at one point there passes what was once an equally important conduit for traffic into and out of Manchester, the Rochdale Canal (Figure 3.1). But standing on the road above the canal there are hardly any markers of this crossing of routes, indeed, historically these two thoroughfares had little relation, moving people and goods north–south and east–west but with no physical celebration of the crossing-point itself. Today – writing in the autumn of 2003 – the area around this crossing point seems inherently quartered, with each quarter in a separate stage of development. What follows is a brief characterisation of these quarters:

3.1
Schematic diagram of the meeting of Great Ancoats Street and the Rochdale Canal in Ancoats, Manchester
Note: To top left is Quarter 1, top right is Quarter 2, bottom right is Quarter 3, and bottom left is Quarter 4

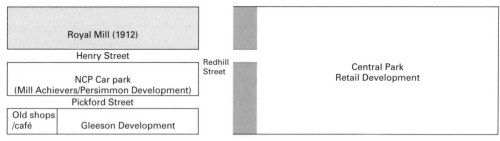

- Quarter 1 (Figure 3.2), to the north-west of the crossing, still has
  many of its pre-twentieth-century buildings standing, but they
  have not yet been regenerated and most are unused. This is the
  area of Ancoats that has been most often represented, largely
  because of a row of early warehouse buildings facing the canal
  along Redhill Street, that are significant both for architectural and
  historical reasons. Two local conservation bodies are centred on
  this quarter: the Ancoats Urban Village Company (AUVC) and the
  Ancoats Buildings Preservation Trust (ABPT) and both coordinate
  with national and local interests.[9] There is much talk of imminent
  development, especially of the historic Murrays Mills, and some
  grant monies have been allocated to speed this process along.
  There is a long way to go, however, before the largely empty
  warehouses in this quarter are suitable for business or domestic
  use, and a master plan has proved impossible to produce because
  the area has so many landowners. What had been for some thirty
  years an empty frontage onto Great Ancoats Street at the corner
  of the quarter has recently had a new commercial property completed on it.
- Quarter 2 (Figure 3.3), on the north-east side, was redeveloped
  some twenty years ago into the Central Retail Park. Everything
  within the boundary walls of the retail park is of the time of its
  making – there appear to be no traces of any past before this. The
  reason for this is that planning permission for the Central Retail
  Park was granted before Ancoats was designated as a conservation
  area and the land had been cleared years previously. Because of
  this, the quarter is now almost entirely detached from Quarter 1

3.3
**View of Ancoats
in 2001, looking
towards the
Retail Park
(Quarter 2)**
Source: Gten
Photography &
Design

3.4
**View of
'Piccadilly Basin'
(Quarter 3)**
Source: Gten
Photography &
Design

3.5
**View of
Brownsfield
Mill and the
Rochdale Canal**
Source: Gten
Photography &
Design

with which, until recently, it once formed a recognisable neighbourhood (indeed, the quarters were indistinguishable before the
digging of the Rochdale Canal).[10] Both this quarter and Quarter 1
stand to benefit from the city council's focus on regenerating outer
East Manchester.

- Quarters 3 and 4, the two quarters on the Manchester side are the
  most closely linked in character although they are divided by
  the canal (Figures 3.4, 3.5). Much of the land in these quarters
  was taken up by wharfs and canal arms for the Rochdale Canal
  Company warehouse as well as for sawmills on the site, and it
  follows that today there is only one landlord for these quarters,
  Town Centre Securities. In the nineteenth century and for much
  of the twentieth century there were also a number of premises
  and a pub/hotel fronting onto Great Ancoats which have since
  been demolished. Quarter 3 has consisted, in some cases since the
  war, of large car parks whose street frontage more recently has
  consisted of hoardings, and now a frenzy of building activity is
  about to be launched on these cleared spaces that will open up
  the canal front to residences and leisure activities – exactly the kind
  of waterfront development that can be found in other areas of the
  city like Castlefield and Salford Quays.

The site as a whole might, then, be described as rather incoherent, with each
quarter being in a separate stage of development: Quarter 1 consisting largely
of Victorian industrial buildings looked over by conservation bodies; Quarter
2 entirely filled with 1980s' buildings with no local element or conservation
interest; Quarter 3, 'empty' for a long time and about to be rebuilt with
contemporary buildings; Quarter 4 also to be rebuilt but less extensively and
taking into account its industrial heritage. Furthermore, the Rochdale Canal,
which defines one of the dividing lines for our quarters, has had different
owners north and south of Great Ancoats Street. This lack of coherence
extends to the way the quarters relate to each other. While the two on the
Manchester side are clearly interlinked, neither has a strong connection with
the other two quarters. For instance, the new waterfront retail units that are
being planned on Quarter 3 have no similarities to buildings on the other
side of the street: the buildings will have lightweight glazed structures, and
while they will be on the front of the street, providing a spectacle of activity
through their glazed walls, their entrances will face across the canal. Indeed,
the development will be further contrasted with the addition of a landmark
tower at the corner of the site. Similarly, the quarters on the east side of Great
Ancoats Street have little connection. The retail park (Quarter 2) conveys no
sense of the site's history and it inherently eschews the notion of conservation.

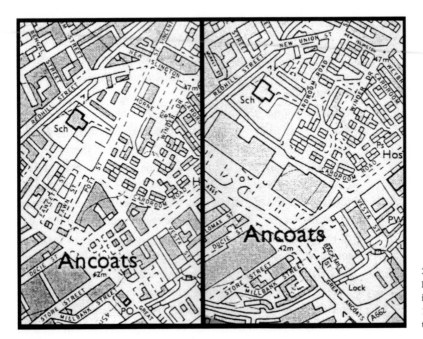

3.6
Maps of Ancoats in 1980 and 1993 (site of the Retail Park)

Where it was previously a site of production and residence, now it is entirely given over to consumption (Figure 3.6). On the other side of the canal from it, the north-western quarter (Quarter 1), despite the fact that many of its buildings face across the water to the unresponsive sides of the Retail Park buildings, is also trying to dissociate itself from its neighbour. The ABPT recently planned erecting a 'beacon' on the intersection of Redhill Street and Great Ancoats as a response to the Retail Park's planned 'tower signs' along its frontage.[11] These would be part of the quarter's claim to be the gateway to the 'real' Ancoats. The real Ancoats would thus be identified as the same as the conservation area and what has become known as Ancoats Urban Village. And of course this beacon would have a strange relation to the sites across Great Ancoats Street and their planned tower: two separate beacons, each demarcating particular spaces less than 100 yards away from one another. Similarly, the two quarters on the Manchester side are of little interest to Quarter 1: they exist outside the conservation zone and are explicitly not the concern of the Ancoats Urban Village Company.

The two quarters on the north side have therefore achieved very marked self-definition and difference from the areas around them. Quarter 1 has until recently (with the redevelopment of the corner site) not had a corporate presence, with non-profit-making companies plus local activists providing a cushion against corporatism. But Quarter 2 is almost equally distinct. Its big sheds lack architectural detail and have the same signage as any other retail park around the country. Their architectural form is therefore easily overlooked simply because it is so pragmatic and ubiquitous (unlike those other, older warehouses across the canal whose pragmatism was so innovatory). Such retail parks must seek to reassure their customers of the consistency of their brands, regardless of where they happen to trade. They are, therefore, inherently placeless. In the context of Ancoats, the Retail Park offers a local polarity: it is not about anthropological place and it is not a place of memory; those are the preserve of Quarter 1.[12] The other main point about this retail park is that it is the most visited of all the four quarters and it is the only quarter that retains a strong and living link to a local working-class community; blindness towards it is therefore only a feature of certain of Ancoats's interested bodies and one that has a distinct sense of a class agenda.

The 'blindness' as regards the Retail Park means that the 'bridge' over the canal which we see as the centre of the larger site seems to offer a view onto the wall of famous mills on the north-west quarter and to ignore everything else. This was always a favoured view for artists making images of Ancoats and its orientation towards the north-west has, if anything, been increased by the lowering of its parapet on the north side. When originally built, these and other similar parapets around Manchester's waterways were upwards of 6 feet high and, as Friedrich Engels observed, they acted 'mercifully' to hide the view of the stagnant and foul-smelling water from those at street level.[13] The parapet that still exists on the south side continues to act as a barrier to easy viewing of the canal on that side from the road.

Across the four parts of the site, then, there is a remarkable variety of urban and architectural elements that bear upon themes of memory and amnesia. Among these we might highlight its small workforce and its residential depopulation (as well as its planned repopulation); the combination of local conservation bodies as well as large regional and national developers; the co-existence of the effects of older attitudes to regeneration (the Retail Park) with newer 'heritage-led' regeneration, both of which have impacted greatly on the current character of the area; the presence of a relatively high proportion of listed buildings, and their co-existence with a high proportion of empty spaces; and, in addition, the continuing attempts to make Ancoats a World Heritage site.

Place

The point where these quarters meet lacks what is commonly thought of as a sense of place and this is partly because it sits astride a boundary, the thoroughfare of Great Ancoats Street. But there is more to this lack of place than merely a wide, busy road. There is little sense of public space across Ancoats and, despite its size and nineteenth-century significance, no major public buildings.[14] The pubs, churches, branch library and dispensary, which once provided the only group of public buildings, have either been demolished or have intermittent use. The schools that once dotted the area had to make extraordinary arrangements for playgrounds, appropriating streets or using their roofs. Once potent senses of community in Ancoats, and the identification of it as a coherent entity, have decreased as more and more people and businesses have moved out of the area and housing has been cleared.[15]

Naming the area, both on the small and large scales, has often been problematic. On the large scale, as part of East Manchester, the area was hardly mentioned until recently in the entrepreneurial narratives that have been constructed around Manchester's regeneration. It was a '"marginal space", the area's communities written out, unnamed, in the envisioning of a New Manchester'.[16] But since the late 1990s the area has been recognised and named – as one consultation document put it, 'New East Manchester, A new town in the city'[17] – as a new abstract space to be redeveloped. On the smaller scale, 'New Islington' was recently announced as a new name for the area around the Cardroom Estate, to the north of the Retail Park.[18] The name revives an older name for the area but deletes one associated with cotton production, presumably because it had come to be identified with a rundown housing estate. Although Ancoats is the name given to Quarter 1 today and, to a lesser extent, to Quarter 2, on a number of nineteenth-century maps the area is called New Cross (after a cross that stood at the corner of Great Ancoats and Newton Lane, now Oldham Road) despite the fact that Police Commissioners named Ancoats as Police District 1 in 1792 with its western boundary as Great Ancoats Street.[19] By the turn of the nineteenth century maps represented New Cross as subsidiary to Ancoats.[20] Whether Quarters 3 and 4 ever qualified for the name Ancoats is more uncertain. There is a Little Ancoats Street just south of Great Ancoats, but the industrial grain of the landscapes on the Manchester side is so different historically that it is easy to imagine this side being unnamed.[21] This namelessness is reflected in current uncertainties about what to call the new development along the canal: from the architects' preferred 'Piccadilly Basin', to the market researchers' 'Waterfront'.[22]

The need to find new names for the area is almost matched by a desire to create spaces that can be readily understood, in contemporary terms, as public. A little further to the north, conservation bodies campaigned a few years ago for the opening up of an Italian piazza beside a Victorian Romanesque church as the heart of an area designated 'Little Italy', and though this has since been scaled down, it remains a key feature of their vision for the area. The Italian-styling of this plan, while it was justified by the historical existence of an Italian community in Ancoats, also linked well with the conservationists' taste for what has become called the 'new urbanism'. It has been suggested, however, that the very size of the originally envisaged piazza would have imposed a false notion of the Italian community's presence, to the detriment of other communities in the area.

Ancoats's historic image is of a tight grid pattern with buildings on the back edge of pavements, the houses and mills so close that life was lived mostly within a small orbit of the workplace. Recently, however, a new concept of place has interposed itself here with the designation of Ancoats as an Urban Village. The designation serves to link Ancoats with a national movement and with a tendency within modern English culture to idealise the village as an intimate, harmonious and orderly community, compact and bounded but also organically related to the national landscape.[23] As deployed here, the concept figures Ancoats as an enclave of civility and community in an industrial wasteland. It emphasises certain aspects of the area's character: St Peter's, for example, is regarded as its natural village hall, and its separation from Manchester by the width of Great Ancoats Street is now part of its distinctive feel, but so too is its proximity to the city centre by foot.[24] Being an Urban Village implies aspiring to being an area where people live, work and play, as well as a more specific set of aesthetic and social aspirations:

> Discussions would be about the quality of the design, the quality of the materials, the massing of the building on the existing site; whether it provides uses that animate the street 24 hours a day or whether it enhances surveillance on the street to reduce issues of crime . . . Are we going to become a residential suburb? . . . We are trying to encourage more commercial use, encouraging workshops, encouraging retail provision and you know café society.[25]

The 'villaging' of Ancoats thus entails demographic and aesthetic changes. One plan is that the small existing population that largely lives in social housing will be fleshed out – actually quadrupled in size – by diversifying tenure and sizes of residential unit. The new urbanism has proposed changes to Ancoats's historic form through the opening up of some areas to provide recognisable public space essentially for recreation and the calming of traffic so that pedestrian activity is less functional. But such opening up only goes so far. In 2000 an electrical shop was demolished on Great Ancoats Street and the demolition unveiled a previously never seen vista of Ancoats; indeed, suddenly the area could be seen as a collection of monuments.[26] However, there was no argument made that this vista should be preserved and the reasons given all depended upon the assumption that certain historical moments had a privileged authenticity.[27] Instead the development that has since filled this space – the new building built by Gleesons – is presented as another beacon or gateway, defining the boundary of Ancoats. Aptly, its raised corner unit will house an upmarket café-bar. Across Great Ancoats, Quarters 3 and 4 will also create public spaces along the new model of outdoor-oriented spaces of leisure. The 'Waterfront' is exactly that – or at least it may be a compromised but still-familiar image of that. Here the Bellway Homes development, an enclave without a new street network to serve it, will have the canal frontage as its centrepiece, thus drawing the line between public and private in favour of privacy even if the canal is still visible to non-residents. Similarly, the return of roving canal boats to the newly styled (private) 'marina' is not likely in the foreseeable future: the 'marina' will be seen as a water-feature not as an accessible area.[28]

Gateways, open piazza-like areas, pedestrian-friendly streets, and café-bars are thus coming to define the public spaces of the new Ancoats. These are all exterior spaces or spaces that orient themselves towards the outside. Although the vision is very far from being realised yet (the cobble-stones may still be present but the carts and horses that would have prevented loungers from hearing themselves speak have long gone), they suggest that public life is best lived as a kind of vacant lingering in the environs of history and that openness, either through being in the open or in a large space, equates with modern freedoms.[29] It is an odd combination in the context of Ancoats, and one that seems to imply a layering, if not an active juxtaposition, of class interests as the area attempts to make its appeal to better-off cus-tomers and residents. In the minds of those who lived in Ancoats, public space was probably very different, mostly centred on churches, markets and pubs. The famous Whit Walks always began and ended at a church, and different communities had their preferred churches and the buildings themselves were important markers of belonging and status. The markets in Ancoats were both general and specialised, just as much gathering places as places of commerce. There were huge numbers of pubs serving the area,[30] and these were often identified with particular communities.[31] But the new vision of an exterior public life is combined with a kind of *nostalgie de la boue*, an almost regressive desire for slums and scenes of labour which despite their privations and poverty are seen as truer than the shams built since.[32] Manchester's regen-eration must retain the old 'satanic mills' image while projecting something new; memory must be seen to be respected but only providing it presents no contradictory or resistant element to change.

Time, heritage and regeneration

On the face of it, the recent past in Ancoats has seen constant tensions between the interests of heritage and regeneration. But this needs imme-diately to be qualified by saying that it is only in Quarter 1 that this is true, since Quarter 2 was almost completely demolished and rebuilt in the 1980s, while although Quarters 3 and 4 have listed buildings in them, they also have sufficient open space (cleared and left to accrue value by being remade as car parks some time ago) to enable development with little interruption from heritage bodies. In Quarter 1, then, the tensions revolve around apparently different visions of change and some examples of this follow. The Ancoats Buildings Preservation Trust regarded St Peter's Church as crucial to its policy of heritage-led regeneration, and it managed to convince the North West Development Agency to give money to cover the building's insurance and security. Over lesser buildings the Trust often argues for the buildings as built records of the local life: in trying to stop the Cotton Tree pub from being demolished, for example, it argued that even though it was not the original Georgian pub nevertheless 'we wanted to record that people lived here, worked here, drank here'.[33] It lost that battle but managed to win another over the Henry Street Bridge which crosses the canal a little way north of Great Ancoats and probably dates back to 1804. (The bridge is actually virtually without purpose now that the route between houses and mills that it used to serve has been erased with the building of the Retail Park.) Here it argued for the retention of the original parapets even though they have become hiding places for muggers, and won the argument with the suggestion that CCTV cameras be placed in the new Redhill Street beacon.[34]

So, by a combination of selective endorsement of details of the existing 'historic' fabric and taking advantage of new developments, the interests of heritage are furthered. Conservation can be seen as preserving the frames (architecture) for historically located forms of social life as if they were eternal: the owner of a local pub, for instance, was not permitted to make changes to the interior so that it could be used for his textile business, the building as a consequence was unworkable and deteriorated until an arson attack in the mid-1990s forced it to be pulled down.[35] Similarly, some recent residents have 'improved' their houses by putting on stone cladding, adding plastic windows or Victorian coach lamps and removing historic features. The ABPT has fought this by pushing for a legal restraint to be applied to Ancoats ensuring that local residents cannot change anything about their house structure or fittings without permission.[36] Conservation also sometimes seeks the most trace-like remains of a building to evoke the whole: in the example of the Coates School on Jersey Street, renovation came too late to save the structure and an old stone sign ('Coates School 1821') in a new building testifies to the ghostly presence of the past. Conservation's chosen objects may also be privileged more because of an historic association than anything intrinsic to the object itself: the Brownsfield Mill, for instance, is a reasonably interesting early nineteenth-century mill whose listing seems more a result of its historical associations (it was partly occupied by the airplane makers AVRO in the early twentieth century) than by any qualities of the building. There is a paradox here, though, because the concrete rendering of the building – most likely added by the Ministry of Aircraft Production in the Second World War – will not be allowed to survive the building's currently planned refitting.

And, of course, conservation can inadvertently inhibit the speed at which regeneration can take place. Landowners believe that they can make a profit from their land because it is in a conservation area that may become a World Heritage-nominated site; and so the best policy seems to be to wait until land values increase. There is an apparent continuity here with the emptying of the area that occurred from the 1960s onwards, with bombsites or demolished buildings replaced by wasteland and then by car parks which particularly abounded on the Manchester side. Here Mancunians were encouraged to moor their cars on the edges of the city centre, the council seeing these car parks as a holding operation to maintain some basic standard of maintenance and a minimum income from charges.[37]

Conservationists often argue that an area has a certain character, best embodied by architectural forms and building materials, and that this should be conformed to in any subsequent development. But in Ancoats's excessive subservience to its existing buildings, pastiche has been explicitly rejected by many of the conservation bodies. The new Gleesons building, for instance, was expected to adhere to the wall-like character of the existing mills along the canal yet not to their function (in that sense the Retail Park buildings are truer to Ancoats) and, while they had a fair measure of red brick, certainly not to their detailing.[38] The bodies themselves disagree over matters like whether new footpath and road materials should be man-made or natural. Here the argument can adopt the idea that the spirit of the place is of a pioneering and pragmatic Victorian ethos that would inevitably have adopted the best materials currently to hand, or the idea that the best thing to do would be to recycle the existing materials both for environmentalist reasons and because the new materials create aesthetic effects that are simply out of keeping.[39] All arguments rest on tests of authenticity, and although there can be disagreement about what this means in practice, there are accepted ideas of what constitutes the character of the area. One of these is the industrial architecture itself, the other is the chief building material – bricks.

Brick (and glass)

Everywhere in Ancoats there are bricks. These are mostly a mixture of the softer red of hand-made bricks and the smoother, harder-seeming manufactured bricks characteristic of the North-west. We argued earlier that the extolling of new public spaces is combined in Ancoats with a *nostalgie de la boue*.[40] While new open spaces are proposed and a life of leisure is imagined, at the same time there is an aesthetics of surfaces, colours and materials that is seen as a continuation with things Victorian. Newer local versions of the dream of sunlight, fresh air and transparency that is still modernism's main legacy, are attached to its old nightmare, the horror of dampness, darkness and unrelenting labour conjured up by the materials of the Victorian city, most notably brick.

Before analysing the contemporary attitude to bricks we turn to an example from a previous period of de-industrialisation in Ancoats. Today, coming across the Daily Express building on Great Ancoats Street still has shock value in the contrast between the red brick walls of the surrounding streets and its streamlined shape, curved corners and smooth sheath of black and translucent glass (Figure 3.7). It seems as if these surfaces will never bear the marks of time (though perhaps they simply bear them differently or need more frequent replacement) and that what was set down here will be, as one observer put it, 'a new building as long as it may last'.[41] Whether new or not, it will certainly always convey a sense of complete difference from the aura of its Victorian surroundings as the embodiment of a new epoch in which a glass and metal architecture offered to erase the traces of memory and to eclipse the presence of the Victorian past.[42] From 1939 when it was finished, the building also brought more than just new materials to Ancoats. Its glazed double-height ground floor windows provided a spectacular sight of the newspaper's presses at work all through the day and, when lit up from the inside, all through the night. This offered a further denial of Ancoats's existing mills which had striven to light up their interiors through open floors and windows regularly punched through their brick walls. Where the mills let light into their interiors, the Daily Express building used light to display its workings to the streets around it. In the Ancoats context the building provided a brilliant discordancy with its industrial surroundings: it was to do with communication and information, it faced away from Ancoats and back towards the city centre, and it offered the pleasures of public display more usually associated with department store consumption. While the Daily Express building still offers some of these pleasures, in the rest of Ancoats, as we have seen, no such spectacular contrasts are planned. Rather, in practice, there is an almost magical blending or merging of elements of the modernist utopia with elements that speak of heritage and memory (and which would have been regarded by modernists as dystopian).

The role of materials in Ancoats's current re-imagining requires further thought. We might start here with the 'bad' everyday of nineteenth-century urban life; its negative, unredeemed modality of daily struggles whose environs have often been associated with bricks.[43] In Charles Dickens's *Hard Times* (1854) the brickyness of Coketown is emphasised repeatedly, and it is

identified both with bricks as the smallest man-made units of the town and with the soul-deadening monotony of work associated with bricklaying. Both these identifications make links between Coketown's material forms, its pollution ('Nature was as strongly bricked out as killing airs and gases were bricked in')[44] and a banal repetition of actions that constitutes its temporality:

> It was a town of red brick or of brick that would have been red if the smoke and ashes had allowed it . . . It had a black canal in it, and a river that ran purple with ill-smelling dye, and vast piles

3.7
Daily Express building, Great Ancoats Street, Manchester (1939). Architect – Owen Williams

of building full of windows where there was a rattling and a trembling all day long, and where the piston of the steam-engine worked monotonously up and down . . . every day was the same as yesterday and tomorrow, and every year the counterpart of the last and the next.[45]

But bricks, as Michael Fried has argued, were also often identified by different artists and thinkers with a 'good' everyday in the nineteenth century. The laying of bricks, an action which of course is preserved in the final appearance of the wall, might be seen as embodying the temporal extensiveness that values 'every single little moment [as] of utmost importance'; a kind of utopian awareness of the positive valence of the everyday.[46]

Clearly contemporary Ancoats has elements of both of these attitudes and in this it epitomises a wider state of affairs. The story of how the good and bad associations of bricks have come together in the present has been particularly well told in Raphael Samuel's essay 'The Return to Brick'. In the 1950s brick was seen as a lowly and somewhat dismal building material, 'cumbersome and heavy, it was the enemy of light and space'.[47] It was associated with 'mean' by-law streets, the squalor of tenements and slums and, we would add, closely identified with the Victorian cities that were beginning to receive their obsequies in the form of extensive demolition. What was most admired in Victorian architecture was largely its beauties of engineering especially as they were achieved through the use of iron and glass. (Concrete at just this same period was coming to be seen as the heroic medium of dynamic modern cities.) Beyond the influence of the Victorian Society and several other factors, Samuel suggests that in the 1960s 'the revaluation of Victorian brickwork was more a collateral effect of the "gentrification" and rehabilitation of erstwhile slum terraces of the inner city by a culturally ambitious if somewhat impecunious stratum of the middle class'.[48] A little later the cultural change became officially recognised: 'conservation areas reflected these efforts rather than initiating them; typically they involved a local council giving the imprimatur of municipal authority to a process already near complete.'[49] So the revival of brick went hand in hand with the recreation of simulacra of past environments or the preservation of environments that had lost their original functions. In the contemporary philosophy of conservation, brickwork has a special place: it represents a craft material in an age of mass production (even when it was not); it is tactile, seemingly individual and even quirky; it has been linked with national virtues; and it seems to mature with age.[50] In all these respects, then, brick seemed to represent the opposite from modernism: 'oldness is all and class discrimination, retrospectively at least, [is] irrelevant.'[51]

Time doesn't flow

Broadly, it might be said that Victorian architects aimed to make their architecture speak directly about historical relationships and differences, and didactically to stimulate the moral sentiments of their architecture's users and viewers by evoking particular remembered associations. But this desire for clear historical relationships in Victorian architecture is largely absent from Ancoats, whose architecture instead embodies a complementary sense of time as regulated around smaller units of productive activity. Bypassed by the civic embellishments of the latter half of the nineteenth century and defined by its industrial functions, Ancoats has been characterised by a mixture of pre-Victorian mills and utilitarian by-law housing and these speak of the framing of time around the working day and the working week – economic space. The arrangement of the mills, epitomised by Murray's Mills and by McConnel and Kennedy's Mills in Ancoats, is largely around courtyards entered via one main portal whose opening and closing would have been rigidly regulated by the working day, with lock-outs defining the start of shifts. The mill yard was a centripetal space often overlooked by the manager's bay window and inside the blocks themselves the workers' actions in time and space were regulated by the working of the looms, defined by the number of picks per minute.[52]

These nineteenth-century ways of understanding the relation between buildings and time are very different from the temporalities that seem to be represented in Ancoats today, now that actual industrial production has been almost entirely erased from the area. The Daily Express building denied both the older economic temporality and the traces and associations of Victorian architecture. The production of daily news, dependent on an actual network of newsgathering, printing and disseminating labour, would be represented by the image of an ever-modern spectacle of tireless machine production. But post-industrial Ancoats seeks a reconciliation between these Victorian and modern positions. Thus, to experience Ancoats in the early twenty-first century is to witness the way that a built environment can seem to manifest time as both receding and approaching at the same instant and with different tempos, as if in a folded and contorted perspective in which the past is never over and done with and the future always arriving. Apparently most diametrically opposed within this perspective are what we might term 'heritage time' and 'developers' time'. In 'heritage time' the most useful metaphors are those of the city as palimpsest – the city as a field of inscriptions, some nearly invisible, some newly written, a delicate matter of layered traces that manifests the 'thickness' of the past but requires care and maintenance – or the city as a spatialised system for recalling the past, a memory theatre. This latter harks back to notions of the traditional city as a 'mental map of significance' and a memorial of itself,[53] and in the case of the heritage industry this is a useful way of avoiding the divisive effects, demographic changes, and economic restructuring of modernity. In the case of Ancoats, however, these metaphors work together to form a generalised idea of remembrance, something that combines the palimpsest and the theatre. The palimpsest's role in this is that it seems to allow for changes since an originating or most-valued historical moment, as well as for additions, distinct but respectful towards that past; it glosses over dislocations or at least contains them within the same medium.[54] In 'developers' time', on the other hand, the city is seen as 'a nowhen . . . a synchronic system' that progresses towards the future flattening out the 'indeterminable and stubborn resistances offered by traditions'.[55] This incessant, interminable march to the future can take in any of the forms of history and modernity so long as they can be absorbed into the flux of change. But perhaps these concepts of heritage time and developers' time, with their seemingly contradictory attitudes to the past – one preserving memory, the other demolishing it – are only apparently opposed.

Of course, all cities change constantly, they have no static moment that enables inventorised description, and their spatial and architectural forms change in myriad ways: rapidly reproducing themselves, in fits and starts, or in the longer *durées* of decay and slow decline. Different paces of change and their associated relations of social power were always evident in nineteenth-century Ancoats; for those who came to it from the country it could not help but be seen as a different world. But change and contrasting temporalities are now evident within Ancoats itself and, we would argue, they are evident in a newly stark way. The starkness seems to have something to do with a desire to mark an epochal change: this is not the industrial city, nor is it the de-industrialised city, it seems to convey – those are both distinctly bracketed out. It is instead the 'post-industrial' city, with all that is implied about both dislocation and the co-location of change. We observe not just the simultaneous traces of many different and non-synchronous periods in the city's history but also a disorienting sense of change in the moment of observation.

'Time doesn't flow', the French philosopher Michel Serres has written, 'it percolates.'[56] In other words, urban time is not like a line, as architectural historians often would have it, a continuous sequence of monuments and events. Rather, in urban time some elements are filtered out, jumped over, left behind or forgotten. Serres uses metaphors like crumpling, folding, and liquid turbulence to capture the complex diversity of time – a multi-temporality that can better be studied by its topology than measured by its metrical geometry or chronology.[57] Thus, buildings themselves, which can be used to represent the most solid, capital-intensive, and slow changing of urban phenomena as well as the rapid changes of demolition and disaster, are revealed to be implicated in a process of constant if erratic transformation, while their representations involve equal displacements or reiterations of priorities and interests. So Ancoats is also not merely 'post-industrial', certain of its industrial forms are no more obsolescent (as a modernist might believe) as its modernisms are anachronistic.

Notes

1 A particularly useful discussion of these issues can be found in Margaret Rose, *The Post-Modern and the Post-Industrial: A Critical Analysis*, Cambridge: Cambridge University Press, 1991, Chapter 2.
2 Helen Hills (with Paul Tyrer), 'The Fetishized Past: Post-Industrial Manchester and Interstitial Spaces', *Visual Culture in Britain*, vol, 3, no. 2, 2002, pp. 103–17.
3 The Prussian architect K. F. Schinkel came to Manchester in 1826 to study mill design in Ancoats, drawing the wall of mills along Redhill Street as well as details of construction: see K. F. Schinkel, *The English Journey: Journal of a Visit to France and Britain in 1826*, ed. D. Bindman and G. Riemann, New Haven, CT: Yale University Press, 1993. In 1835 Alexis de Tocqueville described the conditions of the workforce in Ancoats's mills: Alexis de Tocqueville, *Journeys to England and Ireland*, London: Faber and Faber, 1958, p. 108.
4 One example, rare though paradigmatic, of this philanthropy was the Ancoats Art Museum set up in 1877, among whose exemplary displays were etchings and paintings whose purpose was 'to encourage "righteous discontent" among the residents of Ancoats with their environment': Michael Harrison, 'Art and Social Regeneration: The Ancoats Art Museum', *Manchester Region History Review*, vol. 7, 1993, p. 68.
5 On liberal governmentality, see Patrick Joyce, *The Rule of Freedom: Liberalism and the Modern City*, London and New York: Verso, 2003.
6 There are similarities here with Castlefield, another area of Manchester, whose earlier transformation in the 1980s is often pointed to by Ancoats's conservation bodies as an example of heritage-led regeneration.
7 Richard Rogers and Anne Power, *Cities for a Small Country*, London: Faber and Faber, 2000. For more detailed accounts that adopt the same narrative of improvement, see John J. Parkinson-Bailey, *Manchester: An Architectural History*, Manchester: Manchester University Press, 2000, pp. 292–5; and Clare Hartwell, *Manchester*, London: Penguin, 2001, pp. 273–91.
8 See Parkinson-Bailey, *Manchester*, p. 294. On the marketing of post-industrial Manchester, see Stephen V. Ward, *Selling Places: The Marketing and Promotion of Towns and Cities 1850–2000*, London: E & F N Spon, 1998, Chapters 9 and 10.
9 The AUVC and the ABPT were established as sister organisations in 1996, the former largely focused on the social aspects of the area, especially civic management and promotional activity, the latter on its architectural aspects. The ABPT does have some responsibility beyond the quarter, having a remit to work with the Cardroom Estate across the canal.
10 See Green's 1794 map.
11 Interview with Kate Dixon, Director, Ancoats Buildings Preservation Trust, 8 August 2000.

12 On the relations between non-place, anthropological place and places of memory, see Marc Augé, *Non-Places: Introduction to an Anthropology of Supermodernity*, London and New York: Verso, 1995, pp. 77–9.

13 Friedrich Engels, *The Condition of the Working Classes in England*, London: Penguin, 1987, p. 89.

14 For public space in Manchester, see Karen Evans, Ian Taylor, and Penny Fraser, *A Tale of Two Cities: Global Change, Local Feeling and Everyday Life in Manchester and Sheffield*, London: Routledge, 1996, pp. 84–7.

15 The population of Ancoats accounted for more than a quarter of the city's population in the mid-nineteenth century and now it is down to 400 – in this site there is only one occupied house.

16 Kevin Ward, 'Entrepreneurial urbanism, state restructuring and civilising "New" East Manchester', *Area*, 35: 2, 2003, p. 121.

17 Ibid., p. 123.

18 *The Guardian*, 1 February 2002 and 17 September 2002. The rich ironies of this name, given Tony Blair's identification with Islington in London, have been fully exploited by the press.

19 '"More Than an Example": Ancoats in Historical Perspective', *Manchester Regional History Review*, vol. 7, 1993, p. 3.

20 See 1905 O/S map.

21 The name Brown's Field appears to designate this area on the 1851 O/S map, but it does not appear on any other map.

22 Interview with Dave Green, Ian Simpson Architects, 9 August 2000. By contrast, the names of streets have remained relatively stable over the past 150 years, with many street names still making industrial, commercial and imperial associations: such as Blossom Street, Murray Street, and Bengal Street.

23 The concept is promoted by the Urban Villages Group and a representative of this body was established on the board of the AUVC from early on. Urban Villages are defined by several criteria, including numbers of people (3–5000), pedestrian access, mixed use and mixed demographic profile: see Paul Butler and David Tye, 'Ancoats Urban Village: Old Mills, New Homes', in John Parkinson-Bailey (ed.), *Sites of the City*, Manchester: Manchester Metropolitan University, 1996. On the use of the idea of the village within national culture, see David Matless, *Landscape and Englishness*, London: Reaktion, 1998.

24 There is more than irony here. In the nineteenth century the proximity of working-class areas to respectable shopping and business districts was seen as a threat: Simon Gunn, *The Public Culture of the Victorian Middle Class*, Manchester: Manchester University Press, 2000, pp. 62–3.

25 Interview with Louis Tinker, Ancoats Urban Village Company, 2 August 2000.

26 'You can see the mills, you can see George Leigh Street School, you can see St Peter's church tower, you can see Victoria Square, you can see the Iceplant building, you can see the Express building – it's a great panoramic view.' Ibid.

27 'It was never there originally was it? I mean, you can't sort of say that anything shouldn't be put back onto that site because it's such a great view.' Ibid.

28 Interview with Dave Green, 9 August 2000.

29 This is one of the selling points of loft spaces, regardless of how they might subsequently be subdivided, and in this sense they exemplify the valorization of selected aspects of a fetishized past – surfaces, signs of use, an aesthetic of spartan bareness – with an amnesia concerning others. It might be interesting in this respect to look at previous conversions of mills into dwellings; see Mike Williams and D. A. Farnie, *Cotton Mills in Greater Manchester*, Preston: Carnegie Publishing, 1992, p. 21.

30 In 1920, for example, there were 93 pubs in Ancoats: N. Richardson, *The Old Pubs of Ancoats*, Swinton: Neil Richardson, 1987.

31 Ibid., p. 14.

32 This contrasts very markedly with the immediate post-war period when a drive to reconstruct and modernise entailed representing the existing Victorian city as a place of decay and decomposition; see, for instance, the Paul Rotha documentary *A City Speaks*, 1946.

33 Interview with Kate Dixon, 8 August 2000.

34 Ibid.

35 Interview with Nazir Tahir, 9 August 2000.

36 Interview with Kate Dixon, 8 August 2000.

37 See *City of Manchester Planning and Economic Bulletin*, 6, June 1982.

38 Interview with Louis Tinker, 2 August 2000; interview with Kate Dixon, 8 August 2000.

39 Ibid.

40 This kind of nostalgia for Victorian poverty might be dated back to at least the early 1960s where it has links to an incipient postmodernism. One particularly fascinating and pivotal example of this is the flats designed by James Stirling and James Gowan in Preston in 1961. The flats luxuriate in nostalgia for things Victorian; indeed, the architects even approvingly quote Somerset Maugham writing about Charlie Chaplin's nostalgia for his slum childhood: James Stirling and James Gowan, 'Re-housing at Preston, Lancashire', *Architectural Design*, 31, December 1961, pp. 538–45.

41 Cecil Stewart writing in 1960, as quoted in David Cottam, *Sir Owen Williams*, London: Architectural Association, 1986, p. 115.

42 This contrast was most fascinatingly discussed by Walter Benjamin: see his 'Short Shadows (II)', in *Selected Writings*, 2, 1927–34, trans. Rodney Livingstone *et al.*, Michael W. Jennings, Howard Eiland and Gary Smith (eds.), Cambridge, MA: Harvard University Press, 1999, pp. 701–2.

43 See Michael Fried, *Menzel's Realism: Art and Embodiment in Nineteenth-Century Berlin*, New Haven, CT: Yale University Press, 2002, p. 159.

44 Charles Dickens, *Hard Times*, Harmondsworth: Penguin, 1969, p. 102.

45 Ibid., p. 65. I was alerted to the importance of bricks in Dickens's novel through Fried, *Menzel's Realism*, pp. 174–5.

46 Fried, *Menzel's Realism*, pp. 152–9. The 'good' everyday is also evidently what is behind the value accorded to bricks in the Arts and Crafts movement, as will be apparent from a glance at William Morris's Red House (named after its unrelieved brick exterior) or at his *News from Nowhere* (1890).

47 Raphael Samuel, 'The Return to Brick', *Theatres of Memory* vol. 1: *Past and Present in Contemporary Culture*, London: 1994 Verso, p. 123.

48 Ibid., pp. 126–7.

49 Ibid., p. 127.

50 Ibid., p. 120.

51 Ibid., p. 129.

52 See Richard Biernacki, *The Fabrication of Labor: Germany and Britain, 1640–1914*, Berkeley, CA: University of California Press, 1995, p. 128.

53 Anthony Vidler, *The Architectural Uncanny*, Cambridge, MA: MIT, 1996, pp. 177–9.

54 Much of this can be found in Ruskin and Morris's combinations of admonitions against restoration while fetishising any trace, however blemished – indeed sometimes the more wracked and worn by time the better – of the handiwork of past craftsmen.

55 Michel de Certeau, *The Practice of Everyday Life*, Berkeley, CA: University of California Press, 1988, p. 94.

56 Michel Serres with Bruno Latour, *Conversations on Science, Culture and Time*, Ann Arbor, MI: University of Michigan Press, 1995, p. 58.

57 Ibid., p. 60.

Louis Mercaville,
chef at the Fairmount
Water Works Interpretive
Center, Philadelphia, opens
a parcel which contains
three boxes of organic
Tunisian dates.

Chapter 4

Concrete and memory

Adrian Forty

Nowadays, any middling-sized to large memorial is made of concrete. Think of Peter Eisenmann's Holocaust memorial in Berlin: 11 acres of undulating charcoal grey concrete, made up of 2751 concrete steles from 3 to 15 feet high. The Vienna Judenplatz Memorial to the Austrian Jews: the negative of a book-lined room, cast in concrete. Ground Zero: the exposed concrete slurry walls of the piling of the foundations of the twin towers are the one feature of the as yet undesigned memorial garden we can be sure about. And there are too many other examples to count. Concrete has become the default material for memorials.

What is odd about this is that concrete has, at the same time, been so generally associated with the erasure and obliteration of memory. Concrete makes everywhere the same. It cuts people off from their past, from nature, from each other. This sense that concrete is a symptom, if not a cause, of alienation has been around since the early 1960s, if not for longer. Take, for example, J-L. Godard's 1966 film *Two or Three Things I Know about Her*, in which lingering shots of concrete being poured on the construction of the Paris *périphérique* are accompanied on the sound track by musings on the city's loss of meaningfulness, its demise as a communicative medium. Or another French example, Henri Lefebvre's 1960 essay 'Notes on The New Town', where, despite the absolute clarity and legibility of the functions of the concrete buildings, the result is an utterly impoverished environment: 'Here I cannot read the centuries, not time, nor the past, nor what is possible'.[1] For all its efficiency, its lack of depth makes the concrete New Town irredeemably boring. All this is nicely summed up by graffiti sprayed onto a multi-storey car park in Marburg in Germany in 1992–3 – *'Beton ist Koma'*, 'Concrete is Coma'.[2]

What is it then about concrete and memory? How can a material so generally thought of as anaesthetic, as amnesiac, have become at the same time the material of choice for the preservation of memories? This paradox is not easily answered, and needs considering both in terms of the history of memorials, and from the point of view of concrete, and its history within modernity. Whatever we can say reflects both on memorials and on concrete – it is the intersection of concrete and memory that concerns us.

To take first the memorial. The twentieth century was obsessed with memory, and to commemorate the dead of its many and destructive wars, built more memorials than any previous era of history. At the same time, philosophy and psychology produced more insight into the processes of memory than were available to previous generations – and their general conclusions were to emphasise the aleatory nature of memory, its fragility against the forces of forgetfulness and repression, and to expose the futility of attempts to perpetuate memory by making physical objects to stand for it. In a word, the modern understanding of memory makes it everything that concrete is not.

If popular memorial building activity went against what philosophy had to say about memory, modern artists and architects generally shared the scepticism about memorials. If modernity was about the transient and the ephemeral, about speed, mobility and the abandonment of tradition, what place could there be for static objects that froze moments of the past for perpetuity? More specifically, modernist aesthetics emphasised the immanence of the object, as it presented itself directly to the senses, and was generally hostile to the association of ideas, to the view that aesthetic response occurred through the train of thoughts and images that objects might evoke. Objections to the monument and the memorial erupted periodically during the first half of the twentieth century in modernist architectural circles. A well-publicised instance was the attack in 1929 by the Czech critic Karel Tiege on Le Corbusier's Mundaneum project for a complex of buildings that would enshrine the collective cultures of the peoples of the world, an alternative to the association of governments that was the League of Nations. Tiege attacked both the project, which he saw as ideologically confused, and Le Corbusier's scheme for it, which seemed to him a betrayal of the primary principle of modern architecture – purposefulness. As Tiege put it:

> Monumental and votive architecture, dedicated to whatever memorial of revolution and liberation; all present-day triumphal arches, festive halls, tombs, palaces and castles result in monstrosities. Examples of concrete and utilitarian architecture, as well as omens of a new metaphysical, monumental architecture both show clearly that, at the present time, architecture will fail in so far as it is not dictated by the actual needs of social and economic life.[3]

After attacks like this, modernist architects were understandably uncomfortable about anything with monumental or memorial aspirations.[4]

Yet this suspicion of the memorial and monumental was maintained against a landscape being transformed by the countless war memorials built to commemorate the dead of the First World War put up in the towns and villages of every country that had been involved in the war. The iconography was generally familiar and traditional, and although there was inventiveness in the design of memorials, this inventiveness, except for a brief period in the Soviet Union, owed nothing to the architectural avant-garde. Almost invariably these memorials were made of stone or bronze, the traditional materials of dignity and solemnity. While concrete may have been used for foundations and structure, they were almost always clad in another material; only in a very few rare cases was concrete ever exposed on the surface of memorials, as this would have been considered unbecoming to the memory of the dead.

When after the Second World War the question of the commemoration arose, it proved far more difficult to satisfy than it had been after 1918. Compared to the relatively static nature of the First World War, its deaths relatively easily catalogued, the Second World War was mobile, it took place all over the place, and furthermore the deaths of many of its victims were invisible, deliberately hidden by their perpetrators. As Adorno commented in his *Minima Moralia*, written during the closing stages of the war, one of the peculiarities of the Second World War was that while the general public had the impression, through the presence of cameramen and photographers in front line units, of knowing more, of being more closely involved in the campaigns than had ever been the case in previous wars, it was, on the other hand, far harder to make sense of the strategy of the campaigns.

> The Second World War is as totally divorced from experience as is
> a functioning of a machine from the movements of the body . . .
> Just as the war lacks continuity, history, an 'epic' element, but
> seems rather to start anew from the beginning in each phase, so it
> will leave behind no permanent, unconsciously preserved image
> in the memory.[5]

War left nothing that could be commemorated – or that had not been more than amply recorded as surrogate experience on film.

At the same time, the atrocities of war and of fascism far exceeded those of any previous era, and this too made commemoration difficult, if not impossible. Adorno pointed out that the greatest danger of all was to normalise events, to carry on as before as if nothing had happened. To repeat and continue the extensive memorial-building after the First World War would simply have suggested just such a normality, a return to the status quo and, according to Adorno, have allowed fascism to continue elsewhere in other guises.

From the point of view of the avant-garde architect or designer, any post-war memorial ran the double risk of being both non-modern, not of its time, and of condoning the circumstances of the atrocity. While these strictures did not inhibit people from building memorials, their effect was to raise the level of difficulty in achieving a result that was neither banal nor meaningless. The issues surrounding memorials after 1945 have been extensively written about, particularly in relation to the Holocaust, and no more need be said of them now.[6]

Turning now to concrete, the situation is rather different. Compared to the abundant literature on memorials, little has been said about concrete as a medium for monuments. Most writing about concrete is concerned with its structural aspects; the relatively small proportion of the literature that deals with its aesthetic aspects generally takes the form of an apology, committed to showing that concrete is not dense, dull, grey, monotonous or soulless – all the things that are usually said about it – but that it can be beautiful and inspiring. In these apologies, it is rare to find much mention of concrete's application to monuments. One exception is a book produced for the Swiss Portland Cement Company, entitled *Le Béton dans l'Art Contemporain*, in which we find the following statement: 'It is in the creation of monumental works that the use of concrete fully justifies itself.'[7] Now this is a surprising remark: it is not in bridges, in wide span roofs, or in any other structures that fulfil the ideal of achieving the most effect with the least – the customary measure of justification for a material – but in monuments, which are notorious for displaying serious redundancy of material. It is clear from the illustrations that follow in this section of Joray's book that by 'monumental works' he means purely symbolic objects without utility, apart from commemoration (though not all his examples have memorial purposes). Joray goes on to explain why concrete is especially suited to monuments: first, it is the only material affordable for their necessarily large size, and, second, forms can be produced in it that would be impossible in stone or bronze.

But these explanations are not sufficient. Cost, with memorials is not a factor, or should not be seen to be. Cheapness in a memorial is offensive, offensive to those it commemorates, and therefore concrete could never be chosen simply on the grounds of economy. The memorial is the one form of structure on which, ostensibly at least, no expense should be seen to be spared – and it was for that reason that up until the Second World War, granite or limestone were the almost invariable rule for memorials. Even memorials that might look as if they had been made out of concrete, or imply that they were made of concrete, turn out to have been made of, or at least clad in stone. The war memorial at Como in Italy, built 1931–33 and designed by the rationalist architect Giuseppe Terragni, adapting a sketch by the Futurist architect Antonio Sant'Elia, was not, as one might have expected of a work with these origins, concrete, but was faced in stone. Presumably bare concrete would have been considered disrespectful to the dead, notwithstanding Sant'Elia's and Marinetti's enthusiasm for the material, and contempt for stone architecture.

If cost can be discounted as a sufficient justification for the choice of concrete as a material for memorials, so too can the argument about its structural possibilities. Solidity, mass and weight are the qualities most often implied by memorials; if one were looking for examples of structural ingenuity, monuments are not generally where one would look. As a class, they must in structural terms be among the most conservative of structures – though this is not to deny that there have been individual memorials (and many proposals for memorials) with exceptional structural properties.

If neither economy nor structural possibilities entirely justify the preference of concrete for memorials, what other explanations are there? It is in concrete's association with modernity that the most likely explanation seems to lie, for if the memorial was an inherently non-modern form, concrete offered the aura of being modern. Furthermore, concrete offered a solution to the problem of commemoration after the Second World War, for concrete, as its wartime military uses demonstrated, could be barbaric – and this connotation was of value in the changed circumstances of the post-1945 memorial.

Before considering these questions in any more detail, we should think about what it means to call concrete a 'modern' material. This does not just mean that now it is here, when not so long ago it wasn't. The facts that concrete was only rediscovered in the early nineteenth century, and not until the end of the nineteenth century became widely used as a building material are not what make it modern. Nor does the fact that it created possibilities in the design of structure that had been previously unavailable. The peculiarity of reinforced concrete construction is that it is isotropic – it transmits forces equally effectively in any direction – and the consequence of this is that the distinction between load and support, which had been basic to all previous structural systems, ceased to apply with reinforced concrete. Yet the freedom that this innovation offered to the design of structures is not what constitutes the modernity of concrete. What made concrete 'modern' was that while it has been liberating, it has at the same time been destructive. Its structural possibilities allow us to redirect our destiny, to build bridges and superhighways where none could be built before, to hold back the sea, to join continents, to build cities at densities which would previously have resulted only in unbearable squalor, to reverse or to overcome the forces of nature so that mankind can live in greater comfort and security. In all these senses, concrete has been emancipatory. But the price that is paid for this is the loss of the old ways of life, of the craft skills of stonemasons, of workers in wood and metal. It cuts us off from nature, and eradicates nature: to 'concrete over' is to end nature's dominion over the surface of the earth. And as well as bringing us closer together, it cuts us off from one another – it is part of an irrevocable alteration of relations between people. And these changes are permanent. With concrete, there is no going back. Its indestructability is both one of its most valued, and at the same time most reviled features.

The prospect of the transformation of life, but at the cost of losing what was familiar, is the mark of modernity. Concrete is no more responsible for this process, productive of both excitement and regret than is any other product of science and technology: the motor car or television can be described in identical terms. And like these other instruments of modernisation, concrete also mediates our responses to those changes. Through the very material that transforms the world as we watch, architects and engineers in the way that they use it orchestrate our reactions and feelings about those changes, generally so as to diminish our confusion and misgivings about the whole contradictory process. Where we see this happening most obviously is in the presumption that concrete has no history – it is always new, always fresh. Nothwithstanding that concrete has been around for over a century, longer than the consciousness of anyone living on the planet, we are still now asked to look at every concrete structure as if it were new, the first of its kind, a total innovation. Those who make things out of concrete generally discourage us from seeing it as a historical material, a material that by now has a very considerable past. Its constant newness is one of the more persistent myths that attach to concrete.

In short, what makes concrete 'modern' is that it precipitates all sorts of contradictory responses. It opens up possibilities, but at the same time closes off access to a previous way of life; and every concrete structure, in one way or another, announces this to us. Confronted by a concrete memorial, we face an object that advertises the double aspect of modernity – of a journey into a better future, but which at the same time, as a memorial, reverts to a moment of past time. Considered from the point of view of concrete, then, if we are to find an answer to why concrete justifies itself most fully in the realisation of monuments, it would be that these are the only category of construction in which it is possible for concrete to deal with what convention forbids it to address, namely, the past. Whatever service concrete may be to memorials, it would seem that memorials allow concrete to reveal what otherwise has had to be repressed.

Before turning to some of the cases of concrete memorials, we should comment on what might be called, to borrow a term from nineteenth-century Ecclesiology, the 'sacramentality' of concrete, that is to say, its capacity to bear spiritual or religious ideas. Churches are among some of the earliest concrete buildings. Generally the reason was cheapness: it gave the greatest volume for the least cost. The oldest examples were built in mass concrete: at St Barnabas in Oxford (1869–72) Arthur Blomfield planned to have concrete walls, but substituted rendered rubble walls because it was cheaper; at All Saints, Brockhampton (1901–2), W.R. Lethaby used concrete, as also at his chapel at Melsetter, Orkney (1900); and most spectacularly, in Westminster Cathedral (J.F. Bentley, 1895–1903), the shell and the domes were built of mass concrete. In all these cases, the concrete was covered with other materials, though at Westminster, this was never fully achieved and the marble and mosaic stop short, leaving large surfaces exposed, though this was not intended to be its permanent state. It was in France though that a more explicit connection between concrete construction and religious buildings developed, for among the followers of Viollet-le-Duc, concrete seemed to offer the opportunity to develop the principles of Gothic building beyond those available to the mediaeval mason. Anatole de Baudot's church of St-Jean de Montmartre (1894–1904) represented a refinement of Gothic structural techniques, executed in his own system of reinforced concrete. And at Auguste Perret's Nôtre Dame at Le Raincy (1922–23) where the concrete construction allowed the church to be enveloped in a non-loadbearing honeycomb wall of stained glass, all the concrete surfaces were left bare. Less structurally ambitious, but much larger, and with a bare concrete exterior flank facing on to a main street, was Karl Moser's Antoniuskirche in Basel (1925–27). By 1939, examples from Switzerland and Germany had established concrete as a prime church-building material, and after 1945, the number of new churches in Europe built of concrete is countless. In very many cases the concrete was exposed, for reasons that may either have been to do with a wish to present the church as piece of basic infrastructure, comparable to an electricity substation or a motorway bridge, or to draw attention to the church's desire to project values of humility, simplicity and integrity. 'Concrete', so the Bishop of Brentford once said to a friend of mine, 'is God's gift to religion.'

When we come to memorials, though, the arguments that had justified the use of concrete for churches do not apply. Economy, valid for a church, was not, as we have already seen, acceptable for a monument. Nor was the structural rationalist argument, that concrete was fulfilling architecture's destiny by advancing the principles of mediaeval builders, persuasive with monuments, for these, defined by weight and mass, rarely offered themselves as appropriate subjects for structural innovation. In all of the early cases where concrete was used for memorials, before it had become, as is the case now, the conventional material for memorial building, the choice of concrete relied upon other arguments. Of the possibilities, it might be the relative indestructibility of concrete, increasing the chances that what might otherwise be forgotten will be preserved for perpetuity, that made it the preferred medium: the larger and denser the block of concrete, the safer the memory would be. But this rests on a misplaced power of objects to prolong human memory – it is not the physical decay of monuments that makes them so ineffective at preserving memory. Another answer could be to do with the anonymity, the muteness of concrete, making it particularly suited to mental projection and reflection.

But neither of these explanations are convincing, for they both assume that concrete has some inherent property of signification lacking in other materials. This simply is not acceptable. If there is one thing that emerges from the three cases that we shall now turn to look at, it is that no material, and least of all a modern synthetic material like concrete, has any absolute or immanent value. In none of the three examples was the choice of concrete a foregone decision, but in each one it had to do with the time and place of their making.

Probably the most famous early concrete monument is the memorial to the *Märzgefallenen* in the cemetery at Weimar (Figures 4.1, 4.2), designed by Walter Gropius, then director of the Bauhaus, at that time located in Weimar.[8] The memorial commemorated seven trade unionists who had died in March 1920 resisting the right-wing *Putsch* led by Wolfgang Kapp to

4.1
Märzgefallenen Memorial, Weimar (1922). Architect – Walter Gropius
Source: Photograph by Adrian Forty

4.2
**Märzgefallenen
Memorial,
Weimar, close
up. Architect –
Walter Gropius**
Source: Photograph
by Adrian Forty

overthrow the Social Democratic government. Kapp was supported by one of
the *Freikorps*, the paramilitary associations of ex-servicemen which figured
large in the turbulent history of post-war Germany, and it was in a confrontation with these that the trade unionists had died. The Kapp *Putsch* failed
partly because the trade unions successfully organised a general strike in
support of the government, and the event became an important episode in the
Weimar Republic's short history, because it demonstrated the effectiveness
of organised working-class action in defending the new constitution against
extremists; twelve years later, it was partly the failure of trade unions to
organise in support of the constitutional government that led to Hitler being
able to seize power in January 1933.

The initial design for the memorial was prepared by Gropius late in
1920; construction started in September 1921, and was completed by May
1922. It therefore predates the majority of the memorials commemorating the
dead of the First World War – although the deaths it marks had occurred
after the war – and it was clearly an important aspect of the project that it
not be confused with a war memorial. As a political memorial to working-class
martyrs, it was a type for which there was no model, and no precedent.
(The other, possibly more famous, political memorial of the Weimar period,
the Berlin monument to the Spartacist leaders, Rosa Luxemburg and Karl
Liebknecht, designed by Mies van der Rohe, was built later, in 1925–26.)
The memorial's explicit political significance and place in the martyrology of
the Weimar Republic explain why it was destroyed (with explosives) in 1936,
and then ten years later, in 1946, rebuilt. Its reconstruction in 1946, an almost
precise reproduction of the original, executed with very nearly the same
materials, and by the same processes, must have been one of the very first acts

of reconstruction carried out under the Soviet occupation. What we see today is the rebuilt memorial of 1946: it is a double memorial, a memorial to a memorial.

The large cemetery at Weimar, where the monument stands, is a pantheon of German art and literature: it contains the tombs of, among others, Herder, Goethe, Schiller and Liszt. Although the *Märzgefallenen* is some distance away from these, the design of the memorial, and the choice of the material for it, were nonetheless a sensitive matter. The existing memorials to the great German writers were made of Carrara marble. Gropius's original design for the *Märzgefallenen* was to have been in limestone, a material traditionally used in Weimar for decorative elements of buildings, door and window surrounds, but not for tombs. Gropius's choice of limestone for the memorial was therefore almost as radical as the form – the jagged, crystalline flash; but although limestone was not used for funerary monuments, it was used for their bases, so the choice of this particular stone might have gone some way to making the highly unconventional form more acceptable. Stone was consistent with the principles of the Bauhaus manifesto, the collaboration of artists and craftsmen, for it would have used local artisan labour to execute a work of art. In the event, the memorial turned out to be very much a Bauhaus project: the work was supervised by Josef Hartwig, one of the Bauhaus masters, and some of the labour was provided by Bauhaus staff and students. By early 1921, it was clear that there would not be enough money to build the monument in limestone, so Gropius changed the design to a concrete structure clad in limestone. At the same time, the monument was made larger, and given a more dynamic and unstable shape than would have been possible had it been made from blocks of limestone. This design also turned out too expensive, and Gropius proposed changing the cladding stone to sandstone, which was cheaper – but this produced only a very marginal saving in cost, and finally the decision was taken to build it solely in concrete, in a yet further enlarged version.

Although concrete was chosen primarily for financial, rather than aesthetic or semantic reasons, it nonetheless coincided with the enthusiasm for new materials present in Bauhaus and avant-garde artistic circles in 1921. At the Bauhaus, Johannes Itten's foundation course encouraged experiment with materials to explore their properties, while German and Russian architectural critics were writing about how new materials should generate new forms. And indeed the shape of the memorial did change once it was decided to give it a concrete structure. However, the choice of concrete ran up against the local building code, which prohibited the use of concrete in cemeteries unless it was mixed with natural stone aggregates. Accordingly, when construction began in September 1921, the concrete was made using crushed limestone from nearby quarries, but some terrazzo was also added, thus combining a natural with a synthetic aggregate, a mix that may have appealed to Gropius because it neutralised the traditionalism of the stone aggregate with a more 'modern' addition.

The most skilled part of the production of the monument lay in the finishing of the concrete. The cement surface left from the casting process was removed with hammer and chisel to expose the stone aggregates beneath, and the edges finished, as in traditional stone masonry, with a 5 centimetre wide-tooled margin, leaving narrow ridges perpendicular to the edge. The result is remarkably delicate, showing that despite the coarseness of the material, manual skill could transform it into something refined.

This surface treatment of the concrete, known in German as *Betonwerkstein*, stone-worked concrete, belonged to a continuing debate in German culture, lasting from 1910 to the end of the Third Reich, about the propriety of concrete. Even before the First World War *Betonwerkstein* had been recommended as the best finish for concrete. Josef Petry, the Chairman of the German Concrete Association, writing in 1913, had argued that working concrete in this manner was the way to answer objections to concrete as a low-value material. Petry had insisted that concrete should not be seen as a surrogate for stone, but as a material whose beauty lay in its artificiality – which was best revealed by this manual technique of finishing it. *Betonwerkstein* was used occasionally for other monuments in the 1920s, but acquired greater significance in the 1930s, in the course of National Socialist debates about materials, when it became regarded as the best way of gaining acceptance for concrete.

The Nazis were ambivalent about concrete. On the one hand it was the material that made possible the great infra-structural achievements of the Third Reich, the autobahns in particular; but on the other hand, it was attacked for being unGerman, unnatural and as a synthetic material, not rooted in the German soil, and when it came to making monuments, stone was the invariable choice. Concrete, it was said, failed to give the workman the same feeling of identity with the building as was the case in masonry structures, where he could tell which stones or bricks he had worked and laid. Critics of concrete in the 1930s claimed that it was a cold, grey, colourless material, unworthy of the new structures: compared to natural stone, concrete seemed like working clothes against evening dress. The solution adopted on the autobahn bridges was to hammer away the surface of the concrete and expose the aggregate. Though a relatively expensive process, it was justified on the grounds that it removed all trace of the imperfections of the production process – the imprint of the formwork, variations in the concrete mix – and at the same time endowed the otherwise dead material with the soul and spirit of the workman. The technique gave concrete a patina that made it resemble natural stone, and that would allow it to age like natural stone.

And furthermore, as the General Inspector of Highways commented in 1935, the use of aggregates from a particular locality would express the character of local landscapes, and give the structures a relationship to the places where they stood. The 1936 Four Year Plan, intended to reduce Germany's dependence on imports, enhanced concrete's reputation as a German-made product; the synthetic, artificial nature of cement, a product of human invention, extracted from German soil, and processed with German labour, made it a more respected material. Very occasionally, concrete was even described as an analogy for National Socialism itself: in one far from typical instance in 1934, the concrete of a housing estate was referred to as

> a purely German product, a symbol of our warriors. This concrete block, a product of our newest technological progress, is one of our youngest but best building materials. Like it, our movement [the NSDAP] is the best building material for building the Third Reich, it is our eternal source of energy, that leads to unprecedented ascent. Concrete has the characteristic of becoming harder and harder in the course of time; like this our young movement and its warriors shall come tighter together and become harder in the consciousness of the German people.[9]

But these words were unusual; the prime symbol of Nazism was natural stone, and generally it was stone buildings that were the emblems of the new society, while concrete was regarded as a 'low' material.

At the time that the *Märzgefallenen* was built, little was said about its being made of concrete. Even when it was blown up in 1936, the reason given was simply that it was 'ugly' – though clearly there was more to it than this, for the presence of a memorial commemorating martyrs of the Weimar Republic must have become, under National Socialism, a local embarrassment. Whether the fact it was made of concrete influenced the decision is not recorded.

It is only after its destruction in 1936 that the concrete began to take on significance. When it was reconstructed in 1946, not only was there great care to reproduce the surface finish of the original (though without the addition of the crushed terrazzo to the aggregate), but commentators drew explicit attention to the material, and to the way in which it symbolised socialism. The seamless, unbroken form is not personalised, they said, and shows no traces of individual, only collective effort. Furthermore, the material itself is the result of a chemical bond between the different components, producing a product which is stronger and harder than any of the individual elements, and this could be seen as an analogy for the way that in a socialist society individuals come together to form, with invisible bonds, a collective unity. Unlike stone, which is the result of a long process of sedimentation, concrete is formed the moment it sets, and this might be said to be analogous to the historical formation of the socialist republics, born instantaneously from the shock events of the moment, unlike other regimes that have developed over long periods of time. Yet these sorts of political interpretations were only attributed to it after 1946, and there is no evidence of them in the 1920s, when the political reading of the memorial was more ambiguous. The critic Adolf Behne, though a former colleague of Gropius in the 1918 Arbeitsrat für Kunst, described the monument in 1925 as 'so nervously apolitical that, as a very general symbol of the uprising, it could just as well have been erected by the Kapp forces'.[10] And Gropius himself in 1948, though by then in America, and in the political circumstances of the time presumably anxious not to be connected to anything known to be communist, insisted that the memorial was designed not to commemorate working men, but people of all classes who had died in the upheaval of the *Kapp Putsch*.[11]

With the *Märzgefallenen*, all the evidence is that concrete did not initially signify at all; the choice of the material was made for economic, not symbolic, reasons, and only later did political meanings become attached to it. This should warn us against making any assumptions about concrete having any positive, determinate meaning. In this particular case, it was only over time, and as circumstances changed, that concrete took on a political and memory-bearing iconography.

The second memorial to consider is in Rome, at the Fosse Ardeatine, about two kilometres along the Appian Way, close to some of the Roman catacombs (Figures 4.3, 4.4).[12] The memorial contains the graves of 335 Italians shot by the Germans on 24 March 1944, in reprisal for a partisan attack on an SS column in Rome, killing thirty-three Germans. Hitler himself ordered that ten Italians were to die within 24 hours for every dead German, and the local SS commander, Major Karl Hass, in his haste to carry out the order took the required number, plus an additional five, at random from those who were being held in prisons and police stations in Rome, although none of these were connected with the attack, nor were necessarily even partisans. The victims were taken to an abandoned pozzolana mine at the relatively remote Fosse Ardeatine, shot, and the caves dynamited to create a rock fall to conceal the bodies. Shortly after the German withdrawal from Rome on 4 June 1944, the site of the massacre was discovered, and excavated, and the bodies put in coffins, but left in the caves. In September 1944, while parts of Italy were still under fascist control, a competition was held for a memorial, and two designs were chosen. The two winning teams of architects were invited to collaborate to produce a final scheme, and it was this scheme, under the leadership of Mario Fiorentino and Giuseppe Perugini, that was built, and inaugurated on 24 March 1949, five years after the massacre.

From the start, there was controversy about the memorial. The relatives of the victims wanted the bodies to be left in the caves; but the

4.3
Fosse Ardeatine Memorial, Rome (1949). Architects – Mario Fiorentino and Giuseppe Perugini
Source: Photograph by Adrian Forty

4.4
Fosse Ardeatine Memorial, Rome interior. Architects – Mario Fiorentino and Giuseppe Perugini
Source: Photograph by Adrian Forty

caves were unstable, and lacked the monumental presence felt necessary to commemorate not just the victims but also the event for posterity. The solution was to create a covered mausoleum connected to the caves, and which would be entered through the caves. The mausoleum consists of a shallow excavation, about 1.5m below ground level, containing the tombs of the 335 victims, covered by a single, monolithic slab, 48.5m by 26.65m, and 3 metres high, supported at only six points. Beneath is a dark cavernous space about 2 metres high, compressed beneath the enormous, almost unsupported slab and lit by a light coming through the narrow slit between it and the ground. The slit increases in height from 60cm at the entrance side, to 110cm

both this case, and the next, contributed to the habituation of concrete as a material of memory.

The third memorial is in Paris, the Memorial to the Martyrs of Deportation (Figures 4.5, 4.6). Situated at the eastern tip of the Île de la Cité, it was designed by Georges-Henri Pingusson, who was at work on it between 1953 and 1962, when it was completed. A hundred yards from Nôtre Dame, this is a historically sensitive site, on which construction of any kind would be contentious, let alone a memorial made out of concrete.[18]

Approached across an open garden, it is more or less invisible. Apart from a low wall with an inscription, there is nothing there until you go down the too narrow stairway into a paved triangular court, open to the sky, but otherwise entirely enclosed by 4 metre high concrete walls, except for an opening, covered with a metal grille, through which one can see the moving water of the Seine. The transition is extraordinary. At ground level, you are at the centre of a panorama of the historic centre of Paris; go down into the memorial, and you are cut off from everything except the sky and the water, and only the two unpleasantly narrow and steep stairways allow for any escape. On the same side as the stairs, opposite the apex with the opening to the river, there is a narrow parting in a massive block of

4.5
Memorial to the Martyrs of the Deportation, Paris (1953–62), interior. Architect – Georges-Henri Pingusson
Source: Photograph by Adrian Forty

4.6
**Memorial to the
Martyrs of the
Deportation,
Paris (1953–62).
Architect –
Georges-Henri
Pingusson**
Source: Photograph
by Adrian Forty

concrete, passing through which you feel in imminent danger of being crushed between the two sides; the opening leads to a crypt, in which, through a metal grating, thousands of tiny lights line the walls of an endless corridor, dimly illuminating it.

Of the three memorials discussed here, this is the only one that can be considered a success in memorial terms – and this is partly because it is an inversion of the conventional form of the monument. Not a protrusion, but a declivity; not an object, but a void – and when you are in the void, there is nothing there to look at apart from yourself, the sky, the water, and the unbroken surface of the concrete wall. Pingusson alone of the architects of the three memorials seems to have been aware of the fragility of memory and the general unsatisfactoriness of all attempts to transfer the evanescence of mental recollection into solid matter. (Pingusson begins his own account of the memorial with the words 'It is in the law of all living creatures, beings and things to one day disappear . . . everything will fade away, everything will pass, and to want anything to last is a big challenge.'[19]) Apart from the crypt, there is no *sign* in this memorial; it is pure experience, there is nothing to be read, only the concrete itself.

Of the three memorials, this is the one in which the choice of concrete seems most deliberately calculated, a fully worked out strategy from the start. Once in the memorial, you are surrounded by concrete: the paving is stone, but the walls are pick-hammered concrete, of superfine quality, exposing a dense and rich mixture of aggregates. (The aggregates were chosen from all the mountainous regions of France, giving it, at least to the geologically-minded, a national rather than localised symbolism; the difficulty of making sure that so many different aggregates were evenly distributed can scarcely be imagined.) Pingusson chose concrete, rejecting limestone, sandstone or granite as incapable of expressing the roughness and violence of the Holocaust: but the finish of the concrete is not crude or barbaric, reminiscent of military fortifications, in the way that, say, Le Corbusier's monastery and chapel at La Tourette are. Instead, the emphasis here is on the totally seamless, monolithic effect: Pingusson wanted it to appear that the memorial had been hewn out of a single rock. The concrete facing was poured simultaneously with the structural wall, so as to give an absolute bond between the two, without any evidence of joins. At the Fosse Ardeatine, the surface finish was applied after the structure of the slab was completed, and slight variations in the surface are visible as a result, diminishing the monolithic effect; in the Paris memorial, there is no trace whatsoever of joints between areas of concrete. It was the seamlessness that mattered most to Pingusson about the concrete – though one may add that its other property is to defy nature. Exposed masonry surfaces always show signs of weathering and of time – but this concrete finish is entirely unblemished and seems impervious to the effects of age and weather. There had been an earlier French memorial in concrete, at Verdun, the Monument of the Trench of the Bayonets, constructed in 1920, where concrete was used in preference to stone, so as, the architect said, 'to ensure durability', for a minimum of 500 years. As a contemporary observer explained, 'The Trench of the Bayonets will be everlastingly protected against the attacks of time or the cyclical pillage of the tourists. It will also be saved from the invasion of vegetable growths.'[20] In other words, the purpose of covering the site with concrete was to resist the effects of nature. Pingusson may have had something of the same intention at the Paris memorial – in which case, his choice of finish was infinitely superior to that at the Trench of the Bayonets.

What we see at the Monument to the Martyrs of Deportation is concrete used precisely for the same reasons as it is generally despised – for its anti-natural properties, the fact that it does not succumb to the same processes of ageing and decay as other materials. Pingusson's memorial creates a kind of sensory deprivation, which forces the visitor to concentrate upon the sky, and the present. The concrete surroundings do not invite any kind of reflections on history, or even on the passage of time; memory, if there can be such a thing, is of the moment, it cannot be captured or preserved, and this the permanent newness of the concrete seems to acknowledge. In other contexts, these effects are not generally welcome, and concrete has often been condemned for inducing them. Here, though, they are a major component of the work's memorial function.

Are we any closer to understanding how a medium, concrete, can at once be both a material of memory and of oblivion? Maybe not, but we can at least see the process by which concrete was in certain circumstances made into a memory-signifying material. And what is clear from the cases discussed here is that it was not for any memory-bearing properties as such that concrete was chosen as a medium for memorials, but rather for contingent reasons: for the opportunity it gave to make seamless objects, for its nature-suppressing qualities (ironically the very same reason for which it is so often despised), and for the political associations it has in certain circumstances conveyed. It has to be said that the large majority of concrete memorials betray a naïve optimism about the capacity of solid objects to preserve memory: in too many cases concrete has been used for, apparently, no better reason than that it offers the appearance of dense mass and indestructibility, as if an excess of these properties would be enough to guarantee the prolonging of human memory. It is only in the later generation of Holocaust memorials that there has been a more questioning attitude to this approach, and concrete has come to be used in certain cases more as a material into which memories sink, never to be recovered.

Finally, memorials do give some insights into concrete: above all that concrete does have an iconography, not something generally acknowledged in the circles where concrete is discussed. For the most part, what has been at issue has been how to make concrete stronger, to eliminate its imperfections, to make it smoother and finer. The attitude has been that the problems of concrete are technical: resolve these and it will lose its unpopularity. As a signifying material, it has been treated as neutral, its 'modernity' somehow giving it exemption from the systems of meaning attached to other materials. But the use of concrete in memorials exposes the fact that concrete is not immune to meaning, that it has an iconography. Unlike so-called 'traditional' materials, whose meaning is often said to be inherent and embedded in them, concrete's is fluid and mutable, made by the circumstances of history. It resists the singular, simple meanings that the concrete industry would like it to have, and instead its iconography operates through paradoxes and contradictions. When the architect Louis Kahn said, 'If you're dealing with concrete, you must know the order of nature, you must know the nature of concrete, what concrete really strives to do', what he omitted to mention was that whatever concrete strives to do, it invariably manages to be, at the same time, the opposite.[21]

Acknowledgements

My thanks to Christian Fuhrmeister for his helpful advice and suggestions.

Notes

1 H. Lefebvre, *Introduction to Modernity* (1962), trans. J. Moore, London, New York: Verso, 1995, p. 119.

2 K. Bonacker, *Beton: Ein Baustoff wird Schlagwort*, Marburg: Jonas Verlag, 1996, p. 40 and endnote 164.

3 K. Tiege, 'Mundaneum' (1929), trans. L.E. Holovsky and L. Dolezel, *Oppositions*, 4, 1975, p. 89; reprinted in K.M. Hayes (ed.), *Oppositions Reader*, New York: Princeton Architectural Press, 1998, p. 595.

4 For further discussion of these issues, see A. Forty, 'Introduction', in A. Forty and S. Kuechler, *The Art of Forgetting*, Oxford: Berg, 1999, pp. 1–18; and A. Forty, *Words and Buildings: A Vocabulary of Modern Architecture*, London: Thames and Hudson, 2000, pp. 206–19.

5 T. Adorno, *Minima Moralia: Reflections from Damaged Life* (1951), trans. E.F.N. Jephcott, London: New Left Books, 1974, p. 54.

6 See particularly James E. Young, *The Texture of Memory: Holocaust Memorials and Meaning*, New Haven, CT: Yale University Press, 1993; and James E. Young, *At Memory's Edge: After Images of the Holocaust in Contemporary Art and Literature*, New Haven, CT: Yale University Press, 2000.

7 M. Joray, *Le Béton dans l'Art Contemporain*, Neuchâtel: Editions du Griffon, 1977, p. 107.

8 C. Fuhrmeister, *Beton, Klinker, Granit: Material, Macht, Politik: Eine Materialikonographie*, Berlin: Verlag Bauwesen, 2001. The following discussion of the Weimar Memorial is based entirely upon Fuhrmeister's very comprehensive analysis of it.

9 Quoted in Fuhrmeister, *Beton*, p. 87.

10 Quoted in W. Nerdinger, *Walter Gropius*, Berlin: Bauhaus Archiv, 1985, p. 46.

11 Fuhrmeister, *Beton*, p. 50; also R. Isaacs, *Gropius*, Boston: Bullfinch Press, 1991, p. 74.

12 See A. Aymonino, 'Topography of Memory', *Lotus*, 97, 1998, pp. 6–22, for the fullest discussion of the Fosse Ardeatine in English; and B. Reichlin, 'Figures of Neo-Realism in Italian Architecture (Part 2)', *Grey Room*, 6, Winter 2002, pp. 110–33, contains additional information and useful critique.

13 M. Tafuri, *History of Italian Architecture 1944–1985*, Cambridge, MA: MIT Press, 1989, p. 4.

14 Aymonino, 'Topography', p. 11.

15 See, for example, G.E. Kidder Smith, *Italy Builds*, London: Architectural Press, 1955, p. 176.

16 See Kurt W. Forster, 'BAUgedanken und GEDANKENgebäude – Terragnis Casa del Fascio in Como', in H. Hipp and E. Seidl (eds.), *Architekture als Politische Kultur: Philosophia Practica*, Berlin: Dietrich Reimer Verlag, 1996, pp. 253–71.

17 See P.L. Nervi, *Aesthetics and Technology in Building*, Cambridge, MA: Harvard University Press, 1966, p. 100 and fig. 80.

18 The fullest account of the Memorial is by E. Vitou, 'Paris, Mémorial de la Déportation', *Architecture, Mouvement, Continuité*, 19, February 1988, pp. 68–79; see also B. Marrey and F. Hammoutène, *Le Béton à Paris*, Paris: Picard, 1999, p. 140; and S. Texier, 'Georges-Henri Pingusson, 1894–1977', *Architecture, Mouvement, Continuité*, 96, March 1999, pp. 66–71.

19 G.-H. Pingusson, 'Monument aux déportés à Paris', *Aujourdhui Art et Architecture*, 39, November 1962, pp. 66–9.

20 Quoted in J. Winter, *Sites of Memory, Sites of Mourning: The Great War in European Cultural History*, Cambridge: Cambridge University Press, 1995, p. 101.

21 L. Kahn, 'I Love Beginnings' (1972), in A. Latour (ed.), *Louis I. Kahn: Writings, Lectures, Interviews*, New York: Rizzoli, 1991, p. 288.

The Manager
of the Senoko Fish Market
in Singapore
breaks into a jog
at the junction of
Attap Valley Road
and Admiralty Road West.

Chapter 5

Totemic Park

Symbolic representation in post-industrial space

Paul Tyrer and Mark Crinson

> Totemism helped to smooth things over and to make it possible to
> forget the event to which it owed its origin.[1]

The urban industrial landscape of the past 200 years – stereotyped by images
of L.S. Lowry's towering chimneys billowing smoke, and the hard grind of
heavy machinery right in the centre of cities – has now largely been dismantled, run down or reintegrated into the city for new purposes. This is the
inevitable response to a new domination by post-industrial goods and
services, and their accompanying symbolic and cultural contexts and frames.
Leisure industries, for instance, have become an important driver of not only
what the city does but also how it governs and presents itself. As Mellor points
out, 'In cities in declining regions . . . play and spectacle are increasingly the
crucial elements in reconstituting the city centre.'[2] Such industries 'fuel
the city's symbolic economy, its visible ability to produce both symbols and
space'.[3]

One of the more curious aspects of the British post-industrial city is
its recent reliance upon a symbolic vocabulary that plays on the industrial
past. Thus, there is a tendency not only to emphasise extant industrial form,
materials and symbols in residential, leisure and business settings, but also
to introduce them into new buildings and spaces. This is particularly marked
in Manchester, home of the Industrial Revolution and for a century the

industrial heart of the nation, and now the leading regional city in terms of entrepreneurial and architectural verve and ambition. Loft apartments with stripped floors, vaulted bare-brick ceilings, iron columns and newly exposed pipework have become the norm for aspirational living here, as in other regional cities, but it was Manchester which first converted large chunks of its Victorian architectural infrastructure into modern, desirable accommodation. Manchester's bar and club scene has long been (in)famous for its drugs, dance and guns culture, however outdated all these (aside from the drugs) have become. The city's newest bars have occupied the least opulent, most grimy industrial buildings but have showcased rather than concealed the industrial internal detailing. The most extreme example of this, perhaps, is the über-cool Deansgate Lock stretch of bars, set in railway arches, where industrialesque copper-panelling and substantial piping systems have been enhanced as essentially visible parts of the refurbishment.[4] And service sector businesses, not just those with an arts or architecture brief, have similarly introduced industrial symbolism into the design of their own newbuild premises. The new upmarket Selfridges store, for example, displayed large pieces of industrial machinery in its windows when it opened in 2002. Ferrious, Manchester's most chic independent furniture store, occupies another railway arch. Such spatial and architectural 'collisions' between the post-industrial and the industrial do not apply merely to Manchester – other formerly industrial cities in Britain have been undergoing similar transformations (although perhaps the collisions are most evident here because Manchester effectively defined the industrial city from the nineteenth century). In particular, in this chapter, we are concerned to ask how the use of the industrial symbol within post-industrial cities might be explained and theorized. What cultural and social meanings inform such an appropriation? What does this tell us about architectural practice, the processes of redevelopment, and the importance of the past and memory within such processes?

We will suggest that the theoretical deployment of the term 'totemism' within post-industrial space can make sense of these new developments via a reading of Freud's *Totem and Taboo* (1913). Choosing Freud as a basis for a theoretical model on post-industrial space may appear incongruous, since Freud is writing ostensibly about a tribal society from prehistory. However, both Julia Kristeva and Claude Lévi-Strauss[5] argue that Freud is actually describing his own society rather than making insights into the prehistoric past, and thus this eliding of past and present makes viable the appropriation of Freud's model for contemporary purposes. The theoretical deployment of the totem represents a shift away from the gentrification model of redevelopment championed by Glass, LeGates and Hartman, Laska and Spain, Hartman and Bouthillette[6] among others, which focuses on 'the replacement of lower-status groups by higher-status groups' in private residential neighbourhoods, where property is gentrified by a particular type of middle-class urbanite.[7] Elements of this model do apply to the post-industrial developments we are describing – the economic rationality of the gentrifiers (restoring your house can bring you money) is echoed by the economic goals of the new 'totemisers'. While some gentrification theorists do emphasise that housing is only one facet of a more profound social and economic phenomenon,[8] the mass *introduction* of an industrial symbolism and accompanying materials into new developments is rarely addressed. Sharon Zukin acknowledges this movement in *The Cultures of Cities* (1995) but her emphasis on the American city, and redevelopment via the private sector and its Business Improvement Districts, cannot make space for the significantly different British experience.

Emphasis on the totem also marks a shift away from another academic mode of analysing redevelopment in cities – namely, memory. Partly, the problem with 'memory discourse', as Klein has pointed out,[9] is that there are numerous and conflicting understandings of what this might include – for example, Klein identifies five substantially different versions of memory discourse. A totemic model rejects the notion that 'memory' is a potentially rejuvenating strategy for the city, a view supported by, for example, Benjamin and Boyer.[10] Instead, it sees 'memory' within development as a mechanism of control, exercised by business interests towards the max-imisation of profit. Equally, memory discourse tends to relegate the notion of 'forgetting' to the sidelines of debate, despite the important place forgetting has in producing an unbroken and untroubled capitalist history that enables so much post-industrial redevelopment. A totemic model of analysis gives equal emphasis to both memory and forgetting in the creation and main-tenance of post-industrial space.

Totemic space

Totem and Taboo was written about an ostensibly tribal context positing an ancestor society dominated by an all-powerful tribal Father and a successor society dominated by totemism. Totemism, for Freud, is effectively a system of substitution, where one societal model is replaced by another.[11] The two societies are very different, except that the substitute reproduces exactly in *symbolic* terms what it has replaced. Thus, in relation to symbolism and its meanings, a complete break in history is effectively smoothed over and two radically different societies are represented by those within as one unchanging state. One of the key elements of Freud's analysis is that totemism appears to signal no change (that is, in symbolic terms), but at the same time, in terms of lived experience, a radical transformation of societal relations has taken place.

Freud argues that the tribe takes up the totem – usually though not always an animal – as a substitute figure for the all-powerful tribal Father. He recounts an imagined story in which the Father is violently murdered by a band of his sons, an act driven by resentment about the paternal figure's complete control over the possession and distribution of women. Rather than accepting that the tribe is now Fatherless, the sons take up the totem animal 'as a natural and obvious substitute for their Father' because it was able to occupy his symbolic position seamlessly.[12] This symbolic similarity is reinforced by cultural practice: although there is an absolute taboo on killing the totem, it is nevertheless sacrificed at particular times of the year in a re-enactment of the Father's murder.

The act of parricide, and its subsequent representation in totemic sacrifice, are for Julia Kristeva 'one of the forms assumed by the thetic phase', the thetic being a threshold moment constituted in totemism by an emotional and cultural ambivalence.[13] Freud notes, 'Totemic religion not only comprised expressions of remorse and acts of atonement, it also served as a remembrance of the triumph over the Father.'[14] On the one hand, the sons are remorseful and afraid; on the other, they are delighted to be rid of the oppressive Father. Totemism might in this way be said to have ambivalence at its centre – it is both an avowal and a disavowal of what has taken place, played out through cultural practice in the adoption and sacrifice of the totem. Disavowal emerges as the Father is still, to all intents and purposes, symbolically functional – the totem is honoured and obeyed in exactly the same way and is seen to have the same powers of authority over the tribe – yet dramatically avowed through the tribal re-enactment of the act of parricide in the ritual killing of the totem animal, with great celebration expressed at the attainment of mastery and similarly great mourning about the act that brought it about, constituting an acknowledgement that radical change has occurred. Totemism is founded precisely upon this simultaneous avowal and disavowal, with the totemic society always relying upon the symbolic elements of the previous society to express this dichotomy.

Freud's totemic structure offers a theoretical frame for understanding the particular industrial/post-industrial problem set out earlier. The post-industrial is constituted upon its replacement of the industrial via the violent act of de-industrialisation. De-industrialisation represents a radical break from the previous 150 years of organising and profiting from particular circulations and productions of goods and services. Post-industrialism both avows and disavows this moment by its introduction of a totem – new architectural forms, materials, detailing and other symbols that *reproduce the industrialism that has been torn down.* For Freud, totemism 'helped to smooth things over and to make it possible to forget the event to which it owed its origin'.[15] In terms of post-industrial space, the totem of industrial symbolism helps to smooth over the dramatic rupture between the two periods of economic production. Two distinct historical periods are thus segued together in a seamless fashion, signalling a mastery over history and the past, making the possibility of an imagined second collapse of industrialism a less terrifying prospect.

What makes totemism particularly apt for an analysis of post-industrial space is what it suppresses. The rationale behind the primal parricidal act stemmed from men's power to possess and dispose of tribal women as they chose – the primal Father was killed because he controlled all the women that the sons wanted. Yet women remain absent from the account and similarly totems signalling the lived experiences of working-class labour that made industrial societies possible are notably absent. Totemic spaces suppress that experience, turning formerly working-class spaces into places where the middle classes are always at home. In the following sections, we describe one large and significant post-industrial space where this omission and suppression is evident. This is Trafford Park Village – heavily industrial from the 1900s to the 1970s, and lightly post-industrial since the mid-1990s.

Trafford Park dwellings in industrial Manchester

Since its inception in 1896, Trafford Park has had a central place in the history of industrial Manchester. This, the first industrial estate in the world, was developed in the outskirts of the city in the extensive grounds of the former de Trafford family estate, adjacent to the new Manchester Ship Canal (Figure 5.1). Naming itself 'The industrial Metropolis of England' as early as 1902, Trafford Park was soon seen as the industrial lynch-pin of the region and finally of the nation, as its armaments centre during the Second World War. Some 75,000 people worked here at its peak in 1945, but the impact of changes in industrial production and the subsequent decline of manufacturing led to an abandonment of the estate by many large corporations in the 1960s, the 1970s and the 1980s.[16]

In its early years, the trades established on the estate were heavily industrial, for example, oil refiners, railway manufacturers, chemical manu-facturers, sawmills and shipwrights were all present in 1906. The noise and pollution that such industries brought made Trafford Park 'infamous for its smell'[17]:

> There were some bloody awful smells in Trafford Park. An acrid smell . . . It'd get in your eyes and your throat, your eyes'd smart and you'd choke and wonder where the bloody hell it'd come from. Sometimes the stink was an abomination.[18]

5.1
**Roadside map,
Trafford Park,
Manchester
(1905)**

Despite this, the Trafford Park Estates Company decided very early on to build workers' dwellings in the middle of the estate. These would help to provide a readily accessible supply of cheap labour at the very heart of the estate. A separate company, the Trafford Park Dwellings Company, was established to build and manage the dwellings community. At first, 1,000 houses were planned but in 1904 when house building stopped, 762 almost exclusively terraced properties had been completed.[19]

That these were overwhelmingly dwellings for the working classes is evident from the earliest Manchester directories that list the area. For example, the listed job-titles of residents on the estate in 1904 included labourer, joiner, iron turner, moulder, blacksmith, pattern maker and fitter.[20] And the houses themselves, even when newly built, were typical of the poor-quality accommodation provided for the working-class communities of central Manchester (Figure 5.2). In 1901, Manchester's *Daily Dispatch* newspaper bemoaned that from the outset the dwellings offered:

> the same squat yards, the same narrow streets, the same dreary monotony as can be found in the working class portions of Manchester and when the whole district has been built upon, when the paint on the front doors is no longer new, and when the atmosphere has laid its sooty finger on the brick-work, no great stretch of the imagination is needed to conjure up a picture of the dreariness of what this purely commercial colony will be.[21]

This, then, was not an enlightened approach to building workers' homes. It was modelled neither on the earlier 'chocolate' villages built by Menier

5.2

**People on
Eleventh Street,
Trafford Park
(1910)**

and Suchard (1860s–1880s), nor on the British model villages of Saltaire (1851–1876), Bournville (1878–1906) and Port Sunlight (1888–1909) on Merseyside (this latter featuring 700 houses constructed that 'far exceeded the average for contemporary working-class house design'[22]). The explicitly stated intention of Titus Salt in building Saltaire was to provide 'a paradise on the sylvan banks of the Aire, far from the stench and vice of the industrial city'.[23] The Trafford Park dwellings company failed to match this aspiration; indeed, it failed to extend the radical thinking that led to the construction of the world's first industrial estate to the housing it provided for its labour source. Perhaps this can be explained by the fact that while the other aforementioned model villages were each the product of a philanthropic company, driven by one wealthy individual, Trafford Park was a place of many and often competing businesses, all fixed on profit at the expense of philanthropy, and the dwellings company was more interested in providing a cheap source of immediate labour than a model residential community.

Though the housing itself may have been undifferentiated from the typical northern workers' housing estate, it was contextualised as a place apart in three key ways. First, because the housing was an integral part of the industrial estate – placed at its very centre, providing easily accessible labour for local industry – the community was geographically isolated from the city and its suburbs. For this reason, a number of local amenities had to be provided by the Dwellings Company. Shops sprang up quickly. In 1904, along Third Avenue there were two greengrocers, a tobacconist, two butchers, a supper bar, a hardware dealer, a boot and shoe dealer, a chemist, a clothier and jeweller, and a draper. By 1910, there were three churches, a cinema, a large hotel, a working men's club, a post office, a doctor's surgery and two schools. Over the following two decades, residents benefited from a swimming pool, a park, a children's play area, a library, a health clinic and a wash house. This then was largely a self-contained development. It was, one former resident noted, 'a little community engulfed all by itself'.[24] It was also, mainly because of the lack of transport infrastructure, captive both in terms of its relation to labour and to consumption. Work for those in the dwellings was inevitably within Trafford Park, and what was consumable (and where) was similarly circumscribed.

Second, the streets were named in the traditional American fashion, with numbered streets and avenues – Second Street through Twelfth Street going east to west, and First Avenue through Fourth Avenue going north to south. Houses too were numbered in the style of American blocks: house numbers on Tenth Street, for example, ranged from 1001–1083. Although the rationale for this Americana has never been comprehensively explained, it seems likely that the Trafford Park Estates Company worked to flatter the sensibilities of US industrial companies in order to attract them to the area.[25] In its early years at least, Trafford Park did attract firms like Ford, which built a large factory there for production of the Model T in 1911, and Westinghouse from Pennsylvania, one of the first arrivals in 1901, which constructed turbines and generators. That First Street, the original home of the latter company's headquarters, was renamed Westinghouse Road suggests on its own an interest in choosing flattering street-names. On a different tack, there is significant evidence in Trafford Park publicity materials that labourers in the area were worked in the 'American fashion' following Taylorist practice – a particularly strict and intense working environment to which Mancunian workers were seen as particularly amenable.[26] Taken together, this may explain the system of numbering streets, avenues and houses – a phenomenon unique within Manchester and surrounding towns. It symbolically marked the housing as separate from the rest of the city, and also emphasised the amenability of its workforce, the residents of Trafford Park, to American capital.

Third, the numbered street system effectively differentiated the kinds of housing available and thereby the kinds of work people did. The dwellings were arranged in a hierarchical class system, according to street number, enabling working people to see the possibilities, and limits, of hard work and success. Houses from Second to Fifth Street were two-up-two-downs and had few amenities, no bathrooms, and were therefore cheap to rent. Some had no hot water. One side only of Fifth Street had gardens. Houses above Fifth Street increased in rent, amenities and size, with three or four bedrooms, and bathrooms, according to the street number. Therefore, if a worker secured a better job, s/he might be able to move up the street and from there up the class system. Comparisons between job titles listed for residents of two streets – Fifth and Eleventh Streets – in Slater's 1906 Directory make this clear. Of the 23 residents on Fifth Street, 21 are listed as 'householder' – a title suggestive either of no fixed employment/job title or a difficulty in gleaning this information. The remaining two residents are listed as fitter and engineer. Job titles on Eleventh Street are much more apparent, with just 19 of the 46 listed as 'householder' and remaining job titles including police constable, foreman, electrical engineer, electro-plater, cabinet maker and mechanic. None of these skilled job-titles appear on Fifth Street or indeed on any street below Fifth in this directory.[27]

This system of dividing up the housing was all too apparent to the residents. One told a research team in 1979: 'When you start off, you start off with just two rooms. And there's a boiler in where you lived to boil the clothes and two bedrooms, but no bath and no hot water. And that's the way you lived.' 'Starting off', beginning the process of climbing the class ladder, meant occupying one of the cheaper houses below Fifth. Once skills had been gained and wages increased, houses above Fifth became an option:

> The school sort of divided it . . . she lived down the other end. I was at this end. We knew what we were talking about when we said the 'other end', it meant, you know, you lived in the other half and we had our names for all those things.

> The 'top end' was Eighth Street onwards to Twelfth Street because they were bigger houses, they had more rooms in them.[28]

The 'top end' here represents the limit which the skilled working class could not cross – in Trafford Park at least. This was further emphasised by Fourth Avenue, slightly removed from the rest of the estate and comprising a small number of three-storey, semi-detached properties, sharing tennis courts and extensive back gardens. Here the middle-class professionals who serviced or managed the estate – the rector, a works manager, an estate clerk, and a physician were listed in the 1927 directory – lived. These properties were referred to locally as 'the villas', a name in stark contrast to the humble 'dwellings'. As one former resident noted:

> Then there were the ones in Fourth Avenue which were called the villas. They were pretty big. They were beautiful, they were nice houses . . . The doctor used to live there. We used to have the doctors, the vicar and all those people, the priest before that house was built for him . . . They were a bit uppish in some ways . . . They had a tennis court of their own . . . It gave them a bit of status, you see, having this tennis court that belonged to them four houses.[29]

The geographical placing and symbolism of 'the villas' on Fourth Avenue marked their separateness from the rest of the estate and thus the separation of the classes.

The three factors described above – the community's isolation and reliance on the dwellings company, the residents' apparent amenability to American capital's strict ways of working, and its hierarchical housing system – emphasised the classed nature of the community in a particularly direct fashion. Although other working-class communities were constrained by a similar lack of choice at the time, nowhere in Manchester or the surrounding towns were these constraints more boldly inscribed into the architectural, spatial and symbolic frame. Similar arrangements of houses were apparent elsewhere, for example, Saltaire's larger houses faced each other on a wide main street, while the smaller workers' houses were grouped together on side streets. Yet Trafford Park dwellings were built over fifty years after Titus Salt had laid down plans for his model community and appear much more regressive than that first model development. The arrangement and management of the Trafford Park housing emphasised the expectations, demands and boundaries of the British class-system within the industrial period. Speculation as to a rationale for this is limited by a lack of evidence from the early years of the Trafford Park Dwellings and Estates Companies.[30] However, the development of Trafford Park coincided with an increasing anxiety about Manchester's ability to retain the position of industrial pre-eminence that it had attained in Britain, and further afield, during the nineteenth century. This anxiety is apparent in Trafford Park's harnessing of new 'modern' forms of industrial practice, its attempt to keep up with the times and not be left behind. It is also apparent in the reassuringly 'old' and established forms of class structures and boundaries that pertained in the dwellings.

Although the dwellings community successfully withstood various economic downturns, including the 1930s Depression, experiencing its high point in terms of employment during the Second World War, the properties on the park fell out of favour in the 1960s. Former residents suggest that the worsening pollution and traffic of the adjacent industry, coupled with changing social attitudes about suitable housing conditions, had made the dwellings increasingly undesirable.[31] Stretford Council, which had taken on responsibility for the dwellings, declared the area to be a blight and an increasing number of houses became empty as a result. Three compulsory purchase orders issued by the council between 1973 and 1981 meant that all housing on the estate was eventually demolished, except for the Roman Catholic Presbytery on Fourth Avenue, which still stands today. Demolition took place despite fierce opposition from the remaining residents, many of whom had lived there all their lives, and although the housing has now gone, a strong attachment to the area remains. There are tours and reunions, and many ex-residents still attend the Roman Catholic church (a corrugated iron structure dating from 1904) every week.

The downgrading and demolition of the housing were accompanied by the decline of the industrial estate itself, as Britain slid into a period of relative de-industrialisation. Between 1967 and 1970, many Trafford Park companies either shed large numbers of jobs or closed altogether: Lancashire Dynamo and Crypto closed with the loss of 400 jobs, as did the Leonard Works, Edward Wood and Co, the Lancashire Wire Co, and Truscon Concrete. By 1973, the decline of the estate had produced 15 acres of surplus land, a phenomenon that continued well into the 1980s, with still more closures and significant land vacancies.[32] The redevelopment of the estate under the auspices of a Thatcher Government quango introduced a modern infrastructure that secured the park's immediate future. The area where the dwellings stood was designated as the new service centre of the park and renamed 'The Village'. We will argue that the new 'Village', in its appropriation of the symbolism of the industrial past in a post-industrial setting, is totemic.

Totemic Park

The Trafford Park Development Corporation (TPDC) was established by the Thatcher Government in 1987 and continued its work to revitalise the area until 1998, when it was wound up. Its initial brief was a difficult one: 'When the Corporation was established, the challenge was immense, but self-evident – to transform an outdated, semi-derelict industrial estate into a modern and thriving business location where the world's leading companies would want to invest.'[33] The TPDC soon identified 'the unique Trafford Park Village' as 'its number one priority area which was to be developed as the main business services and amenities centre for the entire Park'.[34] As the leader of the TPDC's Village Project Action Team explained:

> The original vision was that the village was a service centre for the rest of Trafford Park. The thing Trafford Park didn't have was good facilities and services. Even, you know, a butty shop, a pub or whatever. Trafford Park Village had a pub – it had the Hotel that was already there. It had the butty shops along Third Avenue. So it had a focus for the whole of Trafford Park anyway so we thought we'd build on that.[35]

The ensuing development plans produced a very different 'Village' from that which had existed before de-industrialisation and demolition (Figure 5.3). The American flavour of numbered streets and avenues was retained, but only

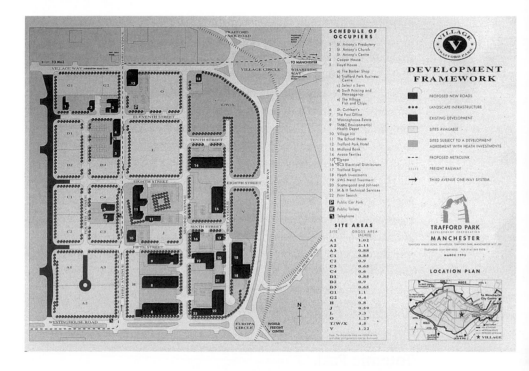

five of the original ten streets survived, and of these most were curtailed or blocked off at one end as a one-way traffic system was introduced. Traditional access points – Third and First Avenues – were closed off and access re-routed through Second and Fifth Avenues, the latter being a new addition to the street system. Fourth Avenue was moved to make space for larger blocks. The new street system meant that traffic moved slowly – thus cutting down on volume and noise – rather than at the frenetic speed of the past.[36] Some original buildings were demolished, but several others were refurbished or significantly rebuilt and given new uses. New facilities – a modern post office and a bank, for example – were introduced. Retail outlets were modernised. Former industrial buildings throughout the village were cleared to make way for light industrial and commercial businesses. By 1998, the TPDC was able to proclaim the Village as:

> A thriving centre with its own post-office, nursery, church, com-
> munity centre, banks, pubs and various retail and food outlets.
> Newly refurbished office space has attracted design, advertising
> and public relations agencies as well as IT consultants and training
> firms which are all ideally placed to serve the Park's 1,400
> companies.[37]

A number of newly introduced design features emphasise the totemic nature of the park, representing both the TPDC's aggressive mastery over the

5.3
Plan of Trafford Park (1998)
Source: Trafford Park Development Corporation, publicity brochure

industrial past and its concomitant defensiveness, shrugging off the possibility of a second wave of de-industrialisation, incorporating industrial symbolism as if no thetic break, no de-industrialisation crisis, has occurred. New landscaping and architectural detail reiterate the construction, organisation and management of the former residential estate – the estate as a business concern. They point to the planning system of the residential area, the cultural origins of Big Business once located there and the original street pattern. For example, imagined tram lines are picked out on the Third Avenue pavement, marking out both where the trams once ran to Trafford Park's big industrial plants and where the metrolink tram system will run in approximately 2005. Bright, blue-starred street signs reflect the original (and maintained) 'American' character of the industrial estate (Figure 5.4). Small square stones erected in the flowerbeds around the borders of the village – each of which is marked out with a carved grid of 9 squares – allude to the American grid system of streets and avenues (Figure 5.5). Red pavures mark where missing streets once intersected with Third Avenue. Elaborate landscaping of the former Trafford Park School, now an award-winning Urban Splash office development, also insistently plays on the notion of the grid, marrying this to markings that evoke Ordnance Survey grids. Large flagstones outside St Cuthbert's Church and outside the public toilets are organised in a pattern, again to evoke a grid system.

However, the nature of the totem is such that working-class memories of the Park are suppressed in the architectural and spatial redevelopment of the Village. Interviews conducted with former residents and community workers reveal their ambivalence with the redevelopment – on one hand, they

5.4
Third Avenue street sign, Trafford Park
Source:
Photograph by Gten Photography & Design

5.5
**Third Avenue
gridblock detail**
Source:
Photograph by
Gten Photography
& Design

were pleased that the Park had been rejuvenated; on the other, they were frustrated and resentful that their working lives had been airbrushed out. Indeed, the TPDC had not felt it necessary to consult former residents about how the place they had lived in was to be redeveloped, arguing that 'the subtlety of some of what we did wouldn't wash with them. They wouldn't have necessarily understood it, why we'd done it.'[38] Although the TPDC overtly linked the development of the Village to notions of protecting workers' heritage, its primary goal was the successful regeneration of an industrial park and this meant that what was able to be included in the new symbolism was inevitably constrained. As the leader of the Village Planning Team commented:

> I think [the new design details] just fitted within what we were trying to do which was to make that area distinctive. And that historical reference . . . with me anyway, gelled quite nicely with what we were trying to do. And I did use all those little ideas to sell the area to potential developers.[39]

Clearly, whereas symbols of the industrial past can be deployed to sell business space, the realities of the working-class labour and accommodation that made that past possible are not to be represented.

The spatial suppression of working-class labour runs through the village redevelopment. Sharon Zukin points out that, 'Developing small spaces within the city as sites of visual delectation creates urban oases where everyone *appears* to be middle-class.'[40] The dwellings area has been reshaped into just such an oasis of middle-class sensibility (Figure 5.6). Red brickwork has been jazzed up by the addition of creamy yellow stone and wooden walkways. Third Avenue's shops that once spilt out a myriad of goods onto the pavement are now dressed in such a way as to echo a traditional (southern) English rural community. Olde-worlde signs hang above shop-doors. Even the chippy has been gentrified with a posh sign and the gleam of new chrome. The British Legion has been renamed the Village Inn. The complex system of one-way streets and cul-de-sacs has introduced the notion of private space into an area where once every street and every property was potentially on view. This is exacerbated by the introduction of gated (business) communities, with the entrances to buildings set back or turned away from the main street, and with boulders set behind iron fences for added protection from an unnamed threat. Even the name that the TPDC used to describe the area, 'the Village', was a suppression of the lived experience of former residents. Village was a term never used by former residents, in spite of TPDC claims for local authenticity. Indeed, our interview data suggest widespread disdain for the term by former residents and community workers.[41] Use of the term 'village' has

5.6
Publicity montage, 1998
Source: Trafford Park Development Corporation, publicity brochure

become common in developments where brownfield sites are being reclaimed, in an attempt to soften the industrial landscape and make it more palatable for residential or post-industrial business use.

'The Village' is a totemic space because it appropriates an industrial symbolism, written into the architectural, spatial and landscaping frame

of the area, that expresses both a triumphal mastery over the past and a defensive drive to resist a second de-industrialisation. But the symbolism itself suppresses many past realities in order to access the capital it needs to promote itself as a success. Memory appears to be written all over the redevelopment through the imposition of the totem, but it is forgetting, in the shape of what the totem can signify, that makes the area curiously history-free. The houses are gone and there is no sign of them. The shops are gentrified. The streets have been re-routed to secure privacy for business. A former community worker told us that former residents frequently get lost on their return because they just do not recognise the place.

Uses of totemism

Many other sites in Manchester are open to similar critiques.[42] Faux-industrialised railway arches have emerged as the most desired spaces for leisure consumption in Manchester. Similarly, in Castlefield, new housing has been built in the style of old shipping warehouses, thus replicating one architectural form of industrial production (so that people can consume this) but not the housing that working people actually inhabited. But analysis which uses totemism is apt for developments across Britain. Formerly industrial premises such as the Baltic Flour Mill in Gateshead and the Bankside Power Station in London have now become leading contemporary art spaces (Baltic and Tate Modern, respectively).

The model of totemic spaces we are proposing contributes to the understanding of post-industrial developments by focusing on elements that standard gentrification analysis and memory discourse do not address. Recognition of the totem enables such development to be viewed critically, particularly in the way it tackles memory and the past. It also enables the currently rather overlooked issue of class, as it is expressed spatially, to be foregrounded and draws attention to the way development fetishises particular elements of industrial production at the same time as it suppresses others.

Acknowledgements

Thanks to Helen Hills, Stephen Hicks and Laura Turney for their comments.

Notes

1 S. Freud, *The Complete Psychological Works of Sigmund Freud*, 13, *Totem and Taboo and Other Works*, London: The Hogarth Press, 1913–14, p. 145.

2 R. Mellor, 'Cool times for a changing city', in N. Jewson and S. Macgregor (eds.), *Transforming Cities: Contested Governance and New Spatial Divisions*, London: Routledge, 1997, p. 56.

3 S. Zukin, *The Cultures of Cities*, Oxford: Blackwell, 1995, p. 2.

4 Helen Hills (with Paul Tyrer), 'The Fetishized Past: Post-Industrial Manchester and Interstitial Spaces', *Visual Culture in Britain*, 3: 2, 2002, pp. 103–17.

5 J. Kristeva, *Revolution in Poetic Language*, New York: Columbia University Press, 1984; Claude Lévi-Strauss, *Totemism*, Boston: Beacon Press, 1963.

6 R. Glass, 'Introduction', in Centre for Urban Studies (ed.), *London: Aspects of Change*, London: McGibbon and Kee, 1964, pp. xiii–xlii; R.T. LeGates and C. Hartman, 'The Anatomy of Displacement in the United States', in N. Smith and P. Williams (eds.), *Gentrification of the City*, Boston: Allen and Unwin, 1986, pp. 178–200; S.B. Laska and D. Spain, *Back to the City: Issues in Neighborhood Renovation*, New York: Pergamon, 1980, pp. 77–94; C. Hartman, *The Transformation of San Francisco*, Totowa, NJ: Rowman and Allanheld, 1984; A.M. Bouthillette, 'Gentrification by Gay Male Communities: A Case Study of Toronto's Cabbagetown', in S. Whittle (ed.), *The Margins of the City: Gay Men's Urban Lives*, Aldershot: Arena, 1994.

7 B. London, 'Gentrification as Urban Reinvasion: Some Preliminary Definitional and Theoretical Considerations', in S.B. Laska and D. Spain (eds.), *Back to the City*, p. 80.

8 Smith and Williams, *Gentrification*.

9 K.L. Klein, 'On the Emergence of *Memory* in Historical Discourse', *Representations*, Winter 2000, pp. 127–50.

10 W. Benjamin, 'Paris: Capital of the Nineteenth Century', in *Charles Baudelaire: A Lyric Poet in the Era of High Capitalism*, London: Verso, 1997; M.C. Boyer, *The City of Collective Memory: Its Historical Imagery and Architectural Entertainments*, Cambridge MA: MIT Press, 1994.

11 We must stress that we are addressing Freud's analysis rather than reflecting others' views of its accuracy. Freud's version of totemism is in contrast to that of Lévi-Strauss, for example.

> Lévi-Strauss has shown that totemism and sacrifice are contrasting and even incompatible. Totemism is constructed as a language, as a system of differential spaces between discontinuous terms – the natural series (plants or animals) understood as globally homomorphic to the social series. Sacrifice by contrast is the reign of substitution, metonymy, and ordered continuity (one victim may be used for another but not vice versa).
>
> (Kristeva, *Revolution*, pp. 76–7)

Freud's interpretation, however, clearly merges these terms and it is this merging that we find theoretically productive.

12 Freud, *Totem and Taboo*, p. 126.

13 Kristeva, *Revolution*, p. 78.

14 Freud, *Totem and Taboo*, p. 145.

15 Ibid., p. 144.

16 R. Nicholls, *Trafford Park: The First Hundred Years*, Chichester: Phillimore and Co., 1996.

17 I. McIntosh, '"It was a very big horrible place with works": Life and work on Trafford Park – 1896–1939', *Transactions of the Lancashire and Cheshire Antiquarian Society*, 90, 1994, p. 80.

18 I. Brotherston and C. Windmill (eds.), *Bridging the Years: A History of Trafford Park and Salford Docks as Remembered by Those who Lived and Worked in the Area*, Salford: Salford Quays Heritage Centre, 1992, p. 20.

19 Reasons for this limited expansion of the residential aspect of the estate are not cited in any archive material.

20 I. Slater and Co., *Slater's General and Classified Directory and Street Register of Prestwich etc.*, Manchester: Isaac Slater, 1904, p. 262.

21 *Daily Dispatch*, 1901.

22 Port Sunlight Village Online, 2000, 'History', http://www.portsunlight.org.uk

23 Saltaire, 2002, 'Saltaire, World Heritage Site', http://www.bradford.gov.uk/tourism/trails/saltaire/saltaire.html

24 Manchester Studies Trafford Park Interviews, 1979, Tape #780, held at Stalybridge Library.

25 It is not likely, as has been suggested elsewhere, that the dwellings were built by an American construction company, as the architect who developed the plans was English and there is no evidence of American building techniques or materials. The claim that the houses were built to flatter American corporations is made by McIntosh ('It was a very big') but he provides no supporting evidence for this.

26 I. McIntosh, 'Ford at Trafford Park: "an Americanized corner of old jog-trot England"', *Manchester Sociology Occasional Papers*, Manchester: University of Manchester, 1991.

27 I. Slater and Co., *Slater's General and Classified Directory and Street Register of Prestwich etc.*, Manchester: Isaac Slater, 1906.

28 D. Russell and G. Walker (eds.), *Trafford Park 1896–1939: A Selection of Photographs and Recollections about Living in Trafford Park*, Manchester: Manchester Polytechnic, 1976, no page number.

29 Ibid., no page number.

30 Although Green Properties plc, the successor company to the Estates and Dwellings companies, has an extensive warehouse of archive material, there is very little that touches on the early years of the dwellings themselves. This in itself is suggestive that the company had little interest in the housing it had developed.

31 P. Tyrer, interviews in Trafford Park conducted November–December 2000.

32 Nicholls, *Trafford Park: The First Hundred Years*, pp. 119–23.

33 Trafford Park Development Corporation, 'Introduction', http://www.poptel.org.uk/trafford.park/CC001.HTM, 1998.

34 Ibid.

35 Interview with the leader of the TPDC's Village Project Action Team, 15 November 2000.

36 The speed and the sheer volume of traffic are evident in clips from the *Trafford Park Centenary Souvenir Video*, Trafford Park Development Corporation, 1996.

37 Trafford Park Development Corporation, 'Village', http://www.poptel.org.uk/trafford.park/4.HTM, 1998.

38 Interview with the leader of the TPDC's Village Project Action Team, 15 November 2000.

39 Ibid.

40 Zukin, *The Cultures of Cities*, p. 9.

41 For example, according to a community worker:

> It wasn't till the investment strategy started to come in and we started looking at solutions for the whole of the park. That what they started to do was to establish key areas and then the term village started to appear cos that's the only way planners could understand it. So when they then started to promote it, they had consultations about 'The Village'. But of course there was sometimes quite a lot of anger from some of the

ex-residents who'd come back here. 'Bloody 'ell', they said, 'it were never the village, it was the Park.' . . . The Village is an alien concept.

42 Hills (and Tyrer), 'Fetishized Past'.

Qudsiyah Saleh
ascends 14 flights
of stairs in order
to check the
anemometer on the roof of
the United Arab Emirates
Meteorological Office.

Chapter 6

Remembering, forgetting and the industrial gallery space

Richard Williams

My concern in this chapter is the meaning of the industrial gallery space. This art exhibition aesthetic has origins in the art scene of 1950s' New York, and its apotheosis can be said to have been reached at the opening in 2000 of Tate Modern, London, the largest gallery of modern art in the world.[1] In between these historical points, the industrial gallery space has proliferated all over the developed world. Examples include the numerous galleries of SoHo, New York City, which flourished in the 1970s to the 1990s; the Hallen für Neue Kunst, Schaffhausen, Switzerland, a former textile mill converted as a *Kunsthalle* in 1984; the Massachusetts Museum of Contemporary Art (Mass MoCA), a converted factory complex in Williamstown (1986); the Liverpool branch of the Tate Gallery, in a mid-Victorian dock warehouse (1988); the Deichtorhallen, Hamburg, another warehouse (1989); the Tramway, Glasgow, an Edwardian tram depot in use as a multi-purpose arts venue since 1989; the SoHo branch of the Guggenheim Museum, a downtown warehouse in New York City (1992); the Andy Warhol Museum, in a former Pittsburgh warehouse (1994); Baltic, Gateshead (England), a converted 1930s' flour mill (2002). Indeed its proliferation in the Anglophone world is such that the industrial gallery space now provides the dominant aesthetic for museums of modern art. As the architecture critic Deyan Sudjic has stated, 'The tidied-up industrial space has become as much the conventional gallery form as the Greek temple used to be.'[2]

But the proliferation of the industrial gallery space has not occurred without change. Once a radical aesthetic, the style of the avant-garde, the industrial gallery space has been wholeheartedly appropriated by the establishment. It no longer signifies marginality, rather the reverse. No aspiring city is without its converted warehouse museum, a badge of cultural respectability signifying its accession to a realm of sophisticated, international urbanity. And this increasing respectability has been accompanied by uncertainty about its future. The SoHo branch of the New York Guggenheim closed to the public in 2001 after only nine years of operation; in Glasgow, the Tramway's future as an art gallery is in doubt at the time of writing, after dismal visitor figures.[3] This is an anxious moment for the industrial gallery space, therefore, poised between hegemony and collapse. It seems an opportune moment to ask the following questions: what is it, or was it, that attracted powerful institutions of art to these buildings in which the past was so clearly visible? What kind of experience did they want to provoke in the visitor? What did they want to remember of the past, or forget?

Origins

Artists in 1950s' New York were probably the first to work and exhibit in industrial spaces. In the latter part of the decade they began to adopt such spaces in downtown for studio use.[4] Later they began to live in them as well, contravening contemporary zoning regulations in the city.[5] The buildings were, for the most part, generic Anglo-American late nineteenth-century warehouses, found from San Francisco to Bombay. Framed in cast-iron, of seven to eight storeys, they had large, unencumbered spaces and decorative façades which aped Renaissance *palazzi* (a New York peculiarity, now celebrated, was the cast iron façade). For artists the advantages were numerous. Large spaces could be had for little money, and their lack of proximity to the normal amenities of bourgeois life did not greatly matter: a fabricator was worth more than a delicatessen. The phenomenon developed in the 1950s with artists such as Robert Rauschenberg and Allan Kaprow. In the 1960s it was closely associated with Minimalism.[6] The American term used to describe such a space was a 'loft'. In contemporary accounts, they were hard, masculine spaces with clear associations of manual labour, and in them the normal distinctions between work and residence were calculatedly blurred. Rauschenberg's loft had the basics of domestic life – a refrigerator, a stove, and a bed – but it was primarily a place of work. It was full of things that might or might not become part of the artist's sculpture – 'a car door, a window frame, a roof ventilator mounted on wheels' as well as (oddly) a 'big, ramshackle wire cage containing a pair of kinkajous'.[7] It was not a homely setting: the big windows let in plenty of light, but also the cold and the roar of traffic. Kaprow's accounts of happenings in New York lofts in the early 1960s similarly locate these buildings as places of urban theatre in which anything might (and probably would) happen.[8]

At first, the loft was a private affair and it would have been unusual for a gallery visitor to be familiar with them, unless they knew artists. But from the early 1960s, the loft space came to be more familiar, consumed as image, if not as fact. Andy Warhol and his entourage occupied a series of industrial buildings, each called 'the Factory' from November 1963 onwards, the first a former hat factory close to the United Nations headquarters on the East River.[9] Warhol's talent for publicity ensured that it, and future Factories, became in effect a theatre set for the New York socialites. With every surface painted silver, and used as much as living room and social space as working studio, Warhol showed the loft's potential for domestication by New York City's upper classes. Nevertheless, the tendency to show art in lofts was underwritten by a belief that they were somehow more 'real'. When the dealer Paula Cooper moved her gallery to a SoHo loft in 1968, she said that she had been motivated by the desire to show her artists in a less precious context than that of the uptown gallery: 'I didn't want to be bothered with all the social trimmings, things that often counted for more than the art itself.'[10] A decade later SoHo had become the prime location for commercial galleries in New York.

Leo Castelli was one dealer who most effectively made the transition from uptown to downtown. As early as 1968, he had experimented with a warehouse space, which he had rented at West 108 Street, initially for storage (Figure 6.1). Its potential as an exhibition space was realised by Castelli artists including Robert Morris, who saw possibilities – especially messy ones – in the raw environment of the warehouse which would have been inconceivable at the gallery's HQ.[11] The group show of new sculpture there in December 1968 was little visited, but much discussed; Castelli formally opened a warehouse gallery in SoHo in 1971.

The increasing visibility of the loft as gallery in the early 1970s led to its appropriation as an aesthetic for residential development: as Sharon Zukin has written, 'the economic and aesthetic virtues of loft-living were transformed into bourgeois chic'.[12] The loft, for some years a sign of bohemia, had been assimilated by that to which it once stood in opposition. This process coincided with its adoption as the standard aesthetic for public art museums in the developed world. The examples I cite above from Gateshead, Hamburg, Liverpool, New York City, Pittsburgh, Schaffhausen, and Williamstown are just a few of the many such spaces that were developed at the time. The translation of the aesthetic from the New York art business of the 1960s, to the American civic art museum, or European *Kunsthalle* of the 1980s nevertheless

6.1
**Castelli
Warehouse,
New York**
Source: Photograph
by Richard Williams

involved some adaptation, particularly as regards the philosophical engagement with the past. As most of these structures were located in areas that
had undergone profound industrial change, to adapt them for cultural
purposes was an ideological act as much as a material one. What I want to
explore here is the meaning of this particular adaptation. What does it mean
to adapt an industrial structure for cultural purposes? What does it signify
about the past? What do these structures mean to remember, and what do
they mean to forget? How should we, as visitors, apprehend them?

Remembering and forgetting

Remembering and forgetting are the key psychological processes that concern me here, as they have increasingly concerned art historians and museologists in recent years.[13] However, my precise interest in the industrial gallery space is its apprehension by the visitor – the subject position the visitor is supposed to adopt in relation to these rehabilitated structures – and for this reason I will call on a different academic discourse. My understanding of the processes of remembering and forgetting is underwritten here less by art history than by anthropology, and in particular the disciplinary distinction made by anthropologists between their practice and that of the historian. There are, I argue, historical and anthropological approaches in play in these former industrial structures, often simultaneously, and it helps to think about these disciplinary problems as a way of working out what is going on. The particular anthropological text I have in mind here is Claude Lévi-Strauss's introduction to *Structural Anthropology*, in which he defines the then new term of anthropology against history.[14] Both are concerned, he writes, with 'societies *other* than the one in which we live'.[15] They share the same subject,

> which is social life; the same goal, which is a better understanding of man; and, in fact the same method, in which only the proportion of research techniques varies. They differ, principally, in their choice of complementary perspectives: history organises its data in relation to the conscious expressions of social life, while anthropology proceeds by examining its unconscious foundations.[16]

This is an important distinction. Transferring this disciplinary schema to the museum, we can imagine an historical approach to the use of space, in which a building from the past is used in ways which identify it with publicly available texts and ideas. A building may be refurbished in order to represent certain ideas about the past, to articulate them publicly, and to change them. It may use architectural forms to consciously evoke the past, leaving, for example, old structures intact so that the past is visible. It may emphasise the distinction between old and new by making stylistic contrasts between the two. It may appear to value the old over the new by rhetorically emphasising the former – it may, for example, relegate the modern parts of a building to non-public, invisible, functions while keeping the old as the public, visible part. All this may be said to demonstrate a conscious concern for history. In the broadest sense, it is evidenced in postmodern styles of architecture, with their historical quotations and incorporation of existing historical structures.

If this can be said to be an historical approach, we might equally imagine an anthropological approach to the art museum. An anthropological approach might emphasise the experience of the visitor in the present.

It might deliberately exoticise its exhibits, or make its viewing conditions uncanny, drawing on *unconscious* factors to create a powerful experience. It would draw on and adapt anthropology's attraction to those subjects which are supposedly more natural, less hidebound by convention, less bound by conscious rules; its attraction to working in what Lévi-Strauss describes as 'exceptionally unfavourable conditions'.[17]

Now, I am not trying to argue that the experience of industrial gallery space is *other* for the westerner in the same way as Lévi-Strauss's encounter in the 1930s with the Tupi-Kawahib.[18] But it has something of this character. As the contemporary anthropologist Marc Augé has argued in his book *Non-Places*, the desire for the exotic has masked the otherness of places closer to home. If the fundamental purpose of anthropology is the description of the exotic in contrast to a supposedly identical 'we', then much of the contemporary 'near' world may be an appropriate object of study.[19] In these modernised anthropological terms, this other may be defined by such things as class, relation to the centre, place, or psychogeography. Thinking of our industrial gallery spaces, one of their major characteristics is their peripheral location, certainly *vis-à-vis* the traditional centres of the art world. The Leo Castelli warehouse, for example, was in a run-down, largely Hispanic area on the fringes of Harlem. Considered 'dangerous' by one critic, it barely received any visitors; reviews concentrated on the rawness of the surround-ings, and the lack of creature comforts.[20] In this broad sense, the warehouse was anthropologically other without being more than a few miles from the centre. We can therefore locate it in terms of an anthropological approach to art experience, as distinct from a historical one.

In fact, this distinction between historical and anthropological approaches to the museum already exists. Consider Nicholas Serota's essay on the 'dilemma' of the modern art museum, *Experience or Interpretation*.[21] Serota does not invoke the terms anthropology or history, but in all other respects the distinction he makes is the same one. His essay revolves around the question of whether the museum should concern itself with an experience of the other in the present ('Experience'), or the remembering of the past ('Interpretation'). The Tate, which Serota directs, evidences both approaches. And, crucially, both approaches are legible in the Tate's employment of the industrial gallery space. The cases I have in mind are of course the two industrial conversions the Tate has made for its displays of modern art, Tate Liverpool, converted by James Stirling and Michael Wilford in 1988, and Tate Modern, converted by Herzog and de Meuron in 2000. While ostensibly similar, the former is much more bound up with 'history' in the sense I have defined it above, and the latter with 'anthropology'.

Let me begin with Tate Liverpool (Figure 6.2). This grand, iron and brick mid-Victorian warehouse by Jesse Hartley was converted by Stirling

6.2
**Tate Liverpool.
Architect –
Jesse Hartley
(1841–45),
conversion by
Stirling & Wilford
(1984–88)**
Source: Photograph
by Richard Williams

from 1984 to 1988, and is suffused with historical imagery.[22] A concept sketch by Stirling from 1984 drew attention to the architect's memory of the Albert Dock immediately after the Second World War, when, badly damaged and more or less abandoned, it was used as a store for ship parts. The central dock was, according to Stirling, a mess of funnels, bridges, railings and ventilators, and his first proposal imagined the entrance to the new Tate through a gangway and a ship's bridge.[23] He went further, inscribing his deepest origins in the history of the Dock: he conceived, he said at the time, of a ship berthed there.[24] Tate Liverpool as realised is no less historical in its approach. The conversion leaves exposed most of the original structural features of this dour Victorian building, showing off its cast-iron columns, brick vaulting, and the spars of its intricate metal roof. Meanwhile the light and ironic character of the contemporary interventions in the structure leave little doubt

127

as to the continuing importance of the Victorian past. The jolly maritime quality of these interventions – all portholes and pastel colours – is itself historically informed, underwriting the city's seafaring history, and continuing the range of references to it in the rest of the Dock.[25] These signs of history are quite conscious, and they suppose an uncomplicated consumption of the past, all Beatles and boats and empire, with Liverpool at the centre of the world. Its staged quality has been much remarked upon, and often lamented, for its interpretation of history is undoubtedly simplistic, and self-serving.[26] But however limited, it is a historical approach, of sorts: as a visitor, one is supposed to consume this highly mediated and unproblematic view of the past.

Tate Modern presents a different scenario (Figure 6.3). It is also a historical building, a great power station in brick, built between 1948 and 1963 by Giles Gilbert Scott: as at Liverpool, the historical structure remains clearly visible.[27] But where Tate Liverpool seems to affirm history, poignantly

reminding visitors of the city's past maritime greatness, Tate Modern is a much more ambiguous representation of the past. The original structure is, for a start, wildly anachronistic, completed in the early 1960s but arguably having more in common with European modernism of the early 1900s. And the architects of the redesign, the Swiss practice Herzog and de Meuron, unlike their counterparts at Liverpool, deliberately blurred the distinction between new and old parts. They incorporated the Gilbert Scott structure as if it was one of their own designs, adding brickwork and metal grilles in a style indistinguishable from the original. The major additions to the structure, the glass pavilions on the roof and inside the turbine hall, announce that an intervention has been made, but the forms and materials they adopt could belong to the original building. The result is a building that superficially has the character of a historical structure, but conspicuously lacks its effect. In a roundtable discussion for the journal *October*, the art historian Alex Potts remarked: 'the whole display is an evacuation of memory and nostalgia . . . the amazingly powerful effect of the whole thing [does] block out associa-tions'.[28] In the same discussion, Julian Stallabrass noted the lack of poignancy about Tate Modern's relationship with the past, a character that contrasted, he argued, with earlier modes of using industrial space[29]:

6.3
**Tate Modern,
London.
Architect –
Giles Gilbert
Scott (1948–63),
conversion by
Herzog and de
Meuron (2000)**
Source: Photograph
by Richard Williams

> If you went to so-called alternative exhibitions of British art in the 1990s, they were often housed in industrial ruins. Many were unrenovated and bore clear traces of their past use. Signs admon-ishing workers, or sinks and other fittings. The feeling of a ghost workplace was still very much present. Personally I don't find that at Tate Modern. There's not that kind of poignant juxtaposition of postmodern products disporting themselves in the ruins of modernity.[30]

In other words, the architects treated the old Bankside power station as simply another one of their structures, and in so doing treated it with no more or less respect.[31] Tate Modern, as a result, supposes no nostalgic engagement with the past. Heritage, as Serota noted in a discussion with one of the project's architects, Jacques Herzog, is not glamorised at Tate Modern: 'the turbine hall is still a quasi industrial space but you don't walk in there and think of it as a heritage object.'[32] Instead of the evocation of history, there is a deep experience in the present moment, a 'profound physical and psychol-ogical impact'.[33] The correct initial response to Tate Modern, it could be said, is to stand dumbfounded on the entrance ramp, astounded by the sheer scale of the building, which could equally belong to the nineteenth or twenty-first centuries. The commissioned projects for the Turbine Hall, that part of the building that most clearly reveals its past, have played on this historical ambiguity. Olafur Eliasson's *Weather Project* (2003–4) is a spectacular

6.4
Olafur Eliasson,
Weather Project,
2003–04
Source: Photograph
by Richard Williams

evocation of the sublime that has nothing whatever to do with the space's industrial history, and everything to do with its immense size (Figure 6.4). The astonishing popular reaction to the piece, in which visitors lay prostrate on the floor of the Turbine Hall, soaking up the rays of Eliasson's giant imaginary sun, showed an industrial relic completely removed from its history.[34]

The curious, unpremeditated, response to *Weather Project* points to another aspect of Tate Modern which indicates its anthropological spatial character. It is conceived in terms of the evocation of unconscious rather than conscious feeling. Herzog alludes to the same thing when he states that outside, it is 'very ordinary, very typically London', but inside 'there is something absolutely extraordinary about it.'[35] However self-serving this statement might seem, it locates the gallery in the realm of the uncanny, an idea which, Herzog elaborates, comes from an appreciation of Hitchcock's films, whose uncanny quality derives from their subversion of the everyday. As he puts it: 'Whatever is scary or beautiful comes out of these very normal situations. You only switch it or shift it a little and other things become visible.'[36] The unconscious affect of the Tate (or at least the intention that it has such an affect) further entrenches its approach in terms of the anthropological.

The last point I will make about the Tate as anthropological experience is perhaps the most obvious one: it concerns its site.[37] Bankside Power Station is remarkable in its centrality. No other capital city can have constructed a major coal-fired power station directly opposite its major cathedral, yet this is what happened at Bankside. It faces St. Paul's over the Thames; the two are barely a quarter of a mile apart, and vie with each other for monumental presence. But this very centrality is misleading, for it is the fact that Bankside lies on the southern side of the Thames in the borough of Southwark that explains its extraordinary position. While physically in central London, Southwark is psychogeographically other; it is its long history as a marginal place, the home of the dispossessed and the poor, and more recently, of industrial London, that permitted the building of Bankside in the first place.[38] Southwark was 'remote', poorly connected to the rest of central London, despite its proximity to it.[39] Foreign and other, a journey to Southwark was a journey, in effect, into darkness. Tate Modern signifies not a journey into history, but into anthropological place.[40]

Tramway

As much as the distinction between history and anthropology is useful in problematising the industrial gallery space, it is nevertheless a rather crude analytical tool. Sharon Zukin has written of the tendency of industrial conversions to distance history, reducing, as she puts it, 'the immediacy of industrial society and its problems'.[41] Taken to an extreme (as in the comprehensive redevelopment of docks undertaken in Baltimore and Boston) it makes it 'impossible to consider a return to any version of the old urban-industrial infrastructure.'[42] Zukin is thinking here specifically of residential redevelopment, but the schemes in the north-eastern part of the USA by James Rouse that she mentions were explicitly a model for Liverpool. In the same context, the planner Peter Hall has written of the obliteration of history by such schemes: despite their attention to the historical façade, they are no more historical than Disneyland's 'Main Street USA'.[43]

I have written elsewhere of the connections in Britain between the industrial gallery space and the picturesque cult of the ruin.[44] This aesthetic, central to the British (particularly English) understanding of architecture and urbanism, was codified in the eighteenth century, but had a profound influence on the country's post-war reconstruction; the pages of the *Architectural Review* contain several important articles during and immediately after the Second World War romanticising the urban landscape left in London, Coventry and Liverpool by German bombing.[45] In 1942, the *Review*'s editor, J. M. Richards eulogised the post-Blitz City of London, with its

> sacrificed surface of blasted walls, the chalky substance of calcined masonry, the surprising sagging contours of once rigid girders and the clear sienna colouring of burnt out brick buildings, their rugged crosswalls receding plane by plane, on sunny mornings.[46]

This aestheticisation of destruction contributed to the choice of the Albert Dock for the northern branch of the Tate Gallery. Long in decline, and damaged, though not badly, by German air raids, it already had a discursive existence as a romantic ruin thanks to Richards, and Nikolaus Pevsner who had declared it, and the nearby St Georges' Hall in Liverpool among the greatest monuments of neo-classicism.[47] Now this aestheticisation of decay, it barely needs to be said, involves an act of forgetting – so, to return to the question of the museum, to declare Tate Liverpool an 'historical' as opposed to 'anthropological' case is too simplistic. As Tony Bennett has argued in relation to the museum of the industrial revolution at Beamish, in County Durham, the heritage museum is an amnesiac site as much as one of remembrance. In order to image the past in a way that may be acceptably consumed, then a great deal must be repressed: there must be nothing on labour or co-operative movements, nothing that detracts from the image of labour as a 'picturesque element' for the enjoyment of the observer.[48] The museum, despite its origins in the profound conflicts of the Industrial Revolution, is (he cites Michel Foucault) 'a place of rest, certainty, reconciliation, a place of tranquilised sleep'.[49]

If Tate Liverpool's acknowledgement of the past is also a sanitising, and therefore a forgetting of it, then Tate Modern is a play on received ideas about the past as much as it is a denial of them. Its Turbine Hall, through the name, and the maintenance of certain pieces of industrial equipment including a crane, is a case in point. It might therefore be more accurate to say that the industrial gallery space therefore presents a scenario of simultaneous remembering *and* forgetting. What I want to do in the final part of this chapter is analyse a case in which remembering and forgetting are especially blurred. This is Tramway, an arts centre on the south side of Glasgow, which has been used for cultural purposes since 1989 (Figures 6.5, 6.6).[50] Owned by the city council, at the time of writing its future as a publicly-funded venue was in doubt, dependent on a Lottery application that would turn it into a rehearsal space for the Scottish Ballet. Much of the debate on its future had to do with identity questions of the kind that have been discussed so far. What kind of a

relation did this place have with the past? How did it remember or forget the past? What does this remembering and/or forgetting tell us about the city in which it exists, its hopes, desires, fears? Tramway therefore bears some detailed analysis, not just as a local instance of an industrial gallery space on the damp north-western periphery of Europe, but as an example of international practices and issues.

Tramway's history is complex. It lies about two miles from the commercial centre of the city, the other side of the Clyde river to the south in

the suburb of Pollockshields. The journey from Glasgow Central railway station to Pollockshaws East is less than five minutes' duration, but takes, in effect two decades: crossing the Clyde, one leaves a thriving, contemporary commercial centre, to a site of abandonment and decay, where little has changed in twenty years. One enters at Pollockshaws an inner city no-man's land, seemingly identical to those found in King's Cross, Manchester, or Liverpool. Here is open space, the ruins of industry, barbed wire, distant tower blocks in low density formations, fragments of older tenements and terraces. The station at Pollockshaws East has four platforms, indicative of traffic which no longer exists. The short walk along Albert Drive reveals a blasted, post-industrial landscape, albeit one that is slowly regenerating; stubby neo-modernist towers rise on Barrland Street. But the overall impression is of a familiar post-industrial stagnation, in which the past still hangs heavy; this is a waste zone of gas works, freight terminal, low-rise industrial estate, council tower block and cemetery. Cut through by busy roads and railway lines, it feels mostly left over. There are fragments of an old city life here – grand Victorian tenements still line the main roads – but away from them, the impression is of emptiness. Here the past hangs heavily over the present.

The building that is now Tramway was opened in 1893 as the Coplawhill depot for Glasgow's trams. It was first abandoned in 1964 when the city's tram network was closed, and subsequently became the city's transport museum, again being abandoned in 1985 when that museum was given new premises in Kelvingrove Park in the city's West End. Threatened with demolition in 1988, it was chosen as the site for a performance of Peter Brook's *Mahabarata*, a theatrical spectacular based on the world's earliest-known text, a Sanskrit account of the origins of Hinduism. The performance had already been realised in a disused theatre in Brooklyn, a gasometer in Denmark, a stone quarry in Adelaide, and a Tokyo office building. It cost £350,000 to stage; some of the cost was met by the city, as a sign of its commitment to being the 1990 European Capital of Culture; there were

6.6
Tramway, Glasgow. Conversion by Zoo Architects (1999–2000)
Source: Photograph by Richard Williams

further contributions from Strathclyde (the metropolitan region abolished in 1992), the Scottish Arts Council, and the Arts Council of Great Britain. The cast of thirty performed in a specially built 700-seat auditorium in the main shed. The audience looked onto a 360-square metre stage made of 75,000 bricks, 250 tons of sand, and 140 tones of clay, sand and rock.[51] It was a gruelling experience for the audience as well as the performers: each performance lasted for nine hours.[52] As a performance, *Mahabarata* was widely reviewed and critically acclaimed. For the *Guardian*, it represented the 'richest and most exciting work that world theatre has to offer'. Meanwhile for Glasgow, it represented the city's accession once more to a place among the 'great second cities of the world, vigorous, handsome, cosmopolitan, fizzing with creative energy and civic pride'.[53]

After the production of *Mahabarata*, Tramway gradually became a venue for the visual arts as well as theatre, programmed by Neil Wallace and Nicola White, and later Charles Esche. As a visual arts venue, it had a number of successes, including, in 1993 the first showing of *24-Hour Psycho* by the young Scottish artist and Glasgow School of Art graduate, Douglas Gordon. Projected continuously on a single 15 by 10-foot cinema screen in the main tramshed, the piece comprised a version of the Hitchcock film slowed down to last for 24 hours. The shower scene alone lasted a gruelling 45 minutes. Gordon's piece and the positive critical response to it set the tone for Tramway as a visual arts venue: the work it showed would be very large in scale, somewhat demanding, and highly theatrical. Visiting an exhibition would be a challenging experience, taking the spectator literally out of the bustling reconstructed centre of Glasgow, and placing them in an unfamiliar, and uncomfortable environment to view uncompromising images. It was not an experience of the everyday; it quickly got its devotees. A retrospective account of the beginnings of Tramway declared that it had been

> all about exhilarating experiences in evocative and forlorn spaces: dark massive rooms with their previous functions, industrial and cultural, stamped into the rough walls, the uneven floors. Always a thrill to visit, it reeked of history . . . Tramway was a bit like going to church – humbling, and not a tremendous amount to do with real life.[54]

During 1999 to 2000, Tramway was refurbished as an arts venue, through a conversion by the Glasgow-based practice, Zoo Architects at a cost of £3.6 million, or roughly £450 per square foot.[55] The aims of the project were to restore the basic fabric of the building, in particular, the leaking roof; to add toilets, a bar, and to improve access. The client asked that the architects leave the industrial character of the building as untouched as possible, so from the outside on the main façade on Albert Drive, it barely appears that any transformation has taken place.[56] A sheet of plate glass appears to signify the presence of modern culture, but the brickwork, although stabilised, has not been restored. Similarly, the rear of the building appears largely unaltered. At the back of the building, glass doors now open out onto a formal garden, which incorporates a tall brick chimney from the original complex. The rear façade of the building itself remains largely scruffy and unreconstructed. Apart from the roof, it is hard at first to see what exactly has been done; the part of the building bordering the busy Pollockshaws Road is a mess of car park and waste ground, sealed by heavy iron gates.

Inside, however, there have been several clear interventions. The major alteration is the introduction of what the architects call the 'Street', an 'art promenade' in the words of the architects, a clear axis from the front to the back of the building, leading from the entrance to the downstairs bar and gardens beyond. Off this axis are the main galleries themselves, which include the largely unchanged tramshed, renamed as Tramway 2. At the rear, between the vast new bar overlooking the garden and the exhibition spaces, there is a ramp leading to the upper level. This is a reconstruction of the ramp for horses that used to allow them to reach the stables at the end of their day. At first floor level, the Street provides upper level access to the galleries (there is a balcony overlooking Tramway 2) and a range of smaller, domestically sized spaces used as workshops and exhibition rooms. These are converted from the former stables – the horses that used to pull the trams were led up a ramp at the rear of the building, which has been restored. The clearest indication of the building's past is the maintenance of the tram tracks in Tramway 2 as a reminder of the building's industrial past (and perhaps its earlier status as a museum of transport). On the ground floor, beyond the large, somewhat bleak, bar there are the Hidden Gardens. This formal garden brings industrial land into cultural use, with contemplative spaces based on artworks referring to major world religions.[57]

A heterotopia

Tramway exhibits, it might be said, some ambiguity toward the notions of historical and anthropological space. Where Tate Liverpool very consciously evokes the past, and Tate Modern obliterates it, Tramway does both simultaneously. It employs tactics of both remembering and forgetting at the same time; the anthropological experience that it evokes is dependent in some way on its condition as a historical ruin. This is quite apparent in critical reactions to it on its re-opening in 2000. The *Independent* on that occasion praised the architects' work for having maintained 'the building's grand scale and utilitarian rough edges'.[58] The *Guardian* talked of 'post-industrial bleakness on a vast, seductive scale'.[59] Zoo Architects said of the building that it was 'generous, simple, Spartan, industrial, linear and orthogonal, invoking a powerful sense of place'.[60] In the condition that they found it, it was 'unkempt' but at the same time 'spectacular and otherworldly'.[61]

Now, all of these accounts of Tramway are preoccupied with the place as a site of memory, as revelatory of the past; as regards its future, they think it essential that its history should be kept visible. There is the attachment to the tramlines, for example, and the restoration of the horse ramp, both features which are essentially useless, indeed, inconveniences: the only purpose they have is to facilitate the memory of the building's past. Now this sense of memory is clearly connected in the minds of the architects, reviewers and artist-advocates of the building with a certain special kind of experience. Its bleakness is 'seductive'; the industrial is a 'feel' or 'feeling'; the architects speak of a 'powerful sense of place', of its being 'otherworldly'. Peter Brook called it an 'industrial cathedral' in 1989, thinking not only of its huge dimensions, but also of the quality of feeling that it produced in him.[62] The Tramway must therefore be situated in a discourse about it as *experience*.

What precisely is the nature of this experience? Is it 'history' or 'anthropology', to use the terms we have put in play throughout this chapter? Is it about memory, or forgetting, or both? All of the accounts of the place suppose a visitor who is fundamentally alienated from their surroundings, for whom the post-industrial south side of Glasgow is as unfamiliar as Delhi. The visitor goes to Tramway for an experience of the extraordinary, that may not be exactly pleasurable: the ordeal of *Mahabarata* is followed by the terror and boredom of *24-Hour Psycho*. Tramway's art, as much as its environment, is self-consciously difficult, unsettling, other – hence the irritation of the *Herald* critic, who complained of the lack of 'background information and explanation' at Tramway, and the 'lack of concern for gallery goers'.[63]

Alienated in this way from the industrial environment, visitors to Tramway bring with them behaviour which belongs to the realm of high culture. In the words of the architects, they 'explore, pause, observe, participate and promenade', the last term 'promenade' perhaps especially indicative of bourgeois cultural experience – not purposeful movement associated with work, but rather walking for leisure in which visual consumption is the key term.[64] Moving through Tramway in this essentially leisured way, they identify with it as an aestheticised image, but not as tramshed. After the experience of the art – which generally makes them feel listless, bored, and finally disappointed – they go to drink coffee in the spacious and well-appointed bar, where they are reassured of their status as visitors. From this comfortable vantage point, they reflect on the peculiar experience they have just had, safe in the knowledge that they may soon return home.

Now a useful term to bring into play here is 'heterotopia', once described in a lecture by Foucault.[65] In short, heterotopia is a site in which the other is temporarily experienced, and the quotidian is temporarily banished.[66] It exists in relation to 'utopia' which (following the correct Greek definition of the term) does not exist in real space.[67] Utopia represents 'society itself brought to perfection, or its reverse' and is 'fundamentally unreal'.[68] The heterotopia is by contrast a real place, but one that stands in distinction to society, one that by definition, has a marginal relationship to it. Foucault describes heterotopias of various kinds: of 'crisis', housing an individual at a critical moment in his or her relations with society (the boarding school, military service, the honeymoon);[69] heterotopias of 'deviance' ('rest homes, psychiatric clinics, prisons');[70] 'chronic' heterotopias, which is to say places that are limited by time (fairs, holiday villages);[71] heterotopias of pleasure (brothels).[72] The function of the heterotopia, Foucault wonders, is perhaps not illusion, but 'compensation' for society's failings; a perfect space that exists in relation to imperfections elsewhere.

The ship, Foucault thinks, is the heterotopia *par excellence*:

> it is a floating part of space, a placeless place, that lives by itself, closed in on itself and at the same time poised in the infinite ocean, and yet, from port to port, tack by tack, from brothel to brothel, it goes as far as the colonies looking for the most precious things hidden in their gardens. Then you will understand why it has been not only and obviously the main means of economic growth . . . but at the same time the greatest reserve of the imagination for our civilisation from the sixteenth century down to the present day . . . In civilisations where it is lacking, dreams dry up, adventure is replaced by espionage, and privateers by the police.[73]

Now why should the heterotopia be an especially appropriate metaphor for the industrial gallery space, and specifically this industrial gallery space? Surely, it might be said, all museums are heterotopias? All museums, after all, perform a compensatory role *vis-à-vis* the culture in which they exist, representing an ordered ideal to which one may retreat for temporary respite from the disorder outside. In this broad sense they are indeed all heterotopic. But the appeal of Foucault's category in this particular case is its elevation of marginal spaces.[74] The heterotopia in his definition is *necessarily* marginal; in the museum world, so too is the industrial gallery: at least this is what it performs.[75] Its historical origin place is (until gentrification) on the edge of the city, away from residence and power and commerce. As I state in the introduction, the industrial gallery may mark a departure in this respect from the dominant western tradition, which has sought to place the museum at the centre of culture, through both architectural form and object collections narrating an official history of state or institutional power. As Carol Duncan has argued, in the traditional scheme of things, the museum outwardly resembles a temple, and museum-going is a secular ritual. The business of the museum here is unquestionably affirmative.[76] Not so the industrial gallery space, which may not only be hard to find, but very likely contain objects or images which stand in obvious critical relation to the surrounding culture. Its job, as it were, is to perform marginality. For Foucault, the heterotopia has immense romantic appeal, shown by his description of the cultural value of the ship (above). As an intellectual, and as a homosexual, Foucault was himself accustomed to a wide variety of heterotopic spaces.[77] The problem of the heterotopia in this context, however, could be said to be its brutal treatment of the past. As Robert Harbison has written of the transformation of the spaces of industry 'commerce is romantic only when it has vanished'.[78] In the case of Tramway, the heterotopia well describes its present function in Glasgow. But its also describes the loss of an earlier culture, which the ostensible presence of the past through architecture does nothing to recover.

Notes

1 This chapter is partly a development of my ideas in Chapter 5 of *The Anxious City: British Urbanism in the Late 20th Century*, London: Routledge, 2004. For more on Tate Liverpool, see that volume.

2 D. Sudjic, 'Industrial Light and Magic', *Observer*, 14 May 2000.

3 Fewer than 100 visitors per day at the time of writing. Details of Tramway's situation in 2003, and the campaign by artists to save it, can be found at the following website: http://mail-archive.com/ambit@mediascot.org.msg01333html/ Accessed 18 December 2003.

4 'Downtown' signifies the area around Houston St. now universally know as SoHo; 'SoHo' itself (South of Houston) was an invention of real estate agents in the 1960s.

5 Much of lower Manhattan was zoned for industry, not residence.

6 The Minimalists I refer to here included Carl Andre, Eva Hesse, Robert Morris, Richard Serra, and Robert Smithson, all of whom lived and worked in downtown loft spaces.

7 Tomkins quoted in S. Zukin, *Loft Living: Culture and Capital in Urban Change*, Baltimore, MD: Johns Hopkins University Press, 1982.

8 Kaprow was responsible for the phenomenon of 'Happenings', vaguely structured performances involving the participation or implication of an audience. They invariably occurred in downtown lofts. See Kaprow's own account in *Essays on the Blurring of Art and Life*, Jeff Kelley (ed.), Berkeley, CA: University of California Press, 1993, pp. 15–26. See also the commentary on Kaprow in R.J. Williams, *After Modern Sculpture: Art in the United States and Europe 1965–70*, Manchester: Manchester University Press, 2000, pp. 93–4.

9 See account in C.A. Jones, *Machine in the Studio: Constructing the Postwar American Artist*, Chicago: Chicago University Press, 1996.

10 Cooper, quoted in R. Greenberg, B.W. Ferguson and S. Nairne (eds.) *Thinking About Exhibitions*, London: Routledge, 1996, p. 354.

11 Morris, letter to the author, 1996. For a more detailed account of the Castelli warehouse, see Williams, *After Modern Sculpture*, pp. 110–13.

12 Zukin, *Loft Living*, p. 2.

13 See S. A. Crane (ed.) *Museums and Memory*, Stanford, CA: Stanford University Press, 2000; G. Kavanagh, *Dream Spaces: Memory and the Museum*, Leicester: Leicester University Press, 2000; also T. Bennett, *The Birth of the Museum: History, Theory, Politics*, London: Routledge, 1995.

14 C. Lévi-Strauss, *Structural Anthropology*, vol. 1, Harmondsworth: Penguin, 1993.

15 Ibid., p. 16.

16 Ibid., p. 18.

17 Ibid., p .8.

18 This is one of the Amazonian tribes he describes in *Tristes Tropiques*, Paris: Librairie Plon, 1955.

19 M. Augé, *Non-Places: Toward an Anthropology of Supermodernity*, London: Verso, 1995, p. 52.

20 See discussion in Williams, *After Modern Sculpture*, pp. 110–13.

21 N. Serota, *Experience or Interpretation: The Dilemma of Museums of Modern Art*, London: Thames and Hudson, 2000.

22 For a longer discussion of Tate Liverpool in the context of the city's economic and cultural decline, see Williams, *Anxious City*.

23 None of these direct references to maritime architecture survived in such a literal form in the building as realised; such nautical references as there were, were abstracted.

24 P. Buchanan, 'Tate on the Mersey', *Architectural Review*, 184: 1097, July 1988, p. 20.

25 The maritime theme is strongly asserted in the street furniture of the Dock.

26 See R. Weston and W. Janusczak, 'Stirling Statement', *Architect's Journal*, 27: 187, 6 July 1988, pp. 32–50.

27 Scott coincidentally had a Liverpool connection, being the designer of the city's Gothic revival Anglican Cathedral (completed 1977); like Bankside Power Station it is extraordinarily vast, and stylistically anachronistic.

28 B. Fer., A. Hudek, M. Nixon and J. Stallabrass, 'Round Table: Tate Modern', *October*, 98, Fall 2001, p. 25.

29 Ibid., p. 24.

30 Ibid., p. 25.

31 The fact that the architects were Swiss is perhaps relevant here. Stirling declared a childhood acquaintance with the Albert Dock, and his interventions in it are presented in partly nostalgic terms. The distant past is a repository of good things here. For Herzog and de Meuron, Bankside Power Station has no such positive associations. It means precisely nothing, except as a spectacular, but redundant structure at the heart of Europe's biggest city.

32 R. Moore and R. Ryan, *Building Tate Modern*, London, Tate Gallery, 2000, p. 44.

33 Ibid., p. 51.

34 For a retrospective account of the reaction from a member of the Tate staff, see Adrian Hardwicke, 'Secret Diary of a Gallery Attendant', *Guardian*, 18 March 2004. Accessed online at: http://www.guardian.co.uk/arts/features/story/0,11710,1171737,00.html

35 Moore and Ryan, *Tate Modern*, p. 51.

36 Ibid.

37 See C. Slessor, 'Art and Industry', *Architectural Review*, 208: 1242, August 2000, p. 44.

38 For a useful discussion of eighteenth-century Southwark in this context, see D. Solkin, *Painting for Money*, New Haven, CT: Yale University Press, 1993, pp. 106–56; J. Brewer, *The Pleasures of the Imagination: English Culture in the Eighteenth Century*, London: HarperCollins, 1997, pp. 357–83.

39 Moore and Ryan, *Tate Modern*, p. 13.

40 I borrow the term 'anthropological place' from Augé, who uses it in distinction to 'non-place'. See Augé, *Non-Places*.

41 Zukin, *Loft Living*, p. 112.

42 Ibid., p. 178.

43 P. Hall, *Cities of Tomorrow*, Oxford: Blackwell, 1996, p. 348.

44 Williams, *Anxious City*. See Chapters 2 and 5 especially.

45 The most important texts here are J. Richards and J. Summerson, *The Bombed Buildings of Britain*, London: Architectural Press, 1942, and J. Piper, 'Pleasing Decay', *Architectural Review*, 102, September 1947, pp. 85–94.

46 Richards, *Bombed Buildings*, p. 3.

47 N. Pevsner, *The Buildings of England*, vol. 36, *Lancashire* vol. 1: *The Industrial and Commercial South*, Harmondsworth: Penguin, 1969, p. 167.

48 T. Bennett, *The Birth of the Museum: History, Theory, Politics*, London: Routledge, 1996, p. 109. The phrase is Gramsci's.

49 Bennett, *Birth of the Museum*, p. 114.

50 My perspective on Tramway is informed particularly by a discussion with Andrew Patrizio from the Edinburgh College of Art.

51 A. Johnson, 'Glasgow's Big Build Up for Indian Epic', *Guardian*, 19 March 1988, p. 4.

52 R. Wishart, 'Ouch Calcutta', *The Scotsman*, 19 April 1988, p. 13.

53 J. MacMillan, 'The Wisest Story Ever Told' , *The Guardian*, 19 April 1988, p. 21.

54 *The Guardian*, 30 May, 2000.

55 This was met mostly from the National Lottery; by their standards it was a small project. The majority of the cost went on replacing the roof.

56 Interview with Peter Richardson, Zoo Architects, February 2004.

57 The gardens were opened in 2003. They were a collaboration between the City Design Co-operative, the 'local community' and 'a team of artists'. Tramway leaflet, Autumn/Winter 2003.

58 S. Wilson, 'Welcome to the House of Fun', *The Independent*, 31 May 2000. Accessed online.

59 E. Mahoney, 'Magical Bleakness Emerges', *The Guardian*, 9 June 2000. Accessed online.

60 S. Dawson, 'Next Stop . . . Art', *Architect's Journal*, 8 June 2000, pp. 40–3.

61 Interview with Peter Richardson, February 2004.

62 A. Wright, 'Epic Space Wins Brook Approval', *The Scotsman*, 12 April 1989, p. 15.

63 C. Henry, 'Burgeoning in Spring', *The Herald*, 30 April 1992, p. 12.

64 S. Dawson, 'Next Stop', p. 40.

65 My use of the term 'heterotopia' here was suggested by Jacques Herzog in conversation with Rowan Moore. Searching for a way to describe Tate Modern's peculiar relationship with the past, he invokes the idea of the heterotopia; however he does not explore it in any detail. See Moore and Ryan, *Tate Modern*, p. 55.

66 M. Foucault, 'Of Other Spaces: Utopias and Heterotopias', in N. Leach (ed.), *Rethinking Architecture: A Reader in Cultural Theory*, London: Routledge, 1997, pp. 350–5.

67 'Utopia', strictly speaking, means 'no place'. See discussion of the term in P. Turner, introduction to his translation of T. More, *Utopia*, London: Penguin, 1965, pp. 7–24.

68 M. Foucault, 'Of Other Spaces', p. 352.

69 Ibid., p. 353.

70 Ibid.

71 Ibid., p. 355.

72 Ibid., p. 356.

73 Ibid.

74 Not all heterotopias are marginal spaces, granted – but a great many are.

75 The industrial gallery space may of course (as I state in the introduction) increasingly signify the reverse of marginality: Tate Modern is an example of such a space adopted by an arm of political power as a symbol of modernity. But such galleries still play with the look of marginality, even if this is actually meaningless.

76 C. Duncan, *Civilising Rituals: Inside Public Art Museum*, London: Routledge, 1996.

77 For more on Foucault's life, especially his homosexuality, see D. Macey, *The Lives of Michel Foucault*, New York: Pantheon, 1994.

78 Robert Harbison, *Eccentric Spaces*, London: Andre Deutsch, 1977, p. 131.

Linda Bamford, a second-year exchange student, waits to be shown around the Faculty of Power Engineering at Tallinn Technical University.

Chapter 7

The future of the past
Archiving Singapore

John Phillips

Last time

 (shang ci)

shang   (above; go up; upward; up; go to; appear on scene or enter category; present; affix; apply; place in position; wind up; upper; first; best; better; superior; previous; before; above; top; summit; on; ascend; mount; board; go to court)

ci   (the next in order; secondary; inferior; lower; vice; deputy (ministers, etc.); a place where one stops for rest on a trip; place; stop at a place; by; at (the feast, table, etc.); in the midst; grade; grading; order; sequence; hypo (chemistry); time (each occasion of a recurring action or event)

Cities like Singapore probably represent the truly generic condition of the contemporary city: history has been almost completely blotted out, the entire territory has become artificial, the urban tissue does not endure in any kind of stability beyond a relatively short period of existence.

(Rem Koolhaas)

> now, the corner cigarette-seller is gone, perhaps dead.
> no, definitely dead, he would not otherwise have gone.
>
> (Arthur Yap)

While both seem to be saying the same kind of thing (the urban landscape in Singapore has replaced the history out of which it once emerged), there is a world of difference between the statements of Rem Koolhaas and Arthur Yap. Leaving aside genre and register (for the moment) the distinction can be grasped, in a preliminary way, with reference to a distinction that Walter Benjamin makes in his review of Franz Hessel's *Spazieren in Berlin* ('On Foot in Berlin'), between studying (*studieren*) and learning (*lernen*). 'A whole world separates these words,' he argues, 'Anyone can study, but learning is something that you can only do if you are there for the duration.'[1] This opposition between studying a city and learning will help to identify the problem inherent in most accounts of Singapore's hypermodernity.[2] To study a city is to take it as an object to be analyzed and otherwise accounted for. To learn, on the contrary, would be to become transformed by experience (not *Erlebnis* – the experience of a remarkable event – but *Erfahrung* – which would be more like an *ethos* or way of being). Benjamin's review of Hessel's book emphasizes two motifs that will gather in intensity throughout the remainder of his career: that of cultural memory and that of the *flâneur*. In their underdeveloped state these motifs remain provocative if perhaps somewhat idealistic. Hessel learns his city, Berlin, by walking its streets and remaining open to the city's random stimulations, suggestible to chance encounters and the involuntary associations that they trigger. A crucial factor in this is Hessel's resident's memory, which is what conjures the senses of change and transformation, as well as the relative permanence and impermanence of people and places, some of which remain while others are palpably – often surprisingly – lost to some principle of renewal or decay. And it is this alternative temporality of cultural memory, Benjamin suggests, that informs the dweller's understanding of his dwelling environment.

Later in 'On Some Motifs in Baudelaire' (1939), which is the culmination of Benjamin's engagement with modern urbanism in general, he harnesses a range of key texts and arguments concerning memory, historicity, modernity and urbanism, and creates what is now one of the single most influential studies of the modern city through a sustained reading of Charles Baudelaire's lyric poetry.[3] Here the distinction between *Erlebnis* and *Erfahrung* has been considerably developed and it allows Benjamin, perhaps for the first time, to outline what he understands as the basic conditions for an adequate, historically informed, engagement with modernity. The fact that he chooses to do this through his own admittedly peculiar form of literary criticism is wholly significant. For in Baudelaire's poetry (Benjamin argues that with Baudelaire this was possible for the last and thus the only time), the lived events of urban life were given the weight of an *Erfahrung*: an experience. It is this experience, otherwise obliterated from the urban dweller's consciousness, that constitutes for Benjamin the cultural memory of late nineteenth- and early twentieth-century urban life.

Already suggested in the Hessel review but axiomatic by the time of the Baudelaire article, the vicarious role of the written text is no less a resource for Benjamin than the supposedly (though never in fact) more direct encounter with the urban environment itself. There are good technical reasons for this, which Benjamin develops out of dichotomies like the studying/learning one, and which involve the mutually exclusive categories of consciousness and memory. By critically engaging with texts of philosophy, psychoanalysis and literature, Benjamin develops an analysis of urban experience that would have eluded any attempt to grasp it directly via the intellect. His analysis is based on what he calls the method of historical materialism.[4] The assumption here is not simply that the written text records or is impressed by experiences (and thus functions as a kind of memory) beyond or even against the conscious intention of its authors. Rather, Benjamin acknowledges an historical privilege to particular works, for their ability to register the shocks or anxieties of their times. For instance, in Baudelaire, the crisis of artistic representation that manifests itself in the nineteenth century through the emergence of photography is registered as a critical urban phenomenon on the level of perception and memory. Both the image of the past and that of the present are radically transformed in ways that are brought to crisis in Baudelaire's lyric. Henri Bergson's philosophy of memory, on the other hand, does its best to avoid (and thus reveals in another way) the historical forces behind it.

Further comparison of Arthur Yap and Rem Koolhaas will help to explicate the distinction. Yap's poems are as crafted fragments, skewed or crippled sonnets, lyrics sculpted out of events drawn from a practice of observation that habitually suspends habitual forms of judgement. The poems emerge like a string of postcards capturing the commonplace uncommonly, which is, after all, the conventional role of lyric poetry. Reading through Yap's selected poems, *The Space of the City Trees*, one follows not only a long career of such observed moments but also a rhetorical consistency that demands, and rewards, careful observation in turn. Here, perhaps, a form of learning – as opposed to study – is mobilized. In contrast, Koolhaas's 'Singapore Songlines: Portrait of a Potemkin Metropolis . . . or Thirty Years of Tabula Rasa', despite its weakly autobiographical and confessional opening gambit, presents itself as a study. If Yap addresses the outside from the partial anthropocentric perspective of inhabitant, then Koolhaas comes across as the outsider looking down on all he surveys.

'Singapore Songlines' has attracted considerable criticism from Singaporeans, partly perhaps because it was, in 1995, a relatively rare serious study of Singapore's urban space and its cultural implications by a well-respected international architect.[5] There are numerous often risibly misinformed impressionistic accounts – travelogues and critiques – as well as some rather serious studies, which attract less intense response.[6] 'Singapore Songlines' is meticulously researched and critically aware. It is informed, moreover, by a (now and probably even then rather old fashioned) post-modern consciousness, appearing in the very hip *S,M,L,XL*.[7] As one would expect, the impossible standards of traditional social science – objectivity, empirical exhaustiveness, descriptive fidelity – are subverted by the resolute generation of metaphorical frames. The twin notions of the article's doubled subtitle, *tabula rasa* and *Potemkin metropolis*, impose a quite fecund theo-retical frame on its topic. Singapore is likened by implication to Potemkin's fabricated elaborate fake villages of the Ukraine and the Crimea, designed to hide the fact that nothing was there beyond their façades. These 'Potemkin villages' appeared elaborate and impressive but in actual fact lacked substance, disguising only the massive poverty of the region. The modern urban equivalent of a Potemkin village would be the Potemkin City, the economically successful urban centre surrounded by overcrowded areas of hopeless poverty. The relationship, then, between Singapore and its imme-diate neighbors (Malaysia and Indonesia) is already strongly implicated but, despite the evidence of a first glance, not quite in a way that is appropriate to the actual economic conditions. The notion of the *tabula rasa* – the blank slate that hypermodernity creates in order to build its history-free edifices – will turn out to be significantly more complex than Koolhaas has allowed. Nonetheless, this is his leitmotif in the 'Songlines' article.

The material basis of the article is relatively straightforward. Koolhaas outlines the accelerating narrative of Singapore's building plan. Focusing on the moment of independence – 1965 – he explores the conditions on which Singapore's bureaucracy 'is now unleashed on a promethean enterprise.'[8] This is the enterprise of the *tabula rasa*, the 'razed plane as the basis for a genuinely new beginning'.[9] He cites from the contemporary UN report, which unintentionally sanctions the project, as well as the statements of Singapore government officials, notably those of the PAP leader, Lee Kuan Yew. But his reading of the situation is built unashamedly on a poetic identification:

> Still firmly marooned in underdevelopment, Singapore's only resources are physical—its land, its population, its geographical position. Analogous to the way poverty can lead to prostitution, Singapore's transformation is conceived again and again in terms

of work *on the body of the island itself*. Its territory—its ground—is its most malleable material; the housing program and the UN vision turn it into an infrastructural manifesto, a palimpsest of Singapore's political evolution. Like the Dutch, who also fabricated their country, Singapore is about selling and manipulation—an ideology, a population, an island. This process starts innocently with New Towns, accelerates with the UN report, and radicalizes with independence in 1965, the official beginning of the Republic of Singapore.[10]

The thoroughness of Koolhaas's study and the detail with which he engages with the island state compel serious attention. And it is probably correct in a metaphorical sense to regard Singapore as the apotheosis of the principles of *tabula rasa* in urban planning. But *tabula rasa* remains a metaphor, ironically re-inscribing what is actually a complex empirical principle as an aim of modernity. The ancient sense, as blank tablet, cannot easily be dissociated from the sense it has gathered as a principle of post-Enlightenment modernity, derived from empirical philosophy, and according to which the mind of a human individual at birth is blank, ready to take the contingent impressions of experience.[11] Koolhaas's identification of the figure of the *tabula rasa* seems to be designed to re-establish a historicity beneath the overt aims of modernity, specifically against the metaphorical empiricism of pragmatic urbanism. Now the analogy of prostitution is in this context yet more significant. Having identified the *tabula rasa* in analogy with Singapore's prostitution of its malleable body, Koolhaas goes on to distinguish Singapore's thirty years as a kind of *doing* – a bureaucratic pragmatism – against an impotent *thinking* – presumably an outmoded rational (as opposed to dynamic hypermodern empirical) solution:

> In Singapore, this moment—1965—represents a showdown between *doing* and *thinking*, won hands down by doing. The civil servants—the bureaucracy of Singapore—are obsessively active. Like the horsemen of the Apocalypse, they will not rest before the entire island is plowed over, made utterly unrecognizable. They force all others, especially those handicapped by a need for reflection (i.e. Singapore's intellectuals) into different degrees of more or less humiliating passivity or complicity.[12]

The argument here is nuanced. Koolhaas's rhetoric (which mobilizes both irony and hyperbole) leaves the exact status of Singapore intellectuals ambiguous. On the one hand, their need for reflection, ironized as a handicap, leaves them outside the sphere of action but not far enough, it would seem, to give them any insight into what is happening:

they underestimate both the determination and the ability of the regime, do not realize that a miracle is taking place before their eyes, that their skepticism now will disqualify them from full participation on anything but the regime's terms: something that offends their sixties sensibilities.[13]

Koolhaas, it might seem, is concerned to distance his own more up-to-date approach from those young 1960s' intellectuals[14] by responding to Singapore's thirty years of *tabula rasa* with an intellectual one of his own. The *tabula rasa* is a metaphor stripped of its historical and intellectual value, useful now as a basis for generating figure after figure, here an ironic identification, there a hyperbolic association. What remains unsaid and unobserved? For Koolhaas this would be *nothing*: an emptiness behind the façade, itself surrounded by the abject poverty of global capital's third world victims.

This diagnosis recreates the rhetoric of a peculiarly western architectural idiom in the history of modernity, which belongs as much to experimental modernists like Le Corbusier and Sant'Elia (and architectural historians like Gidieon and Pevsner) as it does to their current self-styled post-modern heirs. The rhetoric tends to hyperbole about material structure, and leads to an at least implicit overvaluation of the visible environment. For Koolhaas, it is self-evident that the clearing of large aspects of a city's infrastructure can be equated with the erasure of its history. His metaphorical frameworks merely emphasize the prejudice, supporting claims about the emotional, economic and cultural transformation of Singapore with his knowledge of the fate of its buildings and dwellings. The idea that the past, and that memory, can be maintained or transported by a culture's buildings is confronted by an implicit critique in traditions of southeast Asia, and arguably even more so in other regions of Asia, China especially, where the value of a building's material existence even now is a matter of contingency, subordinated nearly always to its designation, its purpose or function.

The ancient Yuyuan Garden of Shanghai, which since 1956 has been the beneficiary of China's drive to preserve its ancient 'cultural relics', is four centuries old and during that time has suffered innumerable forms of deterioration and destruction, as well as transformations of parts of it into schools, markets and residencies. By the time of the establishment of the People's Republic of China (PRC) in 1949, the area was nothing but a heap of broken pavilions, dried ponds and withered roots. The current garden is renovation in part but also reconstruction as well as new construction, linking the Yuyuan with the Qing Dynasty's Inner Garden to make a new integrated whole. As in ancient times, the placard at the entrance reads 'Mountains and Forests in the Heart of the City'. The purpose of the garden (which is excellently served) is to provide a peaceful and beautiful haven from modern urban life (of which Shanghai is arguably anyway a *prima facie* case), though tourists from everywhere, products of the age of exhibition, come away from it with scores of digital images snapped for their own remembrance. Something of the ancient Greek meaning of *tabula rasa* is embodied by the reconstruction of the Yuyuan Garden. A writing tablet needs to be erased before the new inscriptions can be composed. An altar needs to be provided with a flat surface – the *tabula* – before the icons can be placed upon it. But in each case – in the case of writing and in the case of ritual – nothing material is destroyed and, again in each case, the new inscriptions – as a matter of definition – are always repetitions.

Next time

 (xià ci)

xià   (put down; lay; fall; descend; begin; below; under; inferior; lower; next)

ci   (the next in order; secondary; inferior; lower; vice; deputy (ministers, etc.); a place where one stops for rest on a trip; place; stop at a place; by; at (the feast, table, etc.); in the midst; grade; grading; order; sequence; hypo (chemistry); time (each occasion of a recurring action or event)

Turning now to Arthur Yap, Singapore's own most inventive and original poet, from his 1977 collection, *Commonplace*, it is possible to read what at first looks like a similar statement of loss, confirming from the inside what Koolhaas diagnoses from the outside. The poem is littered with the human relics of Singapore's fast fading urban landscape (registered as having disappeared) as well as the signs of its new machinated and motorized modernity (in the register of appearance). The title at fist sight might be taken as an ironic reflection on the regime's by then full tilt *tabula rasa* urbanism. I quote the whole poem:

there is no future in nostalgia

> & certainly no nostalgia in the future of the past.
> now, the corner cigarette-seller is gone, is perhaps dead.
> no, definitely dead, he would not otherwise have gone.

> he is replaced by a stamp-machine,
> the old cook by a pressure-cooker,
> the old trishaw-rider's stand by a fire hydrant,
> the washer-woman by a spin-dryer
>
> & it goes on
> in various variations & permutations.
> there is no future in nostalgia.

The rhetorical dimension of the poem largely determines its content and does so even before the incidence of its first referential context, the disappearance of the corner cigarette-seller. The title and first line together compose and expand upon an *antimetabole* – that kind of chiasmic per-mutation where the words of a first clause are repeated in a second but in reverse order, in this case with the ideas of nostalgia and the future. The following two lines repeat the pattern with the ideas of disappearance and death. If it was not for these rhetorical turns we would be left with nothing but irritating truisms. Nostalgia – triggered perhaps by the rapid disappearance of familiar things – manifests itself in at best a sentimental longing for past or lost times. There would thus be no thought of the future in nostalgia. To make sense of the reversal, however, a new thought must be introduced: there is no nostalgia in the future (a hopelessly utopian or perhaps even a dire thought) becomes no nostalgia in the future of the past (an alarming thought perhaps but one that requires reflection). The thought of the future of the past is thus generated by a need in the rhetoric itself, an absence that produces a realization: that this *is* something of the future of the past. The text now becomes a rhetorical account of time. Replacing the conscious present tense is the unconscious of an empty nostalgia, which the following lines confirm. The disappearance of the cigarette-seller leads to thoughts of death, confirmed by the memory of his unexceptional permanence. The context of permutation is each time a kind of disappearance and its replacement (first, of nostalgia in the future, and then of the cigarette-seller in the present) and this is the case too for the list of replacements that follow. But the form all these permutations take is metonymic. The cigarette-seller is replaced not by a cigarette-machine but – arbitrarily – by a stamp-machine. The poetic context that would seem to have generated the speaker's meditations remains simply circumstantial; by chance a stamp-machine has been placed where the cigarette-seller once stood. The replacements that come after have nothing to do with that context but seem to have been generated arbitrarily, mechanically, by the thought of that arbitrary replacement: the old cook by a pressure-cooker (at best a wry pun); the trishaw rider's stand by a fire hydrant (phonetic echo); the washer-woman by a spin-dryer (contiguity of wash and dry). The rhetoric, which functions mechanically to condition these permutations confirms the thought that it conditions: that people (service providers) have been replaced by mechanical devices. There is fundamentally only – as the last lines unambiguously confirm – the thought of death in the painful longing for the past. The 'variations & permutations' replace this thought with a rhetoric that produces its own future.

A vast difference emerges between Koolhaas's outsider narrative and Yap's meditation, the difference between a metaphorical (as well as hyperbolic and ironic) conception and a series of metonymical and chiasmic permutations. But more than this, the difference lies in how in each case the peopled urban landscape has been addressed, and this is where we can afford to return to Benjamin's essay on Baudelaire. Benjamin's method is simultaneously historical and aesthetic but the notions of history and aesthetics are transformed in the process. The question that underlies Benjamin's text would be as follows: how and to what extent is urban experience determined by historical conditions? The main answer that his readings provide would be that, under the conditions of modern urbanism, the ways in which history determines experience do not become matters of conscious awareness. The proof of this, Benjamin suggests, begins with an acknowledgement of the decline in popularity of lyric poetry. Accordingly, because it is thus reasonable to assume that lyric poetry is now only very rarely in accord with the experience of its readers, the structure of their experience may have changed.[15] Moreover, when one turns to philosophy for an account of the structure of experience (during Benjamin's time there is a proliferation of such 'philosophies of life' as they were known), one finds not just an explanation, but also a symptomatic exclusion:

> Towering above this literature is Bergson's early monumental work, *Matière et mémoire*. More than the others it preserves links with empirical research. It is oriented to biology. The title suggests that it regards the structure of memory as decisive for the philosophical pattern of experience. Experience is indeed a matter of tradition, in collective existence as well as private life. It is less the product of facts firmly anchored in memory than of a convergence in memory of accumulated and frequently unconscious data. It is, however, not at all Bergson's intention to attach any specific historical label to memory. On the contrary, he rejects any historical determination to memory. He thus manages to stay clear of that experience from which his own philosophy evolved or, rather, in reaction to which it arose. It was the inhospitable, blinding age of big-scale industrialism.[16]

Bergson's rejection of any historical determination to memory is symptomatic of the historical conditions that determined his philosophy. And this *forgetting*, this *elision*, is exactly what those conditions would determine. Here in this essay and elsewhere, Benjamin argues for the great consequences that the camera and the photograph have had on both memory and culture. In a startling analogy, rich with the metonymic vocabulary of photography, Bergson's work becomes in Benjamin's description the snapshot of his age:

> In shutting out this experience the eye perceives an experience of a complementary nature in the form of its spontaneous after image, as it were. Bergson's philosophy represents an attempt to give the details of this afterimage and to fix it as a permanent record.[17]

Just as the photograph provides a permanent record of a transient moment, the philosophy of the time fixes on a contingent image of memory and renders it essential. Experience has, then, perhaps become blind to the conditions out of which it arises. If this was the case in 1939 then *either* Koolhaas's identification of the material *tabula rasa* operant in Singapore (which has more or less the same effect) inappropriately selects one version of a general twentieth-century condition *or* Singapore is itself late on the scene and late in a peculiarly literal way. Benjamin admits in his review of Hessel that, 'Baudelaire is the source of the cruel *aperçu* that the city changes faster than a human heart'.[18] The effects that are inadequately named by *tabula rasa* would be nothing striking or new in themselves. Whatever the case, it would seem that Koolhaas has bought into Singapore's mythology of itself, or at least accepted it too easily, falling for, in order to criticize and reproduce, the narrative of Lee Kuan Yew's single-minded macro-management.[19]

Benjamin locates what he sees as an immanent critique of Bergson's terms in the works of Marcel Proust and Sigmund Freud. The distinction in Proust between the *mémoire volontaire* and the *mémoire involontaire* decisively excludes one from the other, making it in theory impossible to access what for Bergson was *mémoire pure* (conscious recollection of the *durée*, the stream of life) through contemplation. Proust, on the contrary, insists on the confrontation of *mémoire volontaire*, which would be a work of the intellect, by *mémoire involontaire*, over which the conscious thinker has no control and which is experienced more often in the register of forgetting. This loss of memory must be surprised or shocked by the uncanny experience, where a minor event appears both strange and deeply familiar. Such an event triggers a forgotten (and thus unconscious) feeling, giving access to a fragment of lost time, which is registered at the level of lived experience. So in Proust the taste of the madeleine pastry transports his narrator to a past that had hitherto been beyond conscious recollection. The Freudian reference is to *Beyond the Pleasure Principle*, where Freud, in attempting to unravel the dreams and associations of trauma victims – specifically First World War victims – notes that 'consciousness comes into being at the site of a memory trace'.[20] What Freud argues, in fact, is that it is not unreasonable to assume that consciousness arises *instead of* a memory trace:

> One might thus say that the Consciousness system has the particularly distinguishing feature that excitation processes do not leave their mark in the form of an enduring alteration of its elements, as they do in all other psychic systems, but simply evaporate, as it were, in the process of entering consciousness.[21]

Consciousness, in other words, functions not for the reception or perception of stimuli – which would in 'other systems' (i.e. the unconscious) become permanent traces and as such the basis of memory – but for protection *against* overwhelming stimuli. Shock, anxiety, trauma – these virtually interchangeable terms in Freud name situations where a source of stimulus has failed to leave any impression that could be recalled. For Benjamin, then, this pattern – not simply a theory to be applied, of course, but also part of the symptomatic textual inscription of the time – is best read directly back into the situation that gave rise to it: the hypermodernity of which the nineteenth-century urban *tabula rasa*, the motorized ravages of the World War, and the ubiquitous clicking and snapping of the camera, were only the most powerful of a whole range of assaults on the human sensorium.

Singapore is certainly *conscious* of its history. There are numerous exhibitions, books and entertaining spectacles in theatre or on television, that in various ways document Singapore's past (photographic images, cartoons, comic books, soap operas, situation comedies, histories made easy, and so on). The paradigm would probably be the a²o website, which provides 'Access to Archive Online, Singapore: 100% pure heritage. The New Element in You' (Figure 7.1).[22] There the interactive menu provides access to online exhibitions as well as sound archives, photographic archives and archives of moving images. The visual elements overpower the textual captions and the main page is dominated by a large drink can painted with the a²o insignia;

7.1
**Detail of the a²o
icon and logo**

bursting from its opened lid a frothy spurt of archival materials spill out over the page: sepia photographs, rolls of film, old postcards, shellac disks, and so on.

The online archive, then, appears to be the fulfillment of the trends deciphered by Benjamin. By foregrounding this endless documentation of history the modern urban environment succeeds in freeing itself from that history, distinguishing the archive from those who would access it but at the same time valorizing it as heritage, another sparkling consumable like the distilled water you can buy from the cigarette-seller. What distinguishes the hypermodern archive would be the modes of instruction aspiring archivists are provided with as a condition of access. Here is the externalized manifestation of the distinction between conscious recall and memory as cultural experience.

Already

 (yi)

Yi   (already; come to an end; finish; complete; finished; stop; cease; used to indicate the past; excessive; very; much; a final particle to add emphasis)

Arthur Yap's 'There is no Future in Nostalgia' can be reassessed on the basis of Benjamin's thoughts on the distinction between *Erlebnis* and *Erfahrung*. So long as consciousness – the human intellect – can remain alert as a screen against stimuli, Benjamin suggests, then the shock impulses of an increasingly hazardous urban environment will remain in the sphere of *Erlebnis*, lived through safely but without registering much as *Erfahrung*, or cultural experience. Benjamin chooses to engage with the historicity of urbanism through the lyric poetry of Baudelaire because this poetry bears the traces – a prosthetic memory for a culture without one – of the poet's struggle against the shocks of city life. Now I do not want to suggest that Yap could be regarded as Singapore's belated Baudelaire (by 100 years). Nevertheless, if Koolhaas's hyperbolic narrative version of Singapore's experimental *tabula rasa* stresses the audacity of the regime and the traumatic effects on its people, then Yap can be seen to be registering some of those effects in a more interestingly subtle and detailed way. The poem registers the experience of absence, undoubtedly. But more than this, the city of replacements that Yap's poem evokes requires skills appropriate to the interminable novelty of modern

7.2
**Self-Service
Automated
Machine,
Singapore**

life. The environment and its variations and permutations keep its dwellers
permanently on their toes. A stamp-machine, for instance, if one keeps the
image in mind, requires instruction on how to use it. And now (nearly
30 years later) the stamp-machine has been replaced by 150 island-wide
Self-Service Automated Machines (SAMs) allowing you to buy postage labels
(which have replaced stamps), pay fines and bills and income tax, and top-
up hi! cards for mobile phones.[23] They of course feature detailed instructions
on their use (Figure 7.2). So, when a person uses a SAM a key mode of social
relation is reproduced.

      Another of Benjamin's observations in his reading of Baudelaire
is confirmed here, that 'technology has subjected the human sensorium to a
complex kind of training'.[24] Benjamin's examples resonate with the experience
of hypermodern Singapore: 'One case in point', he remarks, 'is the telephone,
where the lifting of a receiver has taken the place of the steady movement that
used to be required to crank the older models'.[25] In modern Singapore the
telephone is now ubiquitous and even the hand-phone, which nestles permanently in the palm of its user's hand or rests blinking up at them from the
coffee table, is fast being replaced by micro models that nestle invisibly behind

the user's ear, the mouthpiece discretely hanging down to access the back of the jaw, to receive the barked or whispered instructions that will dial the next address. Increasingly Singaporeans communicate with each other on a day-to-day basis remotely. Two can go shopping though only one will actually be there at the shops. The telephonic Short Message Service has been responsible for a new written language that spreads rapidly into the magazines, newspapers and written reports.

A key quality of Yap's poem, then – its permutations radically extended into a future he did not even need to imagine – is that it bears the imprint of what it does not *consciously* record. This is more a function of its rhetorical style of response than of its identifiable content. The stamp-machine does not *replace* the cigarette-seller functionally speaking. It is just that for the poem's speaker the stamp machine is in the place where the cigarette seller once stood. In fact, there remain cigarette-sellers in kiosks or mini-marts on virtually every corner where people habitually congregate. The trishaw riders also carve out a living ferrying tourists around the central district (an undoubtedly unpleasant and expensive experience on Singapore's wide, fast and busy roads). The poem records a complex series of urban developments and personal responses to them. Missing from the poem's peopled landscape, in terms of its presented images, are the ubiquitous crowds that *use* the new machines. These crowds are nonetheless implicit at the level of the poem's address (the writer/speaker and indeterminate addressees) which absorbs and internalizes the experience of the crowd, who now deal not only with other humans but also more and more with the machines that have cropped up everywhere.

These thoughts might lead us to rethink the notion of *tabula rasa*. Koolhaas is no doubt partially correct to identify the Singaporean urban project in terms of a somewhat belated (and thus historically informed) modernism. But in historical terms he makes two assumptions that are incorrect. The first is that Singapore's urban project can be reduced to the machinations of its regime. In political terms, the PAP has been manifestly successful. In the inescapable context of global economic and military forces, however, this must be regarded as at best good – even creative – management of a situation over which no single entity or ensemble the size of Singapore could have had the least control. Part of the strength of Lee Kuan Yew's grip over the fate of Singapore lies in the mythology – replicated over and over again throughout forty years of independence – of that strength in the face of overwhelming global forces, when in fact this was a team of technologically informed international as well as local experts capable of harnessing those forces. The second is that the historicity of Singapore's migrant people has in some sense been eradicated along with its colonial landscape. We should perhaps talk of idiomaticity – what is idiomatic to a people – as opposed to historicity. For here we can begin to identify something of a no doubt plural and yet tense cultural memory peculiar to Singapore. Two idioms so common – as the commonest of idioms must always be – that they are entirely freed of their history and genealogy, directly concern history and memory. This is how the historical permanence of cultural memory is maintained, after all, through its apparent disappearance in its uncanny repetition (i.e. as a permutation that is neither simple replacement nor literal repetition). In Singapore the idiom 'last time' has the property of a flexibility that allows it many senses, depending on context. Generally it means something like 'in the past' and pertains to situations like 'when we were children' or 'when the family was together'. 'Last time' could also refer, of course, to when the cigarette-seller was always there on the corner. Its complement in 'next time' works in a similar way – as an indicator of some hopefully not too fanciful but nonetheless indeterminate future. 'Next time', one might say, 'we'll have two cats and a garden.' These are English words but not English idioms. In fact, like so much of the English spoken in Singapore, they are Chinese idioms. *Shang ci*, and *xià ci* are respectively the *previous* and the *next* in the order of a recurring set of events or occasions. The idiom identifies the experience of temporality as a hierarchy of repetitions. The hierarchy – forgotten by contemporary usages – concerns the pattern of a key cultural symbol: the tree divided at ground level between branching crown and embedded roots.

上 (previous)

下 (next)

The values of *previous* are also those of superiority, height and ascension while the values of *next* are those of inferiority and falling. The embedded sense of temporality, then, would be time experienced as a falling into the future, something like the inverted repetition of a cultural ascension. Yap's chiasmic formulations of the present and the past replicate the hidden background of the idiom fairly exactly, suggesting that the replacements (which any outsider might be forgiven for misrecognizing as the ongoing march of progress on the raised – or razed – basis of the *tabula rasa*) might better be regarded as permutations that could not have anyway been anything but inferior facsimiles of an unreachable past.[26] The transformation of the urban landscape into what is in effect a dynamic training ground has perhaps had a more profound effect on what we might now refer to as a historical *tabula rasa* than Singapore's building program is supposed to have had. When empiricists like

John Locke and later David Hume adopted the metaphor of the *tabula rasa* to illustrate their assertion that the human mind comes into existence not yet influenced by outside impressions and experiences, they were probably closer in sense to the Singapore *tabula rasa* than Koolhaas has managed.

The point now is not so much to construct a theory of Singapore's peculiar brand of global urbanism but more to attempt to derive the theory that urbanism *already is* for Singapore life. Traditionally such a theory would have been considered as a kind of knowledge or *competence*. And urbanism does indeed require considerable competence on behalf of its dwellers, which is why so much of the experience of urban life seems like training or guidance – a process of drilling. It would be an error to regard this knowledge or training simply as the conditioning of urban subjects by forces external to them. But while this competence does not reveal itself to patient questioning as an *a priori* knowledge, it nevertheless functions *as if it was*. That is the condition of the historical *tabula rasa*.

Presence and absence

Nowhere more than in Singapore does the play of presence and absence figure in the everyday cultural memory of urban inhabitants. The intensity of the working week, interrupted only by fierce activity-filled leisure periods, opens to the abyss of numbing lapses of nothingness that may hit the urban subject without warning amid a dense array of in-the-moment stimuli.

Once again we find hints and gestures of this not just as symptoms to be studied but in the attempts of urban artists and poets to engage this fierce regime head on. The young Singapore poet Cyril Wong's collection, *Below: Absence*, begins with a fantastic conceit. 'Foetus' evokes through its metaphor the work of metaphor itself, bringing something out of nothing and inaugurating a pattern of self reference that is maintained throughout the volume. The final poem, 'Happiness', questions the gathering repetitiveness of false starts, looking back to childhood and forward 'twenty years from now' to imagine the poet 'choked once more with/Poems about hopelessness'. In a tighter, more claustrophobic form, the Singapore chiasmus (last time, next time, already) is affirmed here, an affirmation of emptiness in a time and place where this is barely possible.[27]

It hardly seems enough. The Singapore urban landscape permanently and repeatedly replaces the transcendent object world, thus suggesting it and reliving it spectrally, imposing upon it a designer matrix of spiritual ideals. Memory in Singapore seems to be triggered as a repetition that does away with the instrumental distinction between fact and fiction. That is, fact holds fast and fiction establishes its relative autonomy but both in the same gesture, the same event. The difference between sensory perception – the sights, sounds, tastes, smells and tactile encounters of the urban population – and intelligent engagement – the bigger picture, the long term plan, the place in the world – is played out architecturally in the urban environment itself. And its foregrounding both emphasizes and subtly but drastically subverts it and collapses it in a confusion of instrumentally delegated institutions. There's a time and a place to tell the truth and a time and place to lie but no one knows for certain when or where these times and places are. So much of the strategic interaction is guesswork. There thus remains no functional difference between the two. It's not even a matter of rhetorical skill: only evidence counts . . . the round of sensate encounters . . .

The sheer intensity of electronic media – telephony and entertainment, public and home, theatre, surround, and hi-end (with its ensemble of clinicians),[28] the PC, all contribute to the erosion of distinctions between the personal and the public, between home and work. Exchange, on the other hand, is reduced to its price.

A final example of replacement: the replacement of the Colbar by the Colbar. In July 2003 the Colbar Restaurant was closed for good after 55 years to make way for a new road linking two of the main highways in Singapore. The Colbar (Colonial Bar) belongs to a past that has all but disappeared in Singapore. It once was situated next to an army camp and is still overlooked by black-and-white colonial bungalows. At first it served the British army and expatriates who remained after British withdrawal in 1968. But by 2003 the Colbar had become a well-known eating and drinking oasis in the heart of a heavily built up industrial area. Both expatriate and local regulars are presumably seduced by an ambiance quite unlike anything else currently standing in Singapore and perhaps a sense of a past that few alive could have experienced. The décor and decorative fittings are the 1950s' originals and the owners are too. For something to remain in this way unaffected by change in contemporary Singapore is remarkable in itself. But such was the sense of loss for its impending removal that space has since been set aside for it to be rebuilt – exactly as it was, with the original décor and so on – 300 yards away from its original spot. And so it continues, in 2004, to do the same thriving business that kept it going before (Figures 7.3, 7.4, 7.5).

There remains an immaterial undertow that despite the changes to the built environment inhabits the cultural spaces of Singapore. Every now and then it manifests itself and leaves an impression on the built environment. Standing before the Singapore River on Sunday afternoon looking over at disused warehouses: the Gallery Hotel looms up behind on the right, the architectural equivalent of an Arthur Yap poem, a permutation chiasmatically produced from the environment of which it is a part (Figure 7.6). These

7.3
**The Colbar,
Singapore**
Source:
getforme.com

7.4
**The Colbar
(before
the move),
Singapore**
Source:
getforme.com

7.5
**The Colbar
(after the move),
Singapore**
Source:
getforme.com

7.6
Disused warehouses on the Singapore River; the Gallery Hotel, with bright window frames, behind them on the right
Source: Photograph by John Phillips

warehouses would be in some ways invisible or visible only as wasteland in an unbuilt field. They are far removed in their leafy dilapidation from the meticulously renovated relics of Singapore's colonial past, like Victoria Hall or Raffles Hotel. The unbuilt aspects of urban Singapore are revealed here in this juxtaposition of river, warehouse, and hotel, as remnants of a *last time*. The juxtaposition proposes a time that has not yet arrived: few cyclists and strollers currently use this part of the river walk, which seems to aspire to those of many currently restored city centres – busy thoroughfares of promenading weekend citizens. On this side of the river (from where the photograph was taken) similar warehouses have become chief home to Singapore's club scene: Zouk, the paradigm (if I dare a paradigm here in conclusion) of intense urban leisure. The juxtaposition reminds us that next time, if it comes, and in whatever form it takes, cannot but be something of a possibly uncanny repetition of last time.

Acknowledgements

I would like to thank Chrissie Tan, Ryan Bishop, Anne Seah, Fan Jinghua, and Elspeth Thomson for time and discussions regarding the material in this article.

Notes

1 Published as *'Die Wiederkehr des Flaneurs'* and translated as 'The Return of the *Flâneur'* in Walter Benjamin, *Selected Writings*, 2, Cambridge: Harvard, 1999. pp. 262–267.

2 Including, arguably, this writer's own study written in 1998, 'Singapore Soil: A Completely Different Organization of Space', in Maria Balshaw and Liam Kennedy (eds.) *Urban Space and Representation*, London: Pluto, 2000, and to which this article in part can be regarded as a response.

3 'On Some Motifs in Baudelaire', trans. Harry Zohn in Walter Benjamin, *Illuminations: Essays and Reflections*, ed. Hannah Arendt, New York: Schocken, 1968, pp. 155–200.
A slightly modified version of Zohn's translation can be found in Benjamin, *Selected Writings*, 4, Cambridge, MA: Belknap, 2003, pp. 313–55.

4 See his 'Theses on the Philosophy of History', in Benjamin, *Illuminations*, pp. 253–64, for a late account of his understanding of historical materialism.

5 See Bobby Wong Chong Thai, for example, 'A Few Good Men and their Phallic Jet Stream', in William Lim (ed.), *Postmodern Singapore*, Singapore: Select, 2002, pp. 158–72.

6 For a representative range, see the following: William Gibson, 'Disneyland with the Death Penalty', *Wired*, 1:4, September/October 1993; Stan Sesser, 'Singapore: The Prisoner in the Theme Park', in *The Lands of Charm and Cruelty*, New York: Vintage, 1994; Deyan Sudjic, 'Virtual City', *Blueprint*, 104 February 1994, pp. 41–2; Thomas 2Less, 'Singapore ONE', in *ctheory*, 1998 (http://www.ctheory.net); and Dean Forbes, 'Globalisation, Postcolonialism and New Representations of the Pacific Asian Metropolis', in K. Olds, P. Dicken, P.F. Kelly, L. Kong and H. Wai-Cheung Yeung (eds.) *Globalisation and the Asia-Pacific: Contested Territories*, London: Routledge, 1999, pp. 238–54.

7 Rem Koolhaas and Bruce Mau, *S,M,L,XL*, New York and Cologne: Monacelli Press and Taschen: 1995. *Time Magazine* called *S,M,L,XL*, 'the ultimate coffee-table book for a generation raised on both MTV and Derrida'. Rem Koolhaas, 'Singapore Songlines: Thirty Years of Tabula Rasa', pp. 1008–89.

8 'Singapore Songlines', p. 1031.

9 Ibid.

10 Ibid.

11 The notion of the *tabula rasa* as a kind of matrix (the slate) on which memories and experiences are impressed (as forms of knowledge) has a long and distinguished career. John Locke's *An Essay Concerning Human Understanding* (Oxford: Clarendon Press, 1975) is often considered to be the first attempt to set out an extended philosophical account of it. We also find versions of it in writers as diverse as Immanuel Kant, Sigmund Freud, and Karl Marx, all of whom are concerned in different ways with the formal conditions for experience, knowledge and practical action, which, again in different ways, would be under the influence of external forces acting on a malleable surface. This trio are worthy of note as they also form the key references for Benjamin's own attempts to address the forces that govern experience.

12 Koolhaas, 'Singapore Songlines', p. 1033.

13 Ibid., pp. 1033–4.

14 These young intellectuals and architects include those acknowledged in an endnote for their time and insights: William S. W. Lim, Tay Kheng Soon, Chua Beng Huat and Liu Thai Ker. Koolhaas then adds unnecessarily that 'nevertheless, the ideas and opinions expressed in this text are those of the author', as if by mentioning their names in an article that identifies Singapore's still reigning government as the four horsemen of the Apocalypse he might endanger them in some way.

15 Benjamin, *Illuminations*, p. 156.

16 Ibid., p. 157.

17 Ibid.

18   Ibid., p. 265.

19   Koolhaas does acknowledge the regime's pride in Singapore's *tabula rasa* success. On this issue, see also Paul Rae, "10/12": When Singapore Became the Bali of the Twenty-First Century?', *Focas: Forum on Contemporary Art and Society*, Singapore: University Press, 2004, pp. 222–59, for a scholarly attempt to suggest alternatives to the widespread practice of paradigm formation in readings of Singapore:

> A well-chosen figure of speech can be devastating in the right context, but Singapore has been so multiply metaphored by commentators of all political stripes, and by the PAP most of all . . . that one of the most effective—and most difficult—things to do in Singapore is to Tell it Like it Is.
>
> (Ibid., p. 249)

The demand, here, is for sensitive and independent critical attention to 'the social reality and lived experience' of Singaporeans.

20   Benjamin, *Illuminations*, p. 160.

21   Sigmund Freud, *Beyond the Pleasure Principle: and Other Writings*, trans. John Reddick, London: Penguin, 2003, pp. 64.

22   http://www.a2o.com.sg/public/html/ A link on this page takes browsers to The National Heritage Board homepages, where one can access the Asian Civilization Museum, Singapore Art Museum, Singapore History Museum and the National Archives of Singapore, which holds millions of documents: public and private records; building plans and maps; oral history recordings; and a collection of 1.5 million photographs acquired from both government and private resources. The photographs date from the nineteenth century to the present, and the collection claims to document many aspects of Singapore's history and society. Subjects include landscape; sports; costumes; festivals; architecture; arts and entertainment and transportation.

23   More than 71 per cent of Singapore's population subscribes to mobile services, and dial-up Internet subscribers comprise almost 48 per cent of the population. Singapore's fixed telephone lines exceed 1.9 million or a penetration rate of 48.5 per cent.

24   Benjamin, *Illuminations*, p. 175.

25   Ibid., p. 174.

26   Singapore's pre-migration past in many (i.e. excepting a few rare) cases remains quite blank. The conditions of migration, for the most part, were not conducive to documentation or to keeping in touch with any (if any) friends and relatives left behind in the poverty stricken or war ravaged parts of South Asia and China that historically triggered the various diasporas for which Singapore was a promising target in the mid- to late nineteenth century. Attempts to return to a 'homeland' as such would always now be at best farcical.

27   Cyril Wong, *Below: Absence*, Singapore: First Fruits, 2002.

28   'Hi-End' (in analogy with Hi-Fi) appears to be a term adapted from the so called High End Audio market (established in the 1970s in the USA as the quest for the 'Absolute Sound': high fidelity electronic sound reproduction of live vocal and acoustic music; the idea of 'The Perfect Vision' has since become the adjunct in Hi-End). Hi-end A/V technology promises to bring the quality of both live entertainment and cinema into the homes of aspiring professional urbanites.

Charlie McKell,
Head of Research at the
Department of Agriculture,
places a jerk chicken steak
on the barbeque of her
suburban bungalow in
Gungahlin, Canberra.

Chapter 8

9/11

Neil Leach

Walter Benjamin makes a striking observation about the capacity of certain
dramatic events to act like a flash bulb and imprint particular architectural
environments on the 'photosensitive' plate of our minds. It is as though
buildings sink into the recesses of our consciousness as a form of background
landscape – almost unnoticeable because of their very familiarity – unless
some event happens there that leaves them indelibly imprinted on our minds,
such as a tragic accident or a death in the family:

> Anyone can observe that the duration for which we are exposed
> to impressions has no bearing on their fate in memory. Nothing
> prevents us keeping rooms in which we have spent twenty-four
> hours or less clearly in our memory, and forgetting others in which
> we have passed months. It is not, therefore, due to insufficient
> exposure if no image appears on the plate of remembrance. More
> frequent, perhaps, are the cases when the half-light of habit denies
> the plate the necessary light for years, until one day from an alien
> source it flashes as if from burning magnesium powder, and now
> a snapshot transfixes the room's image on the plate. Nor is this very
> mysterious, since such moments of sudden illumination are at the
> same time moments when we are beside ourselves, and, while our
> waking, habitual, everyday self is involved actively or passively in
> what is happening, our deeper self rests in another place and is
> touched by the shock, as is the little heap of magnesium powder by
> the flame of the match.[1]

The events of 11 September seem to have had a very similar effect on the twin
towers of the World Trade Center.[2] The twin towers had been a prominent

part of the familiar New York skyline, but they remained somewhat anonymous. This was in part a result of their architecture. Although clearly the tallest buildings in New York, the twin towers were relatively featureless, and, as individual buildings, did not seem to capture the public imagination as did the Empire State building with its iconic associations with King Kong, or the Chrysler building with its splendid art deco ornamentation. They were, in Rem Koolhaas's terms, a perfect example of the lessons of 'Manhattanism' unlearnt.[3] The exteriors of Manhattan skyscrapers, which had once conveyed so vividly their rich and diverse occupancy, had become increasingly homogenised, so that they concealed that diversity. Indeed, the deep load-bearing mullions of the twin towers, designed – or so it was thought – to withstand the impact of a 747 jet, and also to allow the interiors to be column-free, helped both to obscure any impression of what was going on inside the buildings, and also to obscure the view out.[4] Moreover, through their sheer scale, the twin towers were an example of a radical approach to urbanism, the ultimate response to Le Corbusier's critique of New York skyscrapers, which he criticised for being too small and too numerous. In their architectural language, the towers were reportedly inspired by the minimalism of Mies van der Rohe, but somehow lacked any of his sensitivity.[5] And certainly their architect, Minoru Yamasaki, had a reputation, following the demolition in 1972 of his Pruitt-Igoe housing project, which had failed on sociological grounds, of not being the most sensitive of designers. Eric Darton even goes so far as to describe their aesthetic impression as 'terroristic', and compares the insensitivity of the design and what they represented in sociological terms to the insensitivity of those terrorists who attempted to blow up the twin towers in 1993.[6] Not everyone took such a negative stance. Indeed, the towers had their vociferous supporters, such as Ada Louise Huxtable, and yet it would probably be fair to say that they remained curiously anonymous within the eyes of the general public.

Of course, the towers played an important role in the social fabric of New York – any vast structure that accommodates so much office space cannot fail to do so – and, on occasions, had caught the world's imagination, such as when French high-wire artist, Philippe Petit, walked on his tightrope between the two towers in 1974. Moreover, there were a number of high profile political scandals associated with their planning and construction.[7] Yet their symbolic presence did not match their physical presence. Tourist shops, crammed full of miniature replicas of the Statue of Liberty and the Empire State building, offered relatively few models of the World Trade Center. It was as though the primary role of the twin towers lay in providing viewing platforms and vast receptacles of office accommodation, while contributing at a collective level to the dramatic Manhattan skyline.

All this changed, however, as a result of what happened on 11

September. The twin towers of the World Trade Center have been suddenly etched on to the minds of the world. They have taken on a different status, and lost any anonymity which they may once have possessed. Through their very destruction they have become recognisable and identifiable objects, symbols of the dangers of terrorism.

I want to argue, however, that these events did more than just transform the twin towers from tourist observation platforms and office blocks into icons of a new world order. I want to argue that the destruction of these towers has had a radical impact on the American psyche, and that it is against the backdrop of the now absent twin towers that a new sense of American national identity seems to have been forged. In so doing I hope to elucidate certain general principles about the potential of buildings and monuments – through either their presence or their absence – to symbolise a set of common values and define a collective sense of identity.

Identification

How, then, can a building – or rather newsreel images of the destruction of a building and its associated events – come to serve as a mechanism of identification for an American sense of self? Indeed, how can any building play a role in the formation of an identity? The answers perhaps lie in exploring how identity itself is constituted through processes of identification, and inquiring as to whether the visual domain has any influence in this process. Here it would be profitable to turn to psychoanalytic theory. For psychoanalytic theorists view identity as a consequence of identification. Identity, as Freud once remarked, is like a graveyard of lost loves and former identifications. Moreover, psychoanalytic theorists would argue that the image plays a crucial role in any moment of identification. Indeed, for them, identity is forged out of an interaction with the visual domain. But how exactly does this identification take place?

One of the key pieces of writing on the formation of identity is Jacques Lacan's essay on the 'mirror stage', where he famously describes the moment when a child recognises its own reflection in a mirror.[8] From this moment the child begins to formulate a coherent sense of self and to develop some coordination by identifying with its own reflected image. The child recognises itself as an object in a world of objects, and, having established its own autonomy, is able to forge identifications with other persons and objects. It is this moment, then, that serves both to consolidate the identity of the individual, and also to set the scene for all subsequent identifications.

Lacan's insightful essay on this crucial stage in the development of the individual has become a seminal text within psychoanalytic theories of identification. But although his model of identification premised on the mirror stage is clearly a visual one, Lacan does little to extend its application into the visual arts.[9] Yet the potential is obvious. The model presupposes a spatialised sense of visual awareness grounded in the notion of the image. Of the visual arts it is film theory, in particular, rather than architectural theory, that has developed a framework for exploring these possibilities. It is therefore to the work of Christian Metz on film theory that we might turn to understand the mechanism by which identification takes place in the aesthetic realm.[10]

What Lacan's model seems to suggest is that identification is always specular. It is always a question of recognising – or mis-recognising – oneself in the other. Christian Metz outlines a series of mirrorings that occur within the cinema. The screen, as site of the imaginary, replicates the real as a form of mirror. But at the same time it never reflects the viewer's own body. On certain occasions, then, the mirror turns into a transparent window. It may therefore be contrasted with Lacan's notion of the mirror-stage. Yet viewing a film depends upon the mirror stage. The spectator must have recognised himself or herself already as an object within a world of objects, and can therefore accept his or her absence from the actual screen.

This produces a series of identifications with actors in the film, and so too with the camera itself. In the former case, by being absent from the screen the spectator does not identify with himself or herself as an object, but rather with 'objects which are there without him'.[11] Here the screen patently does not serve as a mirror. But from the point of view of the spectator as viewing subject there is indeed a form of mirroring in that the 'perceived-imaginary material' is 'deposited' in the viewer as if on to a second screen: 'In other words, the spectator *identifies with himself*, with himself as a pure act of perception (as wakefulness, alertness): as the condition of possibility of the perceived and hence as a kind of transcendental subject, which comes before every *there is*.'[12] In the latter case, the identification is with the camera, since the spectator identifies with himself or herself as viewing subject, 'the spectator can do no other than identify with the camera, too, which has looked before him at what he is now looking at'.[13] More precisely, perhaps, there is an identification between the movement of the spectator's head and the movement of the camera.

What we encounter here is the 'double-movement' of vision – its projective and introjective nature. As one casts one's eye (in a projective fashion) one receives and absorbs (in an introjective fashion) what has been 'illuminated', as it were. Consciousness therefore serves, in Metz's terminology, as a 'recording surface':

> There are two cones in the auditorium: one ending on the screen and starting both in the projection box and in the spectator's vision

insofar as it is projective, and one starting from the screen and 'deposited' in the spectator's perception insofar as it is introjective (on the retina, a second screen). When I say that 'I see' the film, I mean thereby a unique mixture of two contrary currents: the film is what I receive, and it is also what I release . . . Releasing it, I am the projector, receiving it, I am the screen; in both these figures together, I am the camera, which points and yet records.[14]

The spectator is both 'screen' and 'projector'. Likewise the spectator is both absent from the screen 'as perceived', but so too present there 'as perceiver'. 'At every moment,' Metz notes, 'I am in the film by my look's caress.'[15] What happens, then, in the process of viewing is a series of mirror-effects. And through these mirrorings – the recognition of the self in the other, the recognition of the other in the self – a sense of identification emerges. There are, in other words, a series of specular identifications that take place in viewing a film, identifications that are connected with the mirror as the original site of primary identification. What we have in the case of the cinema, however, is a combination of what Metz calls 'primary cinematic identifications' with one's own look (as distinct from 'primary identifications' as such, which they cannot be for 'identification with one's own look is secondary with respect to the mirror'), and secondary or tertiary 'cinematic identifications' with characters.

Architectural identifications

We might attempt to develop Metz's theory for an architectural discourse by looking for equivalent processes of 'mirrorings' that take place within a specific architectural environment. These processes would themselves be dependent on the 'introjection' of the external world into the self, and the 'projection' of the self on to the external world, such that there is an equivalence – the one 'reflects' the other – and identification may take place.

The sense of 'introjection', of the absorption of the external world, described by Metz, is echoed within an architectural context in the work of Walter Benjamin, who presents the mind as a kind of *camera obscura*, a photosensitive 'plate' on to which certain interiors are etched in moments of illumination. Benjamin, however, adds a crucial gloss to these processes of introjection and projection:

Buildings are appropriated in a twofold manner: by use and by perception – or rather, by touch and sight. Such appropriation cannot be understood in terms of the attentive concentration of a tourist before a famous building. On the tactile side there is no counterpart to contemplation on the optical side. Tactile appropriation is accomplished not so much by attention as by habit. As regards architecture, habit determines to a large extent even optical reception. The latter, too, occurs much less through rapt attention than by noticing the object in incidental fashion. This mode of appropriation, developed with reference to architecture, in certain circumstances acquires canonical value. For the tasks which face the human apparatus of perception at the turning points of history cannot be solved by optical means, that is, by contemplation, alone. They are mastered gradually by habit, under the guidance of tactile appropriation.[16]

In Benjamin's terms, buildings are 'appropriated'. They are introjected – absorbed within the psyche not just through vision, but also through touch. We should perhaps extend this to include the full register of senses. Moreover, for Benjamin, these 'appropriations' are reinforced by habit. Here memory plays a crucial role. Over a period of time the sensory impulses leave their mark, traces of their reception. These traces are themselves not forgotten, but constitute a type of archive of memorised sensory experiences. Indeed, life itself can be seen to be conditioned by these impulses, such that it is these that constitute our background horizon of experience.

The second part of the 'double-movement of vision' in Metz's terminology is the projective one. This remains a crucial aspect of the process of identification which involves a twofold mechanism of grafting symbolic meaning onto an object and then reading oneself into that object, and seeing one's values reflected in it. The environment must therefore serve as a kind of 'screen' onto which we would 'project' our own meaning, and into which we would 'read' ourselves. We need to project something of ourselves on to the other in order to recognise – or *mis*recognise – ourselves in the other. This reveals the subtlety of a psychoanalytic account of identity, in which the mechanisms of projection and introjection work in tandem, in a model that replicates the operations of the cinema, in which we become the 'projectors' and the environment the 'screen'.

This projection of personality or intentionality on to an object is one that is overlooked by much mainstream architectural commentary. The investment of meaning not only explains the creative potential of seeing oneself in the other in moments of identification, but it also illuminates the problematic foundation of any discourse of architecture and politics that, as it were, attempts to 'project' a range of political values on to an edifice as though they were a property of that edifice. This would further extend to the question of memorials, and serve to undermine the naïve claims that buildings can be in and of themselves the 'sites of memory'. What I would claim is that buildings, monuments, or indeed any form of memorial, are essentially 'inert'. As Fredric Jameson observes, they do not have any inherent meaning. They need to be 'invested' with meaning.[17] They have to be inscribed within an allegorical narrative that gives them their meaning. This meaning is simply 'projected' on to them.

If we are to look for a model of the way in which content might be understood as a kind of 'projection' we could consider the work of the Polish-Canadian public artist, Krzysztof Wodiczko, who literally projects politically loaded images on to buildings as a commentary on the politics of use of those buildings. The projection of the swastika onto a building raises some interesting questions about the relationship between buildings and politics. His projection of 'content-laden' images on to monuments and buildings echoes the process by which human beings 'project' their own readings onto them, as though on to some blank cinematographic screen.[18] In the hermeneutic moment one tends to read that projection as though it were a property of the object.

Identification with a particular place could be therefore perceived as a mirroring between the subject and the environment over time. Here we might understand the subject, in Metz's terms, as both 'screen' and 'projector'. For in moments of identification we effectively see ourselves in objects with which we have become familiar. At the same time we have introjected them into ourselves. The registering of impulses as a kind of introjection leads to one type of 'reflection' – the recognition of the other in the self. Meanwhile the projection of the self on to the external world leads to a second type of 'reflection' – the recognition of the self in the other. The recognition of the 'other' in the self or the self in the 'other' are – in effect – two sides of the same coin. In both cases what results is a form of mirroring.

From this two-way process a fusing between self and other is achieved. And here we can recognise a second order of mirrorings. For mirrorings occur not only in the engagement between the self and the environment, but also between that engagement and memories of previous engagements. There is an originary experience that is replicated in all subsequent enactments. And in that process of replication there is a reinforcement of the original moment of identification. In this sense habit – as a ritualistic replication of certain experiences – is, as Benjamin observes, precisely that which consolidates the process of identification.

Body building

In principle, then, the processes of introjection and projection may be replicated in our engagement with the built environment. Yet, while Metz's model offers a persuasive account of the processes of identification within the cinema, at first sight it seems to be an inadequate mechanism for dealing with an identification with architecture. First, as Metz himself acknowledges, there is a significant difference between a medium such as film that includes sound, time and movement, and other static, silent media such as photography, sculpture or architecture. Second, Metz privileges a sense of identification with the camera or characters within a film rather than the film set or architectural backdrop.

What needs to be taken into consideration, therefore, is an understanding of how identification may take place with a world of architectural objects. The initial potential for this is already established by the fact that, according to Lacan, at the mirror stage humans recognise themselves as *imagos* – as frozen images or statues of themselves. From this point of view it matters little that architecture is primarily static. If individuals recognise themselves as 'frozen' statues, it is no great step for them to recognise themselves as 'frozen' buildings, even though buildings do not possess human features.

The next step would be to acknowledge the potential for individuals not only to identify with characters in a film, but also to identify with 'buildings'. Here one might posit two distinct, yet related, operations: the potential for human beings to see themselves in terms of buildings, and the tendency for them to see buildings in terms of the self. The first operation could be exemplified by the tendency of human beings to respond to the built environment as though it were a reflection of the self – the tendency, for example, to stand up straight in front of an upright building, and so on. Here it must be recognised that the mirror in the mirror stage is not a literal mirror, in the sense that it does not need to reflect our *actual* image. Rather it acknowledges our capacity to see ourselves in the expressions of others, so that we adjust our behaviour according to their approving or disapproving glances, rather as we adjust our clothes or hair in front of an actual mirror. Nor need there be a literal reflection as in the response of others to our behaviour. We might speak also of the potential for human beings to register the properties of the 'other' – even an expressionless, mute 'other' – and see themselves in terms of those properties. A blank wall may therefore serve as a form of 'mirror', in that we register its straightness, hardness, verticality and so on, and replicate these properties in ourselves.

The second operation would be the capacity for human beings to see buildings as the self, to anthropomorphise them, and to incorporate certain proportions or features based on the human body within their designs. To be sure, human beings will always be prone to recreate the world in their own image, such that they inevitably fashion their gods on themselves, and incorporate within their buildings characteristics traceable to the human form.

Hence we find, for example, in the drawings of Francesco di Giorgio tell-tale signs of the inscription of human figures in the plans and elevations of buildings. And hence, equally, we find the urge to fashion buildings according to the principles of human proportions. As Samuel Butler comments, 'Every man's work, whether it be literature or music or architecture or anything else, is always a portrait of himself.'[19]

There are, moreover, numerous examples of architects posing as their buildings.[20] In the context of New York we might point, for example, to the parade of architects dressed up as the skyscrapers they designed. In 'Fête Moderne: A Fantasy in Flame and Silver', a ball held in New York in 1931, seven architects lined up posing as their buildings. The centrepiece was William Van Alen dressed up as his design for the Chrysler Building in a dramatic display in which architect and building become interchangeable. Van Alen is the Chrysler Building and the Chrysler Building is Van Alen.[21] This scene has been re-evoked recently in *Vanity Fair* with images of Michael Graves and Peter Eisenman impersonating their buildings.[22]

The corollary to reading the self as a building is the potential to read buildings as the self. In the context of New York, Salvador Dali's famous 'paranoid' interpretation of the skyscrapers as representations of Millet's *Angelus*, as animated creatures coming alive at sunset 'ready to perform the sexual act', speaks of this opposite moment. It is this image, surely, that inspired the highly anthropomorphised illustration by Madelon Vriesendorp, *Flagrant délit*, in Rem Koolhaas's *Delirious New York*, depicting the Empire State Building and the Chrysler Building in bed together in a state of post-coital bliss, while the other skyscrapers of New York look on from outside in true paranoid fashion.[23]

New York, for Dali, was not the city of impersonal, rational architecture that Le Corbusier had wanted it to be.[24] For Dali despised Le Corbusier, whose 'abject architecture, the Swiss heaviness of which gave indigestion to thousands of young architects and artists'.[25] 'The world,' Dali noted, 'has had enough of logic and rationalism as conceived by Swiss school-masters. I have nothing against Swiss bankers or cuckoos, on the contrary, but the country ought to stop exporting architects!'[26] The future of architecture, Dali predicted, would be 'soft and hairy'.[27] And in contrast to Le Corbusier's 'tidied up', rationalised proposals for rebuilding New York, Dali revelled in its visceral, fleshy forms:

> The poetry of New York does not lie in the pseudo-esthetics of the rectilinear and sterilized rigidity of Rockefeller Center. The poetry of New York is not that of a lamentable frigidaire in which the abominable European esthetes would have liked to shut up the inedible remains of their young and modern plastics! No!

> The poetry of New York is old and violent as the world; it is the poetry that has always been. Its strength, like that of all other existing poetry, lies in the most gelatinous and paradoxical aspects of the delirious flesh of its own reality. Each evening the skyscrapers of New York assume the anthropomorphic shapes of multiple gigantic Millet's Angeluses of the tertiary period, motionless and ready to perform the sexual act and to devour one another, like swarms of praying mantes before copulation.[28]

Yet within Le Corbusier's architecture there is also an attempt to read the human into the architectural. His inscriptions of the proportions of the Modulor Man into the fabric of his buildings speak of an urge to identify with the tectonic materiality of construction. So too, Yamasaki's declared aim to design the twin towers taking account of the human scale – whether or not he succeeded – signals an intent, at least, to foster a sense of identification with the World Trade Center.

Architecture and national identity

Buildings, then, may be read as the 'self', just as the 'self' can be incorporated into their design. The built environment may therefore serve as a form of 'ground' with which we might identify (Figure 8.1).[29] Through this process of identification, identity itself is formulated, as those identifications leave their traces, like tide-marks on the shoreline. We are, according to this argument, the sum total of the places we have visited, lived in, and formed attachments to.

This process of identification may also operate at a group level, spreading like a virus as individuals identify with other individuals and replicate their behaviour, and in so doing forging a collective identity. At the same time, collective identities will always remain 'contested' identities – hybrid, fractured, conflictual. A mediation will therefore operate between the individual and the group behaviour, such that the individual may either 'buy into' or reject the dominant trends. An obvious example of a collective sense of identity would be national identity. We might therefore ask what role the built environment comes to play in forging a sense of national identity.

Lacanian psychoanalytic theory would hold that national identity is based on more than just symbolic identification. National identity is borne of a relationship to a Thing – towards an *incarnation* of Enjoyment, which is structured through fantasy.[30] In common everyday terms this 'Thing' might be understood as a 'way of life', a somewhat mysterious practice that remains accessible only to a certain group, and that is consequently always under threat from those that do not belong to that group, and who do not subscribe

8.1
**The World Trade
Center, New York**
Source: Photograph
by Neil Leach

to the same 'way of thinking'. It may be circumscribed by the various rituals
and practices that hold that community together. It emerges out of a common
commitment to a 'way of life', and therefore shares certain properties with
religion itself, in that its only real base is a 'belief' in or 'commitment'
to certain shared values that are themselves no more than 'beliefs'. Like
religion, national identity amounts to a 'belief' in a 'belief'. As Slavoj Žižek
observes:

> The national Thing exists as long as members of the community
> believe in it; it is literally an effect of this belief in itself. The
> structure here is the same as that of the Holy Spirit in Christianity.

> The Holy Spirit is the community of believers in which Christ lives after his death; to believe in Him is to believe in belief itself – to believe that I am not alone, that I'm a member of the community of believers. I do not need any external proof or confirmation of the truth of my belief: by the mere act of my belief in others' belief, the Holy Spirit is here. In other words, the whole meaning of the Thing consists in the fact that 'it means something' to people.[31]

What role, therefore, might architecture play in such a set-up? How might the very material condition of architecture relate to what amounts to little more than an immaterial belief system? The answer, it would seem, lies in understanding how the material world is itself inscribed within an immaterial belief system.

National identity is essentially a fantasy structure. National identity, in Lacanian terms, cannot be symbolised. It can only be perceived through an alternative symbolic structure. And for this purpose it relies upon the fantasy structure of the homeland, which becomes, as it were, a vicarious vehicle of identification. To quote Renata Salecl:

> In the fantasy structure of the homeland, the nation (in the sense of national identification) is the element that cannot be symbolized. The nation is an element within us that is 'more than ourselves,' something that defines us but is at the same time indefinable; we cannot specify what it means, nor can we erase it . . . It is precisely the homeland that fills out the empty space of the nation in the symbolic structure of society. The homeland is the fantasy structure, the scenario, through which society perceives itself as a homogeneous entity.[32]

The 'myth of the homeland' therefore becomes a mechanism by which society perceives itself. It becomes the embodiment of that which cannot be symbolised. As Žižek puts it: 'The national Cause is ultimately nothing but the way subjects of a given ethnic community organize their enjoyment through national myths.'[33] From this perspective, in order for any national identity to be perceived, it must take some form of material expression. National identity is therefore *cathected* on to objects. It must be embodied. Hence objects such as national flags come to embody that identity through a process of symbolic association. While national flags themselves have little inherent meaning, they become physical articulations of a certain 'way of life'. The stars and stripes flag comes to stand less for a register of the number of states in the union than for the way that people live within that union. It comes to embody all that it is to share an American 'way of life'. This principle would extend beyond the American flag to all other icons associated with an American lifestyle – the hamburger, the baseball cap, the shopping mall, turkey at Thanksgiving, and so on – all of which collectively signify what it is to be American.

Buildings would fall into precisely this category. Potentially they may become the visible embodiment of the invisible, the vehicle through which the fantasy structure of the homeland is represented. There are obvious examples of this when we consider the way in which certain buildings have come to symbolise a city, or even a country, such as the Golden Gate bridge in San Francisco, or the White House in Washington, DC. Indeed the term 'White House' is now used metonymically to refer to the United States presidency. But in terms of national identity it is perhaps more likely that the common, everyday buildings, the familiar streetscapes of our cities and villages, the farmsteads and the landscape of our countryside, will become the embodiment of what we know as 'homeland'.

Such an argument would also account for the tendency to attack an enemy's physical possessions in times of war, to rape and kill its citizens, to plunder their possessions, and to destroy their buildings and bridges. For to attack an enemy's possessions is not only to symbolically attack the enemy itself. It is also to undermine the very Thing around which the enemy has organised its own Enjoyment, and therefore through which it constitutes itself as a community. To attack an enemy's possessions is to attack the very root of its self-definition as a community. It is to attack its very sense of self. Hence one can understand the logic of destroying an enemy's buildings as a vicarious mode of attacking the enemy itself.

It is here, then, that we can understand national identity as an identity which is forged around certain objects. This highlights and exposes the necessary role of the aesthetic in the formation of national identity. The nation, in effect, needs to read itself into objects in the environment in order to articulate that identity. What we have here, then, is a two-way process whereby a nation projects on to the environment certain values as though on to some blank screen, and then reads itself back into that environment, and sees itself symbolically *reflected* in that environment, invested as it now is with certain values. This reveals how, in a narcissistic fashion, national identity comes to be grounded in a reflection of the values assigned to aesthetic objects around us, in which architecture plays an important role.

USA, USA

From this we can begin to understand the principle of any identity being forged gradually against a backdrop of familiar architecture, such as the New York skyline. We can also account for the tendency to 'anthropomorphise' buildings, and to read them as the self. Human beings can equate themselves with buildings and identify with them. And once a sense of identity has been forged against a backdrop of a certain architectural environment, any damage to that environment will be read as damage to the self.

Here I recall an observation made by the author, Douglas Rushkoff, who witnessed the collapse of the twin towers. He recounted how, as one of the buildings collapsed, he felt as if his whole spine was also collapsing. By extension, one could argue that the attack on the World Trade Center was an attack on the American people as a collective. For although there were a significant number of casualties in this tragic event, the attack struck beyond those suffering as a direct or indirect result of the collapse of the twin towers – those who were killed, and those who were bereaved. The attack struck at the very heart of the American psyche, since it was an assault on one of the very iconic references around which an American 'way of life' had been formulated. The attack on the building was equally an attack on American national identity.

Such an argument about the process of identification could also explain how a new sense of identity could be forged gradually against either the New York skyline now without its twin towers, or even against the very images of their destruction. But it could not account for the sudden reinforcement of a specifically American nationalistic identity that seems to have occurred as a direct result of the events of 11 September. I therefore now want to turn to the role of 'loss' as constitutive of any process of forging an identity.

The curious repetitive nature of the coverage of 11 September within the US media where recorded shots of the impact of the aircraft on the twin towers and the subsequent collapse of those towers were repeated over and over again, can be understood within the logic of psychoanalytic theory, in which the compulsion to repeat remains a fundamental, if problematic concern. One interpretation of this compulsion posits repetition as a means of miming and thereby controlling trauma. Just as the child in Freud's famous example of the *fort-da* game seeks to overcome the anxiety of being abandoned by the mother by 'miming' the process of departure and return in various games involving the throwing away and 'retrieving' of a spool attached to a piece of string, so repetition of certain visual traumas can amount to a kind of overcoming of those traumas. Repetition can lead to a normalisation and consequent familiarisation.[34]

At another level the mere act of trying to comprehend such an incident through the lens of historical precedent – the attack of 11 September as the 'second Pearl Harbor' – speaks of a need to conceptualise and frame the incident within a landscape of familiar incidents. Even if such actions can never fully explain such incidents – for Pearl Harbor remains largely incomprehensible to American eyes – it at least offers the potential of figuring the event within some more generalised tradition of terrorism or aggression towards the American people.

But while psychoanalysis might point to mechanisms for overcoming 'loss', we should not overlook the importance of 'loss' within the process of forging an identity. Psychoanalysis tells us that the development of the identity of an individual is founded on the principle of loss. As Julia Kristeva puts it:

> Psychoanalysis identifies and relates as the indispensable condition for autonomy a series of separations: birth, weaning, separation, frustration, castration. Real, imaginary or symbolic, these processes necessarily structure our individuation. Their nonexecution or repudiation leads to psychotic confusion.[35]

Such a process is an essential part of the development of the subject. Kristeva notes:

> It is well known that the so-called 'depressive' stage is essential to the child's access to the realm of symbols and linguistic signs. Such a depression – parting sadness as a necessary condition for the representation of any absent thing – reverts to and accompanies our symbolic activities unless its opposite, exaltation, reappropriates them.[36]

What this suggests is that loss, whether it is actual or imaginary, or experienced vicariously, can serve to reduce this confusion and reinforce an identity. To some extent these mechanisms are replicated in conventional religion. It is the sacrifice of Christ, Kristeva would argue, that gives Christianity its force. The death of Christ offers Christians a vicarious mechanism of loss. The Christian need not experience that loss directly, but by identifying with Christ's own suffering, may empathise with that suffering, and benefit from the sense of loss that it evokes. In this respect the success of Christianity lies largely in acknowledging the necessity of loss or rupture and recognising that this may be acted out within the realm of the imaginary through an identification with Christ. As Kristeva notes:

> On the basis of that identification, one that is admittedly too anthropological and psychological from the point of view of a strict theology, man is nevertheless provided with a powerful symbolic device to experience death and resurrection even in his physical body, thanks to the strength of the imaginary identification – and of its actual effects – with the absolute Subject (Christ).[37]

This introduces a new dynamic into our understanding of identity. For it suggests that identity is built upon a process of identification, but is consolidated as those identifications are severed or come under threat. For identity is ultimately as much about a process of distinction as it is about identification. It is about relating to, but then – importantly – *distinguishing oneself from* a given background. One can therefore understand identity in terms of *gestalt*, as a figure/ground relationship, a sense of separation that cannot be enacted without first establishing a sense of connection.

The notion that identity is based on loss extends to whole communities. In psychoanalytic theory, as Slavoj Žižek, has observed, even the identity of a nation is based on the 'theft of its enjoyment'.[38] If, as noted above, a nation perceives itself in terms of a nation Thing – as a community of individuals who organise their enjoyment around a certain concern – as opposed to those others who fail to appreciate that concern and are therefore a threat to it, the very being of a nation is based on the 'possession' of a certain sense of enjoyment. Or, put another way, that very being of a nation is defined by the threat to its enjoyment. If the 'other' is a threat to the collective self, the potential threat to the enjoyment of the collective is effectively that which articulates and constitutes the 'other' – the way that the 'other' organises its own 'perverse' Enjoyment. As Žižek observes:

> What is therefore at stake in ethnic tensions is always the possession of the national Thing. We always impute to the 'other' an excessive enjoyment; s/he wants to steal our enjoyment (by ruining our way of life) and/or has access to some secret, perverse enjoyment. In short, what really bothers us about the 'other' is the peculiar way it organizes its enjoyment: precisely the surplus, the 'excess' that pertains to it – the smell of their food, their 'noisy' songs and dances, their strange manners, their attitude to work (in the racist perspective, the 'other' is either a workaholic stealing our jobs or an idler living on our labour; and it is quite amusing to note the ease with which one passes from reproaching the other with a refusal of work, to reproaching him for the theft of work).[39]

Not surprisingly, then, a nation is defined most clearly when it is at war and its very 'way of life' is at risk. Nothing will therefore foster a sense of national identity more than a perceived external threat, whether actual or imaginary. For a threat need not be an actual threat. Just as communities are always 'imagined' communities, so too threats to those communities can be 'imagined' threats.[40] But this extends beyond moments of actual conflict to periods of peace when, in order for some sense of national identity to be preserved, a new threat has to be imagined. Thus, in Eastern Europe, following the collapse of the Cold War, a replacement threat had to be found. Inevitably according to a logic of the soil, or of the community, it is the outsiders – Jews, gypsies, wanderers, anyone not bound to the soil – who are perceived as a threat, fluid insurgents that cannot be controlled. Jews, therefore, become scapegoats in Eastern Europe even if there are few Jews to be found there any longer.

So too, within an American context, once the Eastern Bloc had collapsed, the communist 'other' had to be replaced by an alternative 'other'. Although references to a 'crusade' were soon dropped from official rhetoric, there is ample evidence within popular culture to suggest that 9/11 has begun to foment a significant split between the world's religions. Postcards of the Statue of Liberty in Crusader outfit, porcelain models of fire officers in overtly Christian poses (Figure 8.2), and the presence of a steel memorial cross on Ground Zero itself, all serve to illustrate that, in the eyes of many, this is seen as an attack on the Christian world. The US support of Israel and the high number of Jewish inhabitants in New York itself have ensured that this has been expanded into a unacknowledged opposition between a predominantly Judeo-Christian United States and a Muslim 'other'.

8.2
Models of Fire Officers, New York
Source: Photograph by Neil Leach

Within a postmodern world in which old-fashioned racist values must never be acknowledged, a new p/c racism has evolved – or 'metaracism' as Etienne Balibar has described it – in which ethnic or racial factors cannot be 'named', and yet in which alternative cultural values cannot be accepted.[41] Hence the convenient slogan of the 'war on terror', in which freedom fighters

of different ideological persuasions can only be construed as 'terrorists'. Such a definition exposes its own fragility when the understandings of 'freedom' and 'terrorism' are culturally defined. For the United States, Muslim freedom fighters are 'terrorists', and the United States is 'the land of the free', while for Muslim extremists suicide bombers are volunteer 'martyrs', while the United States is tainted for supporting the 'terrorist' state of Israel. Such arguments are inevitably circular, yet it is worth recalling the title of Stanley Fish's book, *There's No Such Thing as Free Speech – and It's a Good Thing Too*. There is no cultural platform that is not constrained by some ideological imperative, and it is precisely because it is issued from some ideologically freighted platform that a statement has any force. However heavily invested they may be with moral conviction, any definitions of the 'other' must be founded inevitably on a mere belief system – an understanding of what constitutes the self inscribed within its own ideological position.

It is important, then, to recognise that national identity depends on opposition. And the same applies to sport. The recent chants of 'USA, USA' from the debris of Ground Zero in New York – only too reminiscent of the collective chants at a basketball match – reveal how the logic of nationalism follows closely the logic of sport. A team is forged around competition. A nation comes together when under threat. And it is around the victims of this threat – the lost heroes and martyrs – that a kindred sense of identity is forged. Likewise the destruction of the twin towers – the 'sacrifice' of the WTC – seems to have helped to give the United States a new identity. And just as the sacrifice of Christ gave others life and provided the basis of Christianity as an identifiable movement, so too around the heroes of the New York City Fire Department there seemed to coalesce a new vision for the United States.

To this extent, we might begin to understand the way in which the events of 11 September seem to have been prefigured by Hollywood. It is as though the 'terrorists' were writing their own perfect movie script, a combination of *Towering Inferno*, and any of a number of other disaster movies where the well-being of the average citizen is at threat from some dark force of evil, all performed in front of the camera with the most realistic of special effects. The United States is a nation obsessed with its own disaster movies. We can recognise, however, that over the years these disaster movies have served as a key factor in forging a US imaginary identity. Movies of 'cops versus robbers', just as the now discredited 'cowboys versus Indians', serve only to illustrate the need within the United States to delineate a sense of self in terms of good versus evil. Thus it is that within these terms of reference the identity of the actual protagonists is less important than the roles they play. The 'goodies', no less than the 'baddies', are relatively interchangeable. They may be substituted at will. It matters less who represents the forces of good and evil, than the fact that those forces exist, in serving as a mechanism for defining the United States as a force of good. Furthermore, the fact that such scenarios might be acted out within the fictive space of cinema serves only to reinforce the role of fantasy in the forging of national identities.

Osama Bin Laden and the al-Qaida network, along with others, have therefore now come to represent in the United States the so-called 'Axis of Evil'. Clearly, there is a certain reductive process at work here, in the tendency for Bin Laden, like Saddam Hussein, to be perceived as embodying all that is a threat to the US 'way of life'. (And, indeed, to some extent Bin Laden has succeeded, in that throughout American culture a dominant refrain has been that 'things will never be the same' after 11 September. It is not simply that the US self-perception must, by definition, be in a constant state of process. Rather, a radical realignment not least in terms of security has been engendered by events of that day.) At a straightforward strategic level it is clear that any 'network' – as opposed to a hierarchical system – is not dependent upon a dominant figure. Aside from the fact that it is the mark of a network to be self-supporting and to retain its integrity even if one of its members is removed, Bin Laden was clearly not the only figure of authority within the al-Qaida network, even supposing that he was a central figure in the first place. Rather this attempt to fetishise Bin Laden as the figure responsible for the attacks points towards the urge to 'symbolise' the world, and to locate recognisable icons to act as substitutes for and to represent more nebulous concepts.

This thinking is what grounds the attack on the World Trade Center in the first place. The motives for this attack are surely many and various, but presumably one would have been that it was intended as an attack on the values of global capitalism that underpinned Western culture in general and US society in particular. On the face of it the attack – if indeed it was an attack on global capitalism – was absurd. To attack a building is hardly to undermine the force of global capitalism. Better to think the logic of a viral network. It is Microsoft, perhaps, which best epitomises the diffuse, dispersed, gaseous nature of power today. Forget the all-seeing panoptical eye of control. Think the deterritorialised, rhizomatic force-fields of credit. Capitalism exerts its power, as Deleuze and Guattari observe, not through the burrows of the molehill, but through the coils of the serpent. Insidious, invisible, capitalism is everywhere and nowhere. The attack on the World Trade Center can therefore be seen as an attack not on capitalism, but on the symbols of capitalism. But just as al-Qaida's attack on the World Trade Center seems perverse in the context of an attack on global capitalism, so too the immediate American response to single out and 'demonise' Bin Laden speaks of a parallel urge to symbolise and 'envision' the enemy, as though 'terrorism' could be reduced to so simplified a set of symbols. Both the attacks of 11 September and the subsequent war on terrorism have been 'wars of symbols'.

In all aspects of life there is a tendency to reduce the world to a set of identifiable symbols, or at least to icons that constitute temporary, strategic manifestations of a continuous, dynamic process of symbolisation, and this tendency also lies at the heart of the formation of national identity.

What we find, then, in the context of the United States, and, specifically, New York, after 11 September, is that the sense of alterity, which is a necessary precondition of any definition of the self – the distinction of the self from one's surroundings – shifted from being an 'internal' alterity of a society fragmented on race and other lines, to become an 'external' alterity. The sense of opposition that defined identity in the United States shifted from being an internal opposition to an external one. Thus New York seems to have lost its 'meanness', as the external threat transcended all internalized factions to bring a nation together. As a result previously unheard of incidents began to be reported, such as the case of African-American kids helping an old Jewish man to cross the road. A nation came together not under God – for in truth the United States embraces a range of religions – but under an external threat.

This new sense of identity can then be 'projected' on to images of the destruction of the twin towers, and reflected back off them. For the built environment, we must recall, is, in essence, inert. It serves as a 'screen' on to which we 'project' our meaning. Such a 'cinematographic' model of meaning challenges the traditional assumptions about how buildings – or indeed any works of art – can be 'read'. For once the built environment is perceived as 'mute' or 'inert' it replicates the role of the analyst, who remains largely silent, as the analysand talks about his/herself. In other words, in our supposed 'readings' of the built environment, we are in fact not reading the built environment, so much as reading *ourselves*. For the gaze is never innocent. We project a certain 'intentionality' on to the environment as though it were a blank screen. We invest it with something of ourselves. And, as that projection is reflected back off that screen, it serves to reinforce that original sense of intentionality.

Hence, one might recognise a certain 'performativity' of the gaze when rereading such events, where performativity is recognised as being a constitutive component of identity – in a contemporary world of theming and role playing, where we 'are' the roles that we play.[42] For performativity also operates in modes of perception, such as the 'gaze' which, as it were, 'colour' and frame our view of the world, but – importantly – also constitute it. To be 'black' is to view the world with a 'black' gaze.[43] But so too what is 'received' by that gaze serves precisely to reinforce that identity. To be American is therefore to gaze at those newsreel images of the destruction of the twin towers with a sense of being American, but equally to gaze repeatedly at those images is to reinforce the sense of what it is to be American.

The destruction of the twin towers and its reception within the media therefore seem to have played a crucial role in the formation of a new US identity – an identity that is, by definition, always in a state of re-negotiation and never totalising. Not only did the 'loss' of the buildings seem to furnish the United States with a mechanism of self-redefinition as a nation, in a manner that echoed a new sense of British identity that seemed to emerge with the death of Diana, Princess of Wales. But the image of the New York skyline without the now absent twin towers may also present itself as a projective screen on to which that nascent identity might be projected, and in which it might be seen to be reflected.

This is not to limit the forging of identities to the introjection and projection of architectural spaces – for clearly there are other factors – people, gestures and events – that will also contribute to this process. Indeed, human gestures can be far more dominant, in that they can be inscribed within a process of identification more effectively than the built environment. Such gestures may be replicated and serve as clear models of 'good behaviour'. Here one thinks, for example, of the New York City firemen and police officers, many of whom perished in the incident, who served not only as 'forces of good' doing battle with the 'forces of evil', but also later as templates for American forces in their subsequent action in Afghanistan and more recently Iraq.

Nor is this to privilege architectural concerns – the iconic potential of a building to symbolise a set of values – above others in analysing the events of 11 September. Indeed the whole range of human factors – the sheer loss of life, the individual narratives of distress, and so on – must be included within any *comprehensive* account of the events of that tragic day. Rather, it is to recognise the capacity of the built environment to serve as one of the complex threads that may contribute to notions of national identity, and, in the context of 11 September, to recognise how the destruction of an iconic building – made even more iconic by its destruction – might contribute to a radical realignment and reconfiguration of a sense of United States national identity.

Notes

1   W. Benjamin, *One-Way Street*, London: Verso, 1979, pp. 342–3.
2   There is an extensive body of literature on the attacks of the twin towers on 11 September 2001. Some of the most theoretically informed analyses include: Noam Chomsky, *9–11*, New York: Seven Stories, 2001; Slavoj Žižek, *Welcome to the Desert of the Real!*, London: Verso, 2002; Jean Baudrillard, *The Spirit of Terrorism*, London: Verso, 2002; Paul Virilio, *Ground Zero*, London: Verso, 2002.
3   Rem Koolhaas, *Delirious New York*, Rotterdam: 010 Publishers, 1994, p. 291.

4 As Darton comments:

> From inside the WTC, its closely spaced columns produce odd vertical window forms
> that feel prisonlike and chop the expected panorama into dissociative strips. . . From the
> outside, under most conditions, it is hard to tell whether, above plaza level, the towers
> have windows at all.
>
> (Eric Darton, *Divided We Stand: A Biography of New York's
> World Trade Center*, New York: Basic Books, 1999, p. 129.)

5 Ibid., p. 115.

6 According to Darton:

> What the trade center's design prefigured has since become an operative mode: an
> all-consuming global market, polarized wealth and resources and fragmenting cultural
> life into a thousand unpredictable mutations. When this myriad of seemingly random
> energies, multiplying autonomously, shows its destructive face, we experience it as
> terrorism.
>
> (Ibid., p. 130.)

7 For a relatively comprehensive account of the twin towers' history, see Darton, *Divided*.

8 According to Lacan:

> This event can take place, as we have known since Baldwin, from the age of six months,
> and its repetition has often made me reflect upon the startling spectacle of the infant
> in front of the mirror. Unable as yet to walk, or even to stand up, and held tightly as
> he is by some support, human or artificial . . . he nevertheless overcomes, in a flutter
> of jubilant activity, the obstructions of his support and, fixing his attitude in a slightly
> leaning forward position, in order to hold it in his gaze, brings back an instantaneous
> aspect of the image.
>
> (Jacques Lacan, *Ecrits: A Selection*, trans. Alan Sheridan,
> New York: Norton, 1977, pp. 1–2, 493–4.)

9 See, however, the chapter 'What is a Picture?' in Jacques Lacan, *The Four Fundamental
Concepts of Psycho-analysis*, London: Penguin, 1991, pp. 105–19.

10 Christian Metz, *Psychoanalysis and the Cinema*, trans. Celia Britton, Annwyl Williams, Ben
Brewster and Alfred Guzzetti, London: Macmillan, 1982.

11 Ibid., p. 48.

12 Ibid., p. 49.

13 Ibid., p. 49.

14 Ibid., p. 51.

15 Ibid., p. 54.

16 W. Benjamin, *Illuminations*, trans. Harry Zohn, London: Collins, 1992, p. 233.

17 Fredric Jameson, 'Is Space Political?' in Neil Leach (ed.), *Rethinking Architecture*, London:
Routledge, 1997, pp. 258–9.

18 On the work of Krzysztof Wodiczko, see 'Public Projections' and 'A Conversation with
Krzysztof Wodiczko', *October*, 38, Fall 1986, pp. 3–52.

19 Samuel Butler, quoted in Louis Hellman, *Archi-têtes*, London: Academy, 2000, p. 7.

20 Vitruvius provides us with one of the earliest of these with his story of Dinocrates, who
dresses himself up as a model of his own project for Mount Athos in order to present it to
Alexander the Great. Vitruvius, *The Ten Books on Architecture*, trans. Morris Hicky Morgan,
New York: Dover, 1960, p. 36.

21 Koolhaas, *Delirious New York*, p. 129.

22 On this see Mary Macleod, 'Everyday and "Other" Spaces', in Debra Coleman, Elizabeth
Danze, Carol Henderson (eds.), *Architecture and Feminism*, Princeton, NJ: Princeton
Architectural Press, 1996, p. 26.

23 Koolhaas, *Delirious New York*, p. 160.

24 For a discussion of Le Corbusier's vision for New York see Koolhaas, *Delirious New York*, pp. 246–61.

25 Salvador Dali, *The Unspeakable Confessions of Salvador Dali*, trans. Howard Salemson, London: W.H. Allen, 1976, p. 229.

26 Ibid., pp. 229–30.

27 Ibid., p. 230.

28 Salvador Dali, *The Secret Life of Salvador Dali*, trans. Haakon Chevalier, London: Vision, 1968, pp. 334–6.

29 Like Metz's 'primary *filmic* identifications' these are 'primary *architectural* identifications', which likewise operate within the overall realm of secondary identification. As such, architectural identifications may prove to be temporary, strategic identifications. This is what allows us, for example, to transfer the notion of 'home' from one architectural environment to another.

30 For a discussion of the 'Thing', see Jacques Lacan, *Le Séminaire VII*, Paris: Seuil, 1986.

31 Slavoj Žižek, 'Eastern Europe's Republics of Gilead', *New Left Review*, 183, Sept.–Oct. 1990, p. 53.

32 Renata Salecl, 'Ideology of the Mother Nation', in Michael Kennedy (ed.), *Envisioning Eastern Europe*, Ann Arbor, MI: University of Michigan Press, 1995, p. 94.

33 Žižek, 'Eastern Europe's Republics', p. 53.

34 Repetition, in this sense, would be linked to the death instinct, the urge to discharge tensions and return to a state of oneness, evoking the nirvana of the womb. On this, see Richard Boothby, *Death and Desire: Psychoanalytic Theory in Lacan's Return to Freud*, London: Routledge, 1991, pp. 2–3, 74–5, 79.

35 Julia Kristeva, 'Holbein's Dead Christ', in Michel Feher (ed.), *Fragments for a History of the Human Body*, New York: Zone Books, p. 261.

36 Ibid., p. 261.

37 Ibid., p. 262.

38 'Enjoyment', here, as Žižek notes, is not to be equated with pleasure: 'enjoyment is precisely "pleasure in unpleasure"; it designates the paradoxical satisfaction procured by a painful encounter with a Thing that perturbs the equilibrium of the "pleasure principle". In other words, enjoyment is located "beyond the pleasure principle"'. Žižek, 'Eastern Europe's Republics of Gilead', p. 52.

39 Ibid., pp. 53–4.

40 On 'imagined communities', see Benedict Anderson, *Imagined Communities*, London: Verso, 1983.

41 On this see Etienne Balibar, 'Is there a "Neo-Racism"?' in Etienne Balibar and Immanuel Wallerstein (eds.), *Race, Nation, Class: Ambiguous Identities*, London: Verso, 1991.

42 On this see Neil Leach, 'Belonging', *AA Files* 49, pp. 76–82.

43 On the 'racing' of the gaze, see Leach, 'Belonging', p. 78.

David Osbaldeston,
floor manager of JD Sports
on Market Street, is late
for work because of
canal bridge
reinforcement work on
Great Ancoats Street.

Chapter 9

Mnemotechny of the industrial city

Contemporary art and urban memory

Mark Crinson

In 1846, intuiting that modernisation would entail transformations in the function of the aesthetic, Baudelaire defined art as a technique of memorising artistic tradition in the face of loss. The artists who best triggered this 'mnemotechny of beauty',[1] or at least the subliminal artistic afterimages that Baudelaire wanted, were those who found some middle point between an excessive realism and an over-generalised idealism: artists like Delacroix whose strange and melancholy canvases, based on historical and literary themes, 'created deep avenues for the most adventurous imagination to wander down'.[2] As it transpired, or so Benjamin Buchloh has argued, many modernist practices came to embody Baudelaire's fears and to enshrine 'the triumphant annihilation of cultural memory'; when not reflective of industrial technology or mimicking the forms of its commodities, art became assimilated to its associated myths of progress.[3] Recently a mnemonic aspect seems to have returned to many artistic practices, particularly through an interest in the way traumatic experience restructures both history and subjectivity.[4] But, more than a century and a half after Baudelaire, there is another area of material for art that can be distinguished from the trauma of war, genocide and mass migration. The re-structuring of once-industrial cities, together with their evocation of the spectacular pleasures of shopping, culture and sport, has many resonances with what inspired Baudelaire's concern, and once again we find memory placed in an interesting relationship to aesthetic practices.

Rachel Whiteread's *House* (1993) has been the most discussed of recent artworks in this context. Whiteread's figuration of mute mourning using the voids of a Victorian terraced residence as a mould for a newly-cast, blank-windowed concrete house, was located in the highly-charged urban environs of London's East End. As well as evoking the Blitz and post-war planning, *House* attracted Freudian and political interpretations.[5] But, though evocative and emotionally charged, seemingly spectral yet massively weighty, Whiteread's work does not by any means exhaust this subject. Indeed I will argue in this chapter that, nearly a decade after *House*, a new group of works have focused on what we could call the 'mnemotechny of the industrial city' using quite different techniques from Whiteread. If Whiteread's main strategy has been the evocation of the trace regardless of specific commemoration, in these new works the key has been the idea of research, sometimes playful, quizzical, or self-reflexive. They have a more allusive and more withdrawn attitude towards the public realm (or a conventional notion of outside public space) that matches their function as gallery art, but they also reach out through the practice of research. Instead of Whiteread's displacement of void by solid, of brick by concrete, they explore the map, the architect's plan and model, the formalities of slide presentations, techniques of surveillance and the re-evocation of film by video. But this does not necessarily mean they have withdrawn from engagements with the politics of urban memory; rather, that the gallery has become a place of temporary reappraisal where these politics might be opened up through a poetics of form, a place that has a secondary but still dynamic relation to the places that their art evokes.

This chapter will assess a small but contrasting group of these aesthetic techniques of memorialization in the context of the post-industrial city. What the term 'post-industrial' means is itself placed under review by these works, which question what constitutes and marks epochal change and what interests might be at stake in the forgetting of what has gone before as much as in its memorialisation. They are not, however, in any conventional or public sense 'memorials'; rather, they take the contested nature of memory itself as their subject. They avoid setting utopian agendas or reaching dystopian conclusions. They seem to bypass the common economic marriage (whether celebrated or one of convenience) or ideological collaboration between regeneration and public art. Nor are they part of what has been called 'new genre public art' in that an idealised notion of two-way conversation enabled by the artwork is not their concern.[6] Instead they engage critically with the co-optation of memory to the advertising-speak of developers or to the *musée imaginaire* of the heritage lobby. More specifically, they are reactions to a new wave of urban transformation aimed at finalising the projected post-industrial city on the very sites and in the very buildings of the old industrial city: the trumpeting of loft living, of urban villages, of public–private partnerships, of millennium squares, and so forth. And they seem informed by a new generation of writing about art which has questioned and further developed notions like site specificity, democratic public spaces and the ethics of ethnographic practice.[7] All of the artworks discussed here have been made in the last few years and all of them are responses to a new wave of regeneration projects and rhetorics. These works address the disavowals intrinsic in the claim to post-industrialism, they question the interests really at stake in regeneration, they opt for oblique tacks through the archive or deploy the nonsynchronous or the outmoded to question the priorities of regeneration. In particular, they challenge one of the deceits commonly implied by the claim that we live in a post-industrial era: that is, that the main appurtenances of industrialism – goods, labour, sites of manufacture – are easily disavowed. As such, they offer a number of ways of rethinking and re-imagining the relation between memory and the city.

The title of Richard Wentworth's *An Area of Outstanding Unnatural Beauty* refers to the area just to the north of King's Cross Station in London.[8] This is a loud, jarring and hard-edged area, traversed by heavy lorries and dubious transactions, and still riven by the transformations of the nineteenth century. It had been described in Charles Dickens's *Dombey and Son* (1848) as if it had suffered the shock of an earthquake; an area of 'dire disorder' entirely subservient to 'the mighty course of civilisation and improvement':

> temporary wooden houses and enclosures, in the most unlikely situations; carcasses of ragged tenements, and fragments of unfinished walls and arches, and piles of scaffolding and wilderness of bricks, and giant forms of cranes, and tripods straddling above nothing. There were a hundred thousand shapes and substances of incompleteness, wildly mingled out of their places, upside down, burrowing in the earth, aspiring in the air, mouldering in the water and unintelligible as any dream.[9]

In his characteristic transposition of human forms and characteristics onto inanimate buildings, Dickens is here depicting the chaos that accompanies industrialism. Later he detailed what emerged from this mess:

> tiers of warehouses, crammed with rich goods and costly merchandise. The old by-streets now swarmed with passengers and vehicles of every kind . . . The carcasses of houses, and the beginnings of new thoroughfares, had started off upon the line at steam's own speed, and shot away into the country in a monster train.[10]

The juxtaposition of these two quotes implies a cyclical inevitability about capitalist urban development; mess, in short, is necessary to progress, renewal demands destruction. In the 150 or so years since Dickens's book, this area had continued to be shaped around the needs of a railway terminus. By 2002 most of the unused Victorian industrial buildings to the north of the train station were scheduled for demolition to make way for the new Eurostar terminus. Effectively, trans-European rail links were displacing an outdated apparatus of regional goods transfer. It was at this moment seemingly between two epochs, and in this area where the mess of renewal was about to be felt, that Wentworth made *An Area of Outstanding Unnatural Beauty*.

The installation was located in the area itself, inside a temporarily disused plumbing workshop (Figure 9.1). In this hard and makeshift space, still bearing the evidence of its recent use, the work consisted of a collection of maps, games and plans arranged in the space of the workshop. Some of the maps located distinctions in the social profile of the area at certain times; others detailed its wildlife or geology or sewer systems, or described taxi-drivers' routes across London. One map charted the area in braille, while another invited visitors to place a pin to mark where they lived in London. There was also an aerial photograph of King's Cross from 1921, a Victorian balloon view of London, and charts of gas and water conduits as well as of flight paths. Other aspects of the work included TV sets showing the 1955 Ealing comedy *The Ladykillers* or a film contrasting the work of road line painters in the neighbourhood with vapour trails in the sky, a series of talks mapping the area, and a 'self-guided' walking tour. There were full-length mirrors placed around the space, as if from some department store lumber room. In addition, a table tennis tournament took place in the workshop using twelve tables that Wentworth had set out and marked up with some of the local roads and junctions. The only stipulation for those entering this tournament was that they should live or work in King's Cross or regularly travel through it. Clearly, a comprehension of the local and the locality were central to the work. Its maps indicated salvaged archival layers that might be pursued further, sorted or researched and the way the same area could hold different topographies, yielding different maps to different preoccupations, as well as its constantly changing and unfixable aspect. In another context Wentworth has talked about displays as offering a way of thinking aloud: 'the possibility of research . . . a variety of contradictions . . . resonances and associations'.[11] At the same time *An Area of Outstanding Unnatural Beauty* encouraged a playful attitude towards the environs, a drifting across its cluttered urban spaces as much as across its cluttered historical baggage.

Another feature of Wentworth's work was a conning tower set up at the top of a specially erected staircase inside the workshop from which visitors could look down onto the interior and have a 360-degree view over

9.1
**Richard
Wentworth,**
*An Area of
Outstanding
Unnatural
Beauty,* **2002**

the surrounding cityscape from a rotating periscope. The periscope was
virtually invisible from the outside among the clutter of neighbouring signage
and cctv cameras. The periscopic view itself brought several other aspects into
Wentworth's work, including an element of pseudo-surveillance, a measure of
the mock-theatrical, and a reframing of the cityscape through picked out
vignettes (Figure 9.2). And it was above all this last, with its displacing and

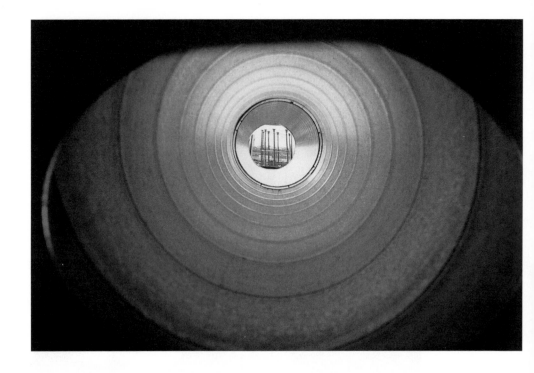

distancing effect on the spectator, that gave the periscope its particular epitomizing role in relation to the rest of the installation. All that multiplicity of maps, and the encouragement to play, with at the same time a refusal to bring together, to fuse or pass judgement, might encourage a multilayered appreciation of the city and might make the totalising aspiration of any map merely relative. But at the same time, with its numerous trajectories across its urban spaces, the installation risked inadvertently foregrounding the numbing or disabling experience of citizenship and reinforcing a sense of powerless insignificance in the face of urban change.

　　　Wentworth has written about maps as attempts to steady us in the face of a city that is 'fugitive, like a very speedy geology . . . all jostling molecules', and similarly of the A–Z as a book whose every page 'is notched with a million map-reading tantrums'.[12] Wentworth's project accepts that knowing the city, let alone directing its forces, is a forlorn task; the artwork can only hope to 'beat the bounds, making new edges, picking up what it finds as it goes'.[13] The table tennis and the periscope pull the installation back towards its site in the changing city and away from any tendency to collapse the workshop into a gallery and 'relax into the fictions which the space proposes'. They reinforce the necessity of thinking of the installation continuously in relation to the railway yards outside, or to the heavy lorries that have lumbered past as one walks towards the workshop.[14]

9.2
Richard Wentworth, *An Area of Outstanding Unnatural Beauty,* **2002**

9.3
Nathan Coley, *I Don't Have Another Land,* **2002**

At first glance, Nathan Coley's *I Don't Have Another Land* is the most immediate of the works that I discuss here (Figure 9.3). It takes the conventional form of an architectural model, an object we might expect in the context of the Centre for Understanding the Built Environment (CUBE), an RIBA-sponsored gallery in Manchester for which the work was made.[15] Architectural models usually represent new proposals for buildings or record certain canonical structures, but not in this case. Coley's model is of the 1960s' Marks & Spencer's building which was badly damaged and eventually pulled down as a result of the 1996 IRA bomb in Manchester. It is neither a new nor a distinctive building, in a strictly architectural sense, apart perhaps from its wavy street-level canopy: as one first-time visitor to the gallery put it,

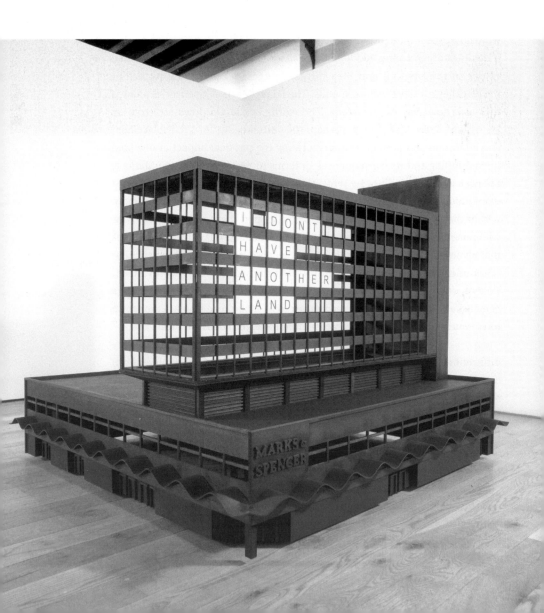

'That's the old Marks & Spencers – I didn't think you had models of buildings like that.' But Coley's work is given a black sheen and it sits almost directly on the gallery floor like a 1960s' Minimalist sculpture or perhaps an elaborate doll's house. (It is actually raised slightly above the floor so that, for instance, its corner pier floats an inch or two above it.) This is a model not as an instrument of design, of architectural development and the erasure of the past in the prospect of the future, as we might expect of the genre and as we might expect of CUBE, usually a place where erasure and new beginnings are displayed. Instead it is a model of re-development or even anti- or ante-development. The architectural model's normal tense has changed from the future ('this will be') to the past ('this has been'), perhaps even, as Barthes claimed of photography, the anterior future ('this has been', with a trace of 'this will be').[16] Its dark sheened surfaces, the stark views through the model, and the words that seem to board up some of its windows like a letting agency, give it qualities of mourning and loss. The black surfaces have no relation to the colour of the original and may instead suggest a blackening by fire or the blackness of sleek high-tech units. The name 'Marks & Spencer' is painted the same as every other surface. The words in the windows are from an anonymous folksong marking, perhaps too portentously, forced displacement and migration and perhaps commemorating the physical impact of one land upon another and its consequences in terms of terrorism. Yet the Marks & Spencer building will not be remembered for its architectural qualities; it would most likely simply disappear from official records and only remain within the living memories of those who shopped there, particularly those who remember it as a local icon of 1960s' consumerism. It is those memories that achieve an interesting displacement because it is the anachronistic that takes unexpectedly physical form through the work's presence in CUBE. Coley's work thus suggests a new kind of urban memorial, one in which a demolished building might be reconstructed as a blackened hulk. Emptied of its commercial functions it becomes a monument to the loss of local time.

On the face of it, Adam Chodzko's *Remixer* (Figure 9.4) takes a very different approach to the question of memory-building and the memorial broached in Coley's *I Don't Have Another Land*.[17] Here Manchester's legendary nightclub of the 1980s, the Haçienda, and the site of the 1996 IRA bomb are linked by a line across the city. Both places could be seen to have had catalytic roles in the regeneration of Manchester: the Haçienda as the best-known of the city's 1980s' nightclubs that led the city's renowned music scene of that time; the bomb as an act of terrorism turned to good by initiating the upgrading of the city's unloved shopping centre. Since these events both sites have had have a curious relation to forms of memorialisation. The Haçienda nightclub, originally named after the Situationists' famous call for a new space for urban culture, has been pulled down and replaced by a swish apartment

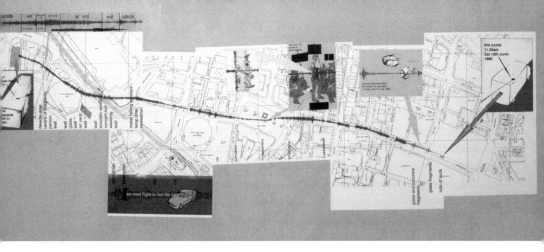

9.4
Adam Chodzko,
***Remixer*, 2002**

complex named after the club it replaced: 'now the party's over you can come home', the Crosby Homes publicity announces.[18] The site of the bomb has become Manchester's glossy shopping centre, a neo-Haussmannized quarter of café-bars, Harvey Nicholls and dressed pavements. Both therefore have become absorbed within developer-led regeneration.

Remixer takes the form of several maps pasted like fly-posters on the walls of the gallery. Accompanying the piece is a recording of a song by A Certain Ratio called *Flight* (1980), to some the unacknowledged Manchester precursor to the dance music/club craze that was one catalyst for the city's urban renaissance. The song's arc of sound is remixed as if it were passing through the materials it might encounter on a direct flight one metre high through the intervening streets and buildings between the Haçienda and the bomb site: stone, steel, glass and flesh; through walls, a car, the body of a street protester in 1991, and even through the flying fragments caused by the 1996 explosion. It also passes Albert Square, one of the city's principal commemorative spaces, with its monuments to Prince Albert, William Gladstone and other Victorian figures, and its history of rallies and protests. In Chodzko's work these various sites are not linked by a piece of psycho-geography or urban writing, a drift across uneven territories of the city which might have been inspired by the deposit of French Situationist thought in some of the music of the 1980s, but by something more like a surveyor's cut across the city, an entirely imaginary vista conceivable only in terms of an inscription overlaid on a map and given mock accurate wavelengths varying depending upon the medium to be passed through. The dictionary reminds us that a vista is not just a view cut across space but a succession of remembered or anticipated events. It therefore combines the idea of a piece of surveyor's or landscapist's rationalism that channels space and organises the view, and also the ordering of time as it is experienced by the individual or community, in this case disparate moments in Manchester's recent history. And yet, looking at Chodzko's 'cut' again, it does have slight but gentle curves, as if a line of flight has provided the blueprint for the surveyor's section.

Remixer joins two seemingly unrelated places in order to pose questions about how we understand urban form and whose memories are prioritised in its history. The sites of commemoration are not in themselves fetishised, nor are hypothetical monuments presented to mark them out. The work even seems to tease us with these ideas by placing drawings of two rectangular blocks (one stands for the Haçienda, the other for the bomb-laden lorry) at either end of its flight path. Chodzko undertakes a kind of capricious urban planning in this work, fastidious in its execution but whimsical in its means, making a cross-section of the city that joins its 'weak' elements of memory and slicing blithely through the steel and glass structures that would otherwise embody its instrumentalism.

Another work by Adam Chodzko, *The Gorgies' Centre*, is in part also a mediation between two places, both of them again beyond the gallery (Figure 9.5).[19] One of these is a gypsy site in Kent which, at the time the work was made, was threatened with relocation because of its purchase by property developers. The other place is Hulme in Manchester, where what the gypsies call 'gorgies', or house dwellers, live. Hulme is notorious for the fact that it has twice been demolished, redesigned and rebuilt since the war. The relocation of Hulme's residents has some parallels with the impending relocation of the gypsies; both can be seen as subject to larger imperatives of land-use, planned environments, and the legalities of ownership, tenancy

9.5
Adam Chodzko,
The Gorgies'
***Centre*, 2002**

and squatting. Chodzko uses his work to mine and interrogate these parallels by arranging to have boxes of official documents relating to one of Hulme's housing developments (led by the architects Mills Beaumont Leavey Channon) distributed to Jo and Bridie Jones, one of the gypsy families whom he got to know. Chodzko's ethnography – his strategy of making his work the collaborating agency between two places, with the aim of empowering the cultural other – is a practice that suggests the possibilities of solidarity between two normally distinct groups of people, implying that those who exist on the margins, or who are most subject to planning, are also those who, because of their intimate awareness of shelter, property and security, have the closest relationship with the city.[20] Beyond this, it also challenges the normal expectation of the ownership of memory, in this case the ownership of the archive. The gypsies become the proprietors and curators of this archive, a potential research centre on the history of Hulme's waves of redevelopment as well as the design of the homes and lifestyles of gorgies in Hulme, but what they might do with this is, seemingly, not the work's concern.

As seen in the gallery, the work is made up of two sequences of slides shown simultaneously. The continuous sequence of images shares the formal logic of a business presentation but the sequence itself lacks easy coherence: the timing of the images, set to rotate every seven seconds, is too fast to dwell long on their sense, they jump between apparently disparate material, and in several instances there are repetitions of what seem to be the least significant images. In their jolts, inexplicable repetitions, switching from black-and-white to colour, and compression of events they are like dreams, or perhaps like the sudden clarities, omissions and ambiguities of memory itself. To take one sequence as an instance of this: flowers are seen with their pollen blowing away, the MBLC archive of papers and plans, blurred black-and-white images of the travellers' encampment, a country lane, the sign for Moate Farm, blurred colour images approaching the camp, images of bees on flowers which have the same colour as the top worn by a traveller boy, the same boy playing with an instrument for stretching barbed wire, the encampment with its flowerbeds and Wendy houses, the MBLC archive seen as half-open files on a table, a rabbit run, adults sitting beside the archive files, pylons, a letter of complaint ('You wouldn't want the horror that comes with the gypsies', we read), Hulme in the 1960s, the new designs for Hulme, blurred images of caravans. Particularly prominent here are the images of rural idyll and of rural embattlement: of flowers and barbed wire, of entering the gypsy site in a manner that implies the visitor is under some form of surveillance, of the careful organisation and maintenance of the encampment, and of the boxes of plans and other documents that constitute the MBLC archive. The labels on these boxes make their ownership by Jo and Bridie Jones clear as well as showing that the boxes contain plans of Hulme in 1955 (that is, in its Victorian manifestation), in 1990 (in its 1960s' manifestation), later guides to its development, and a memorandum of understanding between the city council and housing associations and tenants. But the only way to begin to comprehend these images is to see several rounds of the carousels, in a sense to surrender to their logic of rapidly changing images and cyclical repetition. The format of the timed slide show thus makes comprehension itself subject to a mechanism; it compels an accumulation of imagery from several locations and gathered over a much longer period of time to be viewed individually as equal units of measure; and it makes the number of spaces in the carousel the evidently determining editorial function. Why should this format, which is both a technology and a mechanics of presentation, be important to an understanding of Chodzko's material?[21] And how do both bear upon the issue of memory within a changing city?

To return to the questions raised earlier about *The Gorgies' Centre*, one of the effects of the slide projection format is to use but also to play with the notion of photography as bearing a necessarily documentary function. The slides have been taken as part of a series of meetings, processes and other interactions that led to the creation of the actual Gorgies' Centre. Yet the slides are not transparent to those processes and interactions. They juxtapose images and text, foreground their pictorial devices, and refuse to transform static elements into a narrative drive. They mark a distinction between the engagement in a group of actual events that have led to the transferral of an archive into Jo and Bridie Jones's possession, and the way that these can be marked or recorded within the 'non-site' of the gallery. Therefore, the slides stand for a kind of difference from, or impossibility of, the absorption of art into instrumentality, as well as refusing to allow the viewer the easy position of 'witness'. If the work as a whole can be understood to include that engagement and its overt opposition to matters like the bureaucratic repression of the historical, the demarcation of land ownership through limited legal means, and the movement of populations, then the form it takes in the gallery is necessarily more reflective and fragmented. It registers subjective vision (the blur), the sense of being watched, repetition as a form of willed redundancy, and so on. *The Gorgies' Centre* seeks to displace the official repository of public memory – the archive – so that displacement and transience, as the normally unrecorded aspects of urban policy, are foregrounded. It presents us with a point from outside the dominant culture in which the objects of memory, marked by the archive, can be estranged or displaced while simultaneously trying to avoid the 'ideological patronage' of the invoked other.[22] Such a work seems to ask how we can come to terms, in a way that is not immediately recuperable, with the estranged or marginal circumstances of other people.

Discussing Nick Crowe and Ian Rawlinson's *Explaining Urbanism to Wild Animals* immediately after *The Gorgies' Centre* makes for a very

9.6
**Nick Crowe and
Ian Rawlinson,**
*Explaining
Urbanism to Wild
Animals,* 2002

uncomfortable answer to this question.[23] Crowe and Rawlinson's installation consisted of four large photographs (Figure 9.6) grouped on three walls around four DVD players. The photographs are of country scenes from the area of Cheshire between Manchester and Macclesfield, and each has a matching DVD. The photographs have the scale of sizeable landscape paintings and they represent the countryside head-on as a mass that fills the frame, seemingly not composed or mediated by the photographers. The viewer thus directly faces a bank of nettles, a woody pond, a hollowed-out tree, or a woodland opening. There is no foreground space to create a zone of measurable, distancing room between viewer and scene. The viewer is seemingly already in the woodland yet there is nothing either to register that presence or to explain why it might be significant to find oneself in this place. It is a curious, almost vertiginous experience that has similarities with the desire of Romantic landscape painters to create devices for the absorption of the viewer within the scene: 'you seek confirmation of your arrival, some motivative sign or plot that will explain why you are here . . . although you are placed before nothing that should command your attention, this void, pictured, seems already to imply your gaze.'[24] But the DVDs playing on the four screens puncture this seemingly engrossed experience of contemplating woodland and losing the self in nature's infinities. Now we see two figures who we learn are the artists, tracking through the landscape carrying various pieces of audio equipment and setting them up in the woodland. Absurdly, they place a walkman inside the hollow tree or they wade through the pond slowly swinging loudspeakers across the water as they go. The sound of construction sites emanates from the equipment, mingling with the birdsong and rustling leaves.

One obvious way to understand *Explaining Urbanism to Wild Animals* is as an environmentalist's warning. The landscape polluted by the sounds of the city is an audible portent of what will come. The green belt, for that is where we are, will be eroded by the government's desire to allow house-building within such formerly preserved green field sites. The Romantic's absorption within the miraculous minutiae, density and extensiveness of nature, will become mere reminiscence or fantasy. Yet by thinking about it in relation to Chodzko's *Gorgies' Centre*, several other aspects of Crowe and Rawlinson's work are raised. First, their hilariously earnest tracking through the Cheshire woods takes the idea of mediating between two places into the form of a mock ethnography in which they appear as missionaries setting out to 'explain' an alien faith or warn against an augured cataclysm. They search out marginal and threatened life-forms with whom, if they can ever be found, a conversation can never be staged. These life-forms – the animals – are mute, presumably unaware of government policy, and unable to acknowledge the warning presented by the recordings or unable to do anything about it if they were. The doing of good, or the displacement of the normal conditions of artistic production typical of ethnographic artistic practice, is here shown to be a quixotic venture without even allegorical power. Furthermore, and second, the photographs need not necessarily describe the virgin forest; their framed and symmetrical structure, awaiting perhaps only a *Rückenfigur* to indicate our appropriate response of awe or enchantment, is by now somewhat hackneyed or at least so familiar it is either overpopulated with memories of previous encounters, or the hope of natural plenitude is turned sour by the evidence of litter and pollution. It is, then, possible to suspend the terms of the environmentalist thesis here. Instead, the concrete jungle is the unrepresentable in these scenes; the noise of building construction is the threatening force of another nature that has no consoling memories attached to it.[25]

If relations between permanency and transience or between city and country are the concern of these works by Chodzko and by Crowe and Rawlinson, another concern might be with the way that cities are double-coded. Little Venice, Little Italy, New Amsterdam: through deference and referral the newer area of the city, or the city as a whole, plugs into an older model, seeks glamour by association, or promises the familiar. Names announce this, but so too do certain urban forms. With its industrial eminence diminishing in the late nineteenth century, Manchester sought renewal by building a new ship canal and the world's first industrial park, Trafford Park. As discussed in Tyrer and Crinson's chapter in this volume, Trafford Park became the home for many large factories and warehouses served by docks and new railway lines, and also housed in its centre a small township built on a grid plan and further evoking American prototypes through its numbered street names. Sarah Carne's video projection *High Noon* was made partly as a rumination on Trafford Park's peculiar and uncanny qualities (Figure 9.7).[26] As we will see, in the late twentieth century Trafford Park went through a recession and, suffering a declining population as well as a decline in its industries, Trafford Park's houses became largely uninhabited and were all eventually demolished.

Carne's work takes the classic western *High Noon* (1952) as its source material. In Fred Zinnemann's movie a remote community, Hadleyville, is threatened by a pardoned outlaw, Frank Miller, who is to arrive by the noon train and meet his gang at the climax of the action. But, as the film unfolds and the retired marshal solicits aid from his townsfolk, community spirit deserts the town and the marshal is left alone to face the gunmen, finally defeating them but throwing his marshal's badge in the dust in the last shot of the film. Of any western, Carne's choice of *High Noon* is particularly apt for reworking with Trafford Park because the film is the most urban of westerns, employing no contrast with the wilderness and having an empty main street and railway lines as its most memorable settings. In Carne's

9.7
Sarah Carne,
***High Noon*, 2002**

video the film's script is spoken by office workers and others whom the artist approached in Trafford Park and cajoled and stage-managed into reading their parts from cards. Facing the camera, they read the script completely straight, without play acting, mostly in Manchester accents but with the occasional southern or Australian accent evident. In one scene the 'actors' are shown singing the Battle Hymn of the Republic inside Trafford Park's corrugated iron church. In another the film's famous theme tune, 'Do not forsake me, Oh my darling', is played against an image of the street sign for Third Avenue, the 'main street' of this township. Occasionally the video cuts to an ominous view down the empty vista of Trafford Park's railway line, as if the expected train from *High Noon* might arrive. The scenario is, of course, absurd: the 'actors' are mostly stiff and disjointed and the text only holds together at times because the movie is so well known and its mythic resonances so engrained.

Carne's work shares something with the recent use of video as a kind of archaicising medium, or at least a medium whose cheaper, cruder and more personalised qualities are linked with the forensic focus expected of the gallery experience to enable an unpicking or estranging of the smooth edits and industrialised techniques of the classic Hollywood film.[27] The 'actors' are mostly filmed speaking their lines direct to a static camera as in the 'video diary', the favoured confessional form of much current television. They are seen as animated portraits against the 'set' of Trafford Park and framed by the old school or a Rentokil van, beside a postbox, or inside a pub. Although they have become familiar in contemporary television these are essentially archaic aesthetic forms, similar in their effects to what Hal Foster has called 'the outmoded'.[28] Particularly relevant is the question that Foster raises about whether these forms have now become so recuperated within mainstream media that their juxtaposition with the Hollywood western stimulates merely a humorous frisson, which is evidently one reaction to Carne's video. The critical element here is the relation of the outmoded to what Foster (citing Benjamin) calls the 'wish symbols' of the past. For Foster/Benjamin such wish symbols can be found in urban forms like arcades and international exhibition buildings, but I would extend them to include newly mythical types and scenarios. In Zinnemann's *High Noon*, the wish symbol of the tight-knit, interdependent community of propinquity is ultimately and necessarily replaced by another wish symbol, that of the good but flawed, brave yet reluctant man (perfectly embodied in the casting of an ageing Gary Cooper) who transcends his weaknesses and those of his community through a kind of desperate integrity. In the Cold War era this offered twin and related allegories: of the existentialist man standing out from the cowed populace of witch-hunting America; and of America reluctantly going to the aid of Korea against communism, and despite the opposition of American isolationists.[29]

The changing land-uses, the custodianship of heritage, and the processes of redevelopment in Trafford Park over the past thirty years have been described earlier in this volume. In sum, the successive waves of changes in the area have now arrived at a post-industrial state in which industrial and residential space has been subtly re-formed and co-opted. The illusion of continuity and the progress of investment have to be maintained together: the newly named 'village' lives on without its residents, the grid and its tramlines are consciously evoked in the newly designed street furniture. There are the appurtenances of an organic community without the community being present: the church, the pub, the chiselled masonry that marks boys and girls' entrances into the school. These provide less a theatre of memory in Trafford Park than the management of amnesia.

In this local context many exchanges in the original script of *High Noon* take on charged meaning: 'If you're smart, you'll get out too'; 'This is just a dirty little village in the middle of nowhere'; 'Now people up north are thinking of this town . . . sending money to build schools, factories and houses', 'I've got no stake in this', 'That wasn't here five years ago', 'When he dies this town dies too', and so on. But if Trafford Park has become Hadleyville, what is it waiting for? What is going to come down that disused railway line? The video does not seal this ending for us. The static camera and the inactive recitation of the script seem to allow us to apply the film's messages to any period of Trafford Park's history, so that the coming of Miller could represent the Development Corporation, recession, even the original American firms that settled in the area. Essentially, though, this inaction (in which even the marshal is trapped) and the video's consequently open-ended allegorisation, is formally different from the inaction of Hadleyville's town's folk. It both results from and also stands for a numbing of reflexes and a form of historical dislocation and oblivion that is part of the dubious achievement of the post-industrial city.

In Carne's *High Noon* the wish symbols of the community and the hero that are imported with Zinnemann's film are thus refracted and left unresolved. The recitation of these symbols in the video creates a curious sense of mythic structures cascading into the local politics of place or, to put it in an entirely different way, the nonsynchronous confronting the progressive narrative of redevelopment. Nevertheless the video proceeds as if preordained, recalling as it continues some of the contradictory relations that Trafford Park has had with America but also evoking a sum of collective memories of the American West – theme tunes, mythic structures, scraps of dialogue – now deeply inscribed in British popular culture. The very evocation of these memories acts as a way of reinscribing working-class consciousness back into the de-industrialised and gentrified cityscape.

At the start of this chapter I suggested that the relation of these artworks to urban memory is distinct from several other contemporary forms of the co-optation of memory to urban thinking. Benjamin Buchloh has identified this instrumentalism as the use of memory 'as a cultural retrieval system, an aesthetic means of legitimizing a political present that has long lost its legitimation'.[30] Also, whatever else they do, the works discussed here are not primarily involved in the kind of memorialisation of aesthetic precedents and typologies that Baudelaire had espoused as central to his 'mnemotechny of beauty'. But if, in Baudelaire's scheme, an aesthetics of memory depended upon an 'institutional relay' between the artistic study and the museum,[31] as the mine of precedent and tradition, then with the 'mnemotechny of the industrial city' we might assume a similar relationship, though here the city itself becomes the museum or archive that is threatened and that must be mined. However, this is not all that these works are concerned with. The crucial tack taken here, and the one that both links them to a Baudelairean mnemotechny and also helps them avoid the instrumentalism of memory, is to treat acts of evocation, reminiscence or double-coding as technologies in themselves. By doing this they accept that their relation to the city is largely channelled by these intermediary actions and practices. These are now the 'deep avenues' that viewers' imaginations wander down. And it is in relation to such technologies that these new works act as searching supplements and oblique commentaries.

Acknowledgements

I would like to record particular thanks to Natalie Rudd and Richard Williams for their comments on this chapter.

Notes

1 Charles Baudelaire, 'The Salon of 1846,' in *Selected Writings on Art and Artists*, Harmondsworth: Penguin, 1972, p. 77.
2 Ibid., p. 64.
3 Benjamin Buchloh, *Neo-Avantgarde and Culture Industry*, Cambridge, MA: MIT Press, 2000, pp. 141–2.
4 See Hal Foster, *Design and Crime*, London and New York: Verso, 2002, pp. 130–5.
5 See James Lingwood (ed.), *House*, London: Phaidon Press and Artangel Trust, 1995.
6 See Suzanne Lacy, *Mapping the Terrain: New Genre Public Art*, Seattle: Bay Press, 1995.
7 See, for instance, Alex Coles (ed.), *Site-Specificity: The Ethnographic Turn*, London: Black Dog, 2000; Rosalyn Deutsche, *Evictions: Art and Spatial Politics*, Cambridge, MA: MIT Press, 1996; Hal Foster, *The Return of the Real*, Cambridge, MA: MIT Press, 1996.
8 *An Area of Outstanding Unnatural Beauty* was shown at the Old General Plumbing Supplies, King's Cross, London from 4 September to 17 November 2002.

9   Charles Dickens, *Dombey and Son* (1848), Harmondsworth: Penguin, 1986, p. 121.

10 Ibid., p. 289.

11 Richard Wentworth, *Thinking Aloud*, London: Hayward Gallery, 1999, pp. 6–7. These quotes come from the catalogue of an exhibition curated by Wentworth. Although the exhibition consisted of objects collected by Wentworth and *An Area of Outstanding Unnatural Beauty* was presented as an installation by Wentworth – that is, an artwork – I find the distinction unimportant here. Both 'works' are concerned with the resonances between objects – how physical proximity or remembered nearness works on our understanding of objects taken away from their normal functions.

12 Letter from Wentworth to James Lingwood 20 June 2002, published in K. Ivy (ed.), *Off Limits: 40 Artangel Projects*, London: Merrell, 2003, p. 113.

13 Ibid.

14 Ibid., p. 71.

15 The work was commissioned for the exhibition *Fabrications: New Art and Urban Memory*, held at CUBE, Manchester, 11 September–2 November 2002. See also Mark Crinson, Helen Hills and Natalie Rudd, *Fabrications: New Art and Urban Memory in Manchester*, Manchester: UMIM, 2002.

16 See Roland Barthes, *Camera Lucida*, London: Vintage, 1993, pp. 76–7, 96, 99–100.

17 *Remixer* was another work commissioned for the exhibition *Fabrications: New Art and Urban Memory*, held at CUBE, Manchester, 11 September–2 November 2002. See also Crinson *et al.*

18 *The Guardian*, 29 August 2002.

19 The work was commissioned for the exhibition *Fabrications: New Art and Urban Memory*, held at CUBE, Manchester, 11 September–2 November 2002. See also Crinson *et al.*

20 On the ethnographer paradigm in recent art, see Foster, *Return*, pp. 173–203.

21 For more reflections on the slide projection as a device in contemporary art, see Buchloh, *Neo-Avantgarde*, pp. 152–6.

22 Foster, *Return*, p. 173.

23 *Explaining Urbanism to Wild Animals* was exhibited at Tmesis Gallery, Manchester, 21 September to 1 November 2002.

24 Joseph Leo Koerner, *Caspar David Friedrich and the Subject of Landscape*, London: Reaktion, 1995, pp. 5–6.

25 Such an interpretation is to some extent legitimated by another work by Crowe and Rawlinson in collaboration with Graham Parker. In their *Project for the River Medlock* (1998), the removal of a panel in a parapet enabled a view onto one of Manchester's 'hidden' rivers, while nearby speakers played recordings of the river burbling at its source in the hills beyond the city. Although apparently a reversal of *Explaining Urbanism to Wild Animals*, again it was the traditionally 'natural' that was the consoling and familiar element and the city that was unknown and newly displayed. As Richard Williams has pointed out to me, Crowe and Rawlinson's title refers directly to Josef Beuys' 1965 performance *How to Explain Paintings to a Dead Hare*, which involved the artist in three hours of shamanistic conversation with the dead hare. Needless to say, there is nothing shamanistic about Crowe and Rawlinson's woodland adventure.

26 The work was commissioned for the exhibition *Fabrications: New Art and Urban Memory*, held at CUBE, Manchester, 11 September–2 November 2002. See also Crinson *et al.*

27 I am thinking of works like Douglas Gordon's *24 Hour Psycho* (1993) and Stan Douglas's *Journey into Fear* (2001).

28 Foster, *Design and Crime*, pp. 138–9.

29 See, for instance, Will Wright, *Sixguns and Society: A Structural Study of the Western*, Berkeley, CA: University of California Press, 1975, pp. 75–7, 82–5; and Philip French, *Westerns*, London: Secker & Warburg, 1977, pp. 34–5. Carl Foreman, whose screenplay was his last for a Hollywood film, was later blacklisted.

30 Buchloh, *Neo-Avantgarde*, p. 212.

31 See Foster, *Design and Crime*, 2002, p. 68.

The Brazilian President
leaves the
Teatro Nacional Claudio Santoro
and returns to his vehicle
which is parked
some distance
away.

Index

Index

Herzog J. 129–31; and de Meuron 126, 129
Hessel, F. 146; *Spazieren in Berlin* 146
heterotopia 138–9, 141n65
hi-end 165n28
Hills, H. 50
Himid, L. 24, 25, 28, 31, 32–3: *Cotton.Com* 28–30, 31, 33
history xii–xiv, xvi, 9, 11–13, 15, 17, 23–4, 32, 35, 37, 40–1, 43, 50, 55, 60, 67, 77, 125–6, 128, 131, 136, 137, 145, 146, 150, 153, 155, 156, 159
historical materialism 147
Hitler, A. 83, 87
Hollywood 186, 210
Holocaust xviii, xix, 11–12, 13–14, 24, 36, 37, 42, 78, 93, 94
Homes for Heroes 35
housing estates 35, 42, 58, 86, 105
Hulme 3
human body: and the city xiii, xviii; and architecture 44n9
Hume, D. 160
Hussein, S. 187
Huxtable, A.L. 170
hypermodernity 146, 148–9, 155, 156

identification 171–6, 178, 180, 182–4, 189, 191n29
identity xiii–xiv, 5, 171, 174, 182–4, 188–9; national identity 171, 178–182, 184, 186–9
ideology 44n2
image 171–2, 176
immigrant workers 4
imperial city xvii
imperial imagery 89
industrial city 4, 49, 67, 100–3
industrial estate 103–4, 109
industrial gallery space 121–39
Industrial Revolution 99, 132
industrial symbolism 100–1
industrialism 153, 197
interstitial spaces 50
introjection 173–5
Iraq 189
Ireland 7
Isle of Dogs 34
Israel 186
Italian community in Ancoats 58–9
Italian Republic 89
Italy 89–90: Como, Casa del Fascio, 90; Como,

war memorial, 79; Udine, Resistance memorial 90; *see also* Rome
Itten, J. 84

Jameson, F. 175
Japan xix
Jerusalem, Yad Vashem memorial 90
Jews 184–5; Austrian 75; Berlin xix
Joray, M. 78: *Le Béton dans l'Art Contemporain* 78

Kahn, L. 94
Kapp, W. 82–3, 87
Kaprow, A. 122–3
Klein, M. 101
Koolhaas, R. 145, 146, 147–50, 151, 153, 154, 156, 158, 160, 170; *Delirious New York* 177; 'Singapore Songlines: Portrait of a Potemkin Metropolis . . . or Thirty Years of Tabula Rasa' 147–50
Kracauer, S. 5–6 'Street without Memory' 5–6
Kristeva, J. 100, 102, 183

labyrinth xviii, 7, 8, 35
Lacan, J. 171–2, 176; theory 178–80
LaCapra, D. 15
Lanzberg, L. 4
latency 14, 15, 25, 43
Leach, E. 38
Le Corbusier 150, 170, 177–8; monastery and chapel at La Tourette, 93; Mundaneum 76–7
Lefebvre, H.: 'Notes on the New Town' 75
Lethaby, W.R.: All Saints, Brockhampton 81; Melsetter, Orkney 81
Lévi-Strauss, C. 38, 100, 115n11, 125–6; *Structural Anthropology* 125; Tupi-Kawahib 126
liberal governmentality 51
Libeskind, D. xviii–xix
libido 44n1
library 16–17
lieux de mémoire xiii–xiv, 50
listed buildings 57, 60
Liverpool 31, 123, 128, 132, 134; Albert Dock 127–8, 132; Tate Gallery 121, 126–8, 132, 136
Locke, J. 159–60; 164n11
loft spaces xi, 69n29, 100, 122–3
London xvii, 34, 35, 39, 114, 121, 130–1, 132; Bankside Power Station 114, 129, 131;

post-Fordist 49

post-industrial city xi, 1, 3, 18, 49–51, 66,
67–8, 99–103, 109, 113, 134, 136, 137,
196–7, 211

postmodern architecture 125

posturbanism xi, xv, xix–xx

Potemkin city/metropolis/village 148

Potts, A. 129

power station 128, 131

prairies of history xix

pre-Oedipal 43: gender 39

preservation 50, 65

Preston 70n40

Princess Diana 189

projection 173–5

prostitution 149

Proust, M. xv, xvi, 5, 7, 154

public space 57–60, 62, 196

pubs 60, 61

Putsch 82–3, 87

racism 185

railways 15, 19n36: railway arches 50, 114;
railway lines 209, 211; railway stations
14, 15–16; *see also* waiting rooms

Rauschenberg, R. 122–3

Rawlinson, I.: and N. Crowe's *Explaining
Urbanism to Wild Animals* 206–8, 213n25;
N. Crowe, and G. Parker's *Project for the
River Medlock* 213n25

reconstruction 90; post-war reconstruction
132

regeneration 49, 51, 57, 60, 62, 112, 196–7,
202, 203; heritage-led regeneration 57,
61, 68n6

religion 183

repetition 182, 190n8, 191n34, 206

retail park 53, 55, 57

RIBA bookshop 27, 201

Richards, J. M. 132

Rogers, R. and A. Power: *Cities for a Small
Country* 51

Romantic absorption 206–7

Romantic landscape 207

Rome xvii, 87, 89; Fosse Ardeatine Memorial,
87–91, 93

Rossi, A. xiii: *The Architecture of the City* xiii

Rouse, J. 131

Rückenfigur 208

ruins 131, 132, 134, 136

Rupert Bear 39

Rushkoff, D. 182

Ruskin, J. xvii, xviii, 70n54

sacrifice 115n11

Salecl, R. 180

Salt, T. 105, 108

Saltaire 105, 108

Samuel, R. 65: 'The Return to Brick' 65

San Francisco 122; Golden Gate bridge 181

Sant'Elia, A. 79

Sawyer, M. 39, 44n14

Schinkel, K.-F. 68n3

Schockerlebnis see shock experience

Sebald, W.G. xv, xvi, xx, 1–4, 5, 6–8, 10, 12,
15, 18, 24–5, 37, 40; *Austerlitz* 12–17, 24,
37, 40–2; *The Emigrants* 1, 5; Ferber, M.
1–5, 6, 7–8, 9, 13, 15, 18; *The Rings of
Saturn* 7; Wadi Halfa 2, 3, 6

Second World War xiii, 37, 62, 77, 78, 79,
103, 108, 127, 132, 155

Serota, N. 126, 129; *Experience or
Interpretation* 126

Serres, Michel 67

Shanghai 151; Yuyuan Garden 150–1

ship, as heterotopia 138

shock experience xviii, 5, 6, 8, 14, 147, 155,
156, 197

Simmel, G. xv

Singapore 145, 146, 148–50, 151, 154, 155,
156, 157–61, 163; Colbar (Colonial Bar)
161; Lee Kuan Yew 148, 158; in relation
to Malaysia and Indonesia 148; Raffles
Hotel 163; Victoria Hall 163; Zouk 163

Situationists 202–3

slavery 24, 25, 31–3

slide show 205–6

slums xi–xii, 50, 60, 65

smell 103

Social Democratic government 83

socialism 86–7

Soviet Union 77

space: abstract space 58; economic space 66;
marginal space 58

sport 186

Stallabrass, J. 129

stamp-machine 157–8

Stirling, J. 70n40, 126–7; and M. Wilford 126

Stockport 52

stone 84–6, 90

street-naming xxxi n22, 69n22, 106

Stretford Council 108